D1614974

KING ALFRED'S COLLEGE
WINCHESTER

To be returned on or before the day marked
below :—

29. MAR 1982

PLEASE ENTER ON ISSUE SLIP:

AUTHOR   SMITH

TITLE   Land and politics in the England of Henry
VIII

ACCESSION No. 57631

Land and Politics in the England of Henry VIII

THE WEST RIDING OF YORKSHIRE: 1530-46

BY

R. B. SMITH

LECTURER IN HISTORY
SCHOOL OF ORIENTAL AND AFRICAN STUDIES
UNIVERSITY OF LONDON

CLARENDON PRESS · OXFORD

1970

Oxford University Press, Ely House, London W. 1

GLASGOW NEW YORK TORONTO MELBOURNE WELLINGTON
CAPE TOWN SALISBURY IBADAN NAIROBI DAR ES SALAAM LUSAKA ADDIS ABABA
BOMBAY CALCUTTA MADRAS KARACHI LAHORE DACCA
KUALA LUMPUR SINGAPORE HONG KONG TOKYO

PRINTED IN GREAT BRITAIN
BY SPOTTISWOODE, BALLANTYNE & CO. LTD.
LONDON AND COLCHESTER

FOR
MY MOTHER

PREFACE

THIS study was the outcome of a three-year apprenticeship in Tudor history, having been first prepared as a doctoral dissertation in the University of Leeds. Both in writing the dissertation and in revising it for publication I have incurred innumerable debts of gratitude. I am deeply indebted, above all, to my supervisor Mr. G. C. F. Forster of the University of Leeds, whose encouragement and advice have been invaluable at all stages. I also owe a great deal to Mr. J. W. Cox, who first taught me how to handle medieval estate records without forgetting that they are ultimately about 'pigs and sheep'. My thanks are also due to Professor A. G. Dickens, Professor M. W. Beresford, Professor J. Le Patourel, and to various members of Professor S. T. Bindoff's seminar at the Institute of Historical Research during the sessions 1960–63. In particular I benefited greatly from Dr. R. S. Schofield's expertise in Tudor financial records and from Dr. Christine Black's understanding of county administration. Last, but very far from least, I owe thanks to Dr. Robin Swales, now of Regina University, Saskatchewan, without whose encouragement no final manuscript would ever have reached the publisher; he was, moreover, kind enough to read the final version in its entirety and suggested many valuable improvements. The deficiencies which remain are of course my own responsibility

London, 1969.

R. B. SMITH

CONTENTS

LIST OF MAPS

LIST OF TABLES

INTRODUCTION

IT is unfashionable these days to include chapters of both economic and political history within the covers of a single monograph. The present experiment therefore may seem to require a few words of justification. The relationship between land and power has occupied the minds of a number of students of sixteenth- and seventeenth-century England, since Tawney's celebrated article on the 'rise of the gentry' in 1941.[1] But the questions which Tawney set out to answer in that article cannot be satisfactorily settled by an economic approach alone. For historians who reject the cut and dried relationships of Marxist theory, it is necessary at every step to relate economics pragmatically to the institutional framework of society. By leaving institutions on one side for only a brief moment, Tawney, in that article, laid himself open to the just criticism of Professor Hexter that it was absurd to conduct a debate on the role of the gentry in politics without making any mention of Parliament.[2] For Tawney this was an uncustomary aberration. His study of the changing pattern of landownership between 1558 and 1640 was but one small part of a much wider *oeuvre*, which had begun thirty years earlier with *The Agrarian Problem in the Sixteenth Century*, a study of the decline of manorial custom as the basis of agrarian relationships under the impact of the great inflation. In *Religion and the Rise of Capitalism* he went on to identify both the intellectual and the economic roots of the 'spirit of capitalism' whose effects on Anglican social thought he so much deplored. Whilst no one would pretend that he said the last word on either of these subjects, Tawney took English scholarship a good way along the road towards understanding the fundamental changes which came over English society, both its economy and its institutions, in the two centuries between 1500 and 1700. He sought to observe the changing position of the gentry as landowners against this wider background of social

[1] R. H. Tawney: 'The Rise of the Gentry', *EcHR*, xi (1941).
[2] J. R. Hexter: *Reappraisals in History* (London, 1967).

transformation. The starting-point of the present essay is the desire to take the study of these changes one small step further.

To relate economics to institutions and politics means more than casually linking the economic history of small localities to the political history of the nation. The same people, whether in London or in some remote corner of the realm, must be studied simultaneously from an economic and a political point of view. The time is not yet ripe for a study which would embrace at one fell swoop the economic life of the whole kingdom and also a survey of national politics, under Henry VIII or any other Tudor sovereign; at least, it lies far beyond the competence of the present writer to attempt it. One must be content for the time being to relate the economy of a small selected region to the institutions and politics of that region. My original reasons for choosing the West Riding were largely fortuitous, but as it turned out few English counties could have been more appropriate for this purpose. The size and diversity of the Riding made it possible to study a number of quite different social and economic patterns at once, and to attempt a comparative analysis of the evidence from different regions within it. The diversity was not merely geographical but also institutional. For the period chosen, moreover, the West Riding is exceptionally well-endowed with public records. And although the *Victoria History* of the West Riding has not even been begun, the area has been well-served by recent writings on specific aspects of its history.[1] An additional advantage was the fact that the Riding (together with other northern areas) was the scene of a major political upheaval during the period chosen.

However, despite the importance of relating politics and economics within a single perspective, this essay cannot claim to be a study of every aspect of West Riding society under Henry VIII. It will say little about the cultural and intellectual history of the area. Professor Dickens has said perhaps as much as can be said, using specifically Yorkshire sources, about the religious beliefs and intellectual aspir-

[1] In particular, Professors A. G. Dickens and M. W. Beresford, and for the medieval period, Mr. T. A. M. Bishop; their works will be cited in frequent footnotes.

ations of the early Tudor North. Beyond that one can
observe simply that Yorkshire participated in an English
culture that was already to some extent national, and that
the best hope of discovering what ideas preoccupied the
minds of educated Yorkshiremen is to read such classics of
the age as More's *Utopia* or Halle's *Chronicle*. To borrow a
phrase of Professor Dickens, 'the remoter provinces of
Tudor England were as far as possible from being hermeti-
cally sealed'.[1] One of the results of the present enquiry has
been to dispel the impression of another writer on the period
that Yorkshire can be dismissed as 'an historical anachro-
nism whose greatness lay in the already misty past of the
middle ages and whose present posed chronic and occasionally critical administrative, political and religious problems'.[2]
By writing in that vein Professor Jordan under-estimated the
North's degree of social and cultural development, and
probably at the same time over-estimated the extent to which
more southerly parts of England had become 'modern' by
the mid-sixteenth century. England was still a medieval
country at this time, compared with what she was to become
after about 1650.

The process of social transformation did not begin suddenly with an act of Parliament in 1534 or 1536. English
society under Henry VIII was very much the product of its
past, and anyone trying to describe it will soon find himself
being drawn back into earlier periods. Tawney himself was
conscious of this when, in his *Agrarian Problem*, he analysed
the decline of manorial custom as the framework of tenure
and of rural social structure. But at that time (1912) he felt
safe in the assumption that the main outlines of medieval
society had been satisfactorily traced by Vinogradoff and
Maitland. Later, the work of the Russian scholar Kosminsky
(first published in the 1930s but not fully translated into
English until 1956) was to challenge that assumption.[3]

[1] A. G. Dickens: *Lollards and Protestants in the Diocese of York 1509–1558* (Oxford,
1959), p. 4. The assertion is substantiated in greater detail in the same author's 'The
Writers of Tudor Yorkshire, *Trans. Royal Hist. Soc.*, 5th ser., xiii (1963).
[2] W. K. Jordan: *The Charities of Rural England 1480–1660*) (London, 1961),
p. 215.
[3] E. A. Kosminksy: *Studies in the Agrarian History of England in the Thirteenth
Century* (English translation, ed. by R. H. Hilton, Oxford, 1956).

He showed that the research of Maitland and his contemporaries relied too much on the manorial records of large private estates. By using royal records such as the hundred rolls of 1279, Kosminsky himself demonstrated that what was true of the great ecclesiastical and noble estates was not necessarily true of those of smaller men, and that one cannot hope to grasp the full complexity of an agrarian society except by studying a whole region thoroughly, and not just its principal estates. It was Kosminsky indeed who discovered the economic origins of the gentry. It is as much his work, and that of other recent historians of medieval England, as research on the sixteenth and seventeenth centuries that has placed some of Tawney's work in need of revision. Tawney's disciples and critics have concentrated on the century between 1540 and 1640 to such an extent that it has come to be known (often affectionately) as 'Tawney's century';[1] much valuable research has emerged in consequence. But one must be careful not to take too much for granted the condition of English society at the beginning of that century: further research is needed there too. It is for this reason that in the present study I have resisted the temptation to look forward in time, and have tried to set the West Riding of Henry VIII against its medieval background.

It proved impossible to make a static analysis of the economic and political structure of West Riding society in the single year 1540. The sources do not all relate to a single year, and in any case the situation of that time was a state of flux following upon the Henrician reformation. I decided therefore to concentrate on the period from about 1535 to the end of Henry's reign, and to consider the changes which occurred in the interval, as well as the social and political framework itself. The first three chapters of the study are concerned with the economy and the social structure; the three latter chapters deal with the political framework and with the detailed changes which took place within it, including the rebellion known as the Pilgrimage of Grace.

[1] The term was coined by Professor Trevor-Roper, but see F. J. Fisher: 'Tawney's Century' in *Essays in the Economic and Social History of Tudor and Stuart England in honour of R. H. Tawney* (Ed. F. J. Fisher, London, 1961).

The order of the chapters should not be taken as an indication that I believe economic activity to be more fundamental than politics; it was simply more convenient to describe it first. Politics was indeed often a major factor in economics, and if the changing ownership of land during the sixteenth and seventeenth centuries was an important cause of political change, one should not forget that one of the principal reasons why so much land was on the market after 1540 was a largely political decision by the King to do away with the religious orders.

The difficulties of social description and analysis are too often underestimated by historians of pre-Industrial England. It is a discipline which requires more than simply seizing upon this or that set of documents and counting everything in sight. And if the first rule is that one must always have a framework of significant questions to ask, the second is that one must never try to stretch the documentation too far. An important reason why the techniques of social study have made progress in the past few decades is that much more is now known about Tudor government. The documents of social history can now be read in their administrative context and it is possible to say with more confidence whether or not they will bear the strain of interpretation which the historian wishes to place upon them. Appendix I will discuss some of the problems arising from the use of certain source materials, and try to set them onto the plane of administrative analysis on which Dr. Elton and Dr. Schofield have so successfully specialized.[1] Let us beware of too much self-congratulation on this point however. Perfection in these matters is beyond attainment, and the reader must bear in mind Tawney's remarks that:[2]

Historical statistics should be regarded with more than ordinary scepticism, inasmuch as they cannot easily be checked by comparison with other sources of information, and it may reasonably be asked whether it is possible to obtain figures that are sufficiently reliable to be

[1] As in G. R. Elton: *The Tudor Revolution in Government* (Cambridge, 1952) and innumerable articles; and R. S. Schofield: *Parliamentary Lay Taxation 1485–1547* (unpub. thesis, Ph.D., Cambridge, 1963).
[2] R. H. Tawney: *The Agrarian Problem in the Sixteenth Century* (London, 1912), p. viii.

2

used with any confidence. Often it is not possible. The strong point of surveyors was not always arithmetic. The forms in which their information has been cast are sometimes too various to permit of its being used for the purposes of a summary or comparison. Even when the figures are both accurate and comparable, the student who works over considerable masses of material will be fortunate if he does not introduce some errors of his own.

It would be rash indeed to forget this warning. But for all their shortcomings statistics are essential to the writing of social history. To put new wine into an old bottle is dangerous, but to try to do without the bottle altogether is to risk disaster.

THE WEST RIDING AND ITS ECONOMY
ABOUT 1530

I

THE physical setting of the society which is the subject
of this study was one that the reader familiar with
present-day Yorkshire may find difficult to envisage.
There are no doubt a few parts of the West Riding which
have changed little since medieval times, and even earlier:
the wanderer over bleak moors and limestone crags is likely
to be more conscious of geological than of historical time.
But those are not the areas occupied by villages and towns,
which are the real concern of the student of the sixteenth
century. It requires no small effort of the imagination to
picture the one-time agrarian landscape of regions now
dominated by vast conurbations, where mill-chimneys,
slag-heaps, and acre upon acre of suburban housing coexist
uneasily with pastures and rhubarb plots. And even beyond
these urban concentrations, the countryside has been transformed in the past century or more by railways and metalled
roads; whilst practically all the houses have been rebuilt at
least once since the middle of the sixteenth century.

A twentieth-century explorer in the West Riding of that
time would—if such an exploration were possible—be
struck immediately by two essential features: its poverty,
and its sparsity of folk. The standard of living was low, even
by comparison with the seventeenth or eighteenth century:
its level cannot be statistically measured, but it is evident
enough from what we know of the character of ordinary
peasant housing. The period with which we are concerned
was before the 'housing revolution' about which Professor
Hoskins has written, and there are few if any houses
surviving to-day that can be called ordinary dwellings of that
period. If we want an indication of the character of such
dwellings, we must look to the excavations of deserted

medieval villages such as that which has taken place at Wharram Percy on the East Riding Wolds. That village was deserted soon after 1500. Of the six dwellings that had occupied the first house-site to be excavated, in the two centuries between 1300 and 1500, the topmost layer represented a peasant house of Henry VII's reign.[1] It was a 'long-house', consisting of two rooms with space for livestock at one end; and it had walls of timber, wattle and daub, built on a rough foundation of chalk. Of course building materials would vary according to the locality, and stone would be used in the hill country, but the villages of early sixteenth-century Yorkshire must have been made up of groups of houses of this kind, with just a few more imposing buildings such as the church and the manor-house. Linking the villages would be 'roads'—often no more than muddy lanes—and here and there would be found a large settlement almost worthy to be called a town. Population at that period can only be guessed; England as a whole was, by present standards, not very densely populated. Professor J. C. Russell's estimate of 3·22 million people in England in 1545, which for all its shortcomings is the best any-one can do, implies a density of between sixty and sixty-five persons to a square mile.[2] As for the West Riding, the few statistical clues available suggest that its population about the year 1540 may have been as high as 100,000, but was probably not much higher: a density of thirty-six people per square mile would therefore seem a reasonable guess.[3]

[1] J. G. Hurst: 'Medieval Britain in 1956' and similar articles for 1957, 1958 and 1959, in *Medieval Archaeology*, i (1957), 166–8; ii (1958), 205–7; iii (1959), 324; iv (1960), 161. The excavations were conducted by Mr. J. G. Hurst and Professor M. W. Beresford, to whom I am indebted for information and for an opportunity to participate in the excavation.

[2] J. C. Russell: *British Medieval Population* (New Mexico, 1948), pp. 270–2. His comparisons between the taxed population of 1377 and the chantry survey estimates of 1545, however, are not very helpful as far as Yorkshire is concerned, since the units he uses are not comparable: the former figures relate to townships, whereas those of 1545 relate to parishes, which in Yorkshire were often much larger. (cf. *infra*, p. 7).

[3] In 1377 the poll-tax receipts indicate a total of 48,150 contributors in the West Riding, which implies at least 75,000 inhabitants: see note by J. Topham, *Archaeologia*, vii (1785), p. 337. In 1603 the total number of communicants in the Diocese of York was estimated at 214,470, of which perhaps a third lived in the West Riding; that would suggest a total population of around 110,000 souls in that year: see B.M., Harl. MS. 280, f. 170, cited in A. G. Dickens, 'Recusancy in Yorkshire in 1604', *Y.A.J.*, xxxvii (1951) 32.

This population was not evenly distributed. But then, the West Riding was, as it still is, a very diverse region: it includes within its boundaries as wide a variety of physical conditions as is to be found in any county of England. An obvious distinction may be made between highland and lowland zones, which are very approximately divided by a line drawn between Ripon and Sheffield. The hill country is both wetter and stonier than the lowlands, as well as more remote from the county town of York. But this distinction is only a superficial measure of the Riding's diversity: a more discerning eye will distinguish at least eleven different physical regions, each with its own peculiarities which found reflection in the agrarian pattern of the sixteenth century. A brief description of these regions, which are illustrated in Map I, will form a framework for much of what follows.[1]

The Coal Measures: The heart of the Riding is the broad belt of country which, because of its seams of coal, now contains most of the industry and has the greatest density of population. In the sixteenth century its importance was less striking, and since the unity of the area is geological and industrial rather than agricultural, it was probably at that period not so much a single region as a sort of intermediate zone between uplands and lowlands. Agriculturally indeed there is quite a contrast still, between the arable land around Pontefract (said to be the richest in Yorkshire) and the bleaker, wetter country to the west of Leeds, Barnsley and Rotherham. The area would, however, have one unifying factor in the pre-industrial era: its sandstone, which was useful for local building and drystone-walling, although too soft to be worth transporting for use elsewhere. Presumably this would give the area some unity in appearance at least.

The Magnesian Limestone Belt: The same may be said of the area immediately to the east of the coal measures, where the buildings and walls are of limestone, whose grey-white contrasts sharply with the sandstone to the west and the

---

[1] The principal sources used for this summary are: S. H. Beaver: *Yorkshire, West Riding* (in *Land of Britain* series, no. 46, London 1941), 84–99 and 146–67); and G. Rennie, R. Broun and J. Shireff, *A General View of the Agriculture of the West Riding of Yorkshire* (Board of Agriculture, 1794), passim.

quickset hedges further east. The building qualities of this stone have long been widely recognized, and William Vavasour of Hazlewood included in the panegyric of his homecountry he wrote in 1620, the observation that Aberford stone had been used to build York Minster, Selby

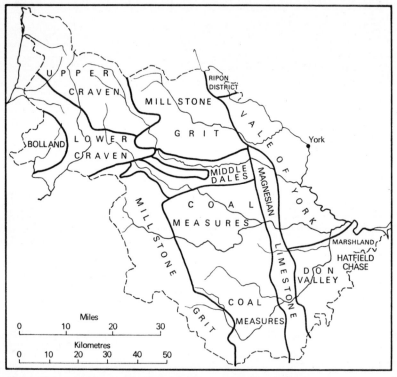

Map I. Physical Divisions of the West Riding

Abbey, and Saint Mary's Abbey at York.[1] Quarrying must therefore have been an important activity there by the sixteenth century. The area stretches from just north of Wetherby south to Tickhill, Maltby and beyond. Agriculturally it is good arable country, and thus forms a natural continuation of the coal measures.

The Vale of York: Further east again we find the vale country which stretches as far as the River Ouse and beyond, with

[1] B.M., Lansdowne MS. 900, pp. 1–4.

an undulating landscape little different from that of more southerly parts of the English lowland zone. It has little stone and no minerals, and is still dependent on agriculture: mostly arable farming, with some enclaves of pasture, as in the sixteenth century.

Marshland and the Don Valley Lowlands: To the south-east the vale flattens out and becomes far less suitable for arable. This region has by now been extensively drained, but in the sixteenth century it must have been liable to frequent flooding and would be more suitable for pasture; however, the degree of agricultural specialization was not so great then as now, and there was probably a good deal of poorish arable there.

Hatfield Chase: Beyond the Don lay an area so wet that (before drainage) much of the land was useless for agriculture of any kind; even to-day part of it goes by the name of Hatfield and Thorne Waste. Conditions in the sixteenth century were probably not unlike those described in Dr. Thirsk's study of the Lincolnshire fens, where the people had to rely for a regular part of their food on fishing.[1] The area also had venison and game, having been set aside for hunting at an early date, and the King himself hunted there on his visit to the North in 1541.[2]

The Ripon Area: To the north of the Vale of York conditions likewise become rather less favourable to arable husbandry and the proportion of pasture is somewhat greater. The country round Ripon is a sort of transitional area between the lowlands of the Vale and the millstone-grit uplands, for here neither magnesian limestone nor coal measures intervene to separate them. Once again the absence of stone and minerals should be noted, and there is no important industry there to-day.

Millstone-Grit Areas: A considerable part of the upland zone of the West Riding is taken up by four areas of millstone-grit, separated from one another by the middle dales of the Wharfe, Aire and Ribble. With high rainfall and little good

[1] Joan Thirsk: *Fenland Farming in the Sixteenth Century* (Occasional papers in English Local History, Leicester University Press, no. 3, 1953).
[2] *L.P.*, xvi, 1540–41, no. 1130.

soil they are agriculturally the poorest region of the Riding, the poorest part of all being Bolland Forest which lies furthest to the west and gets the most rain. Large parts of the region were set aside by medieval lords as hunting-grounds: Knaresborough Forest, part of Nidderdale, Barden Forest, Bolland Forest, and extensive areas of Sowerbyshire and Hallamshire. These were the latest areas of the Riding to be populated and many settlements appear to have originated as cow-farms on forest estates. Except for Sowerbyshire, which developed a cottage cloth industry, and Hallamshire which was an important cutlery centre, none of these four areas could support a very dense population. The presence of industry was due partly (but not, as we shall see, wholly) to the fast-flowing upland streams which could drive water-mills. The millstone-grit rock is itself distinctively hard, and derives its name from its early use in the grinding of corn. In places there are rock-outcrops of scenic beauty, notably at the 'Cow and Calf' above Ilkley, at Brimham Rocks near Ripon, and in the Rivelin Valley not far from Sheffield.

Airedale and Wharfedale: Two of the three dales lying between the millstone-grit areas can be regarded as a single region, where lower land and lighter rainfall made some arable farming possible, though it has long since been abandoned. The economy of the dales villages was, however, closely bound up with the proximity of the millstone-grit moorlands, for the latter provided them with extensive common pastures. Rombalds Moor for example, lying between these two dales, was shared by the villagers of eleven townships.

Lower Craven: The middle dale of the River Ribble, together with part of upper Airedale, is distinguished by the presence of carboniferous limestone, which is once again conspicuous in buildings and stone walls. The soil is noted for its good grassland, and was so in the sixteenth century; but at that period much of the land was under crops, oats being much more easily grown than wheat.

Upper Craven: In the uplands of the north-west of the Riding millstone-grit gives way to carboniferous limestone, again with good grassland despite the greater altitude. In the sixteenth century and earlier the area was valued especially for its summer pastures, and much of it was used in that way by the monasteries of Fountains, Furness and Bolton before the Dissolution. Another part of the area, Langstrothdale Chase, was once a Percy hunting-ground: but by this period it was occupied mostly by cattle farms. Upper Airedale and Upper Wharfedale, and also (beneath the grit) Upper Nidderdale, have deposits of lead (sometimes with silver) which was mined from Roman times onwards.

The Dent-Sedburgh Area: Lastly, in the north-western tip of the West Riding, we come to an area where the limestone gives place to the Silurian rocks of the Howgill Fells. The grassland was less rich than in Craven, but otherwise its agriculture was probably not very different. It was a somewhat remote area, and will not figure very prominently in this study; socially and politically it tended, as we shall see, to look to Westmorland rather than to Yorkshire.

II

It is not enough, however, for the purposes of the present study, to distinguish in outline the physical regions of the Riding. If we would understand the relationship between landscape and society we must look at conditions in individual townships. The township should not be confused with the village, for although it very often contained only one village and its fields, that was not the only pattern of settlement found in it: sometimes it might include both a village and several hamlets, sometimes only a number of scattered farmsteads. Nor was the township the same as the parish, an ecclesiastical division which might well embrace two, three, or even more townships; some village communities have never at any time had their own parish church. The township was in fact the smallest administrative division of sixteenth-century England, and there were about six hundred of them in the West Riding at this period. They varied greatly both in population and in extent. A few had settlements that were really small towns: Ripon, Pontefract and Doncaster were the largest, and we can guess fairly confidently that Ripon's population in 1532 was around 2,000.[1] Other places with over 1,000 inhabitants probably included Leeds, Wakefield, Rotherham, and perhaps also Sheffield, Halifax, Bradford and Selby. At the other end of the scale were townships with well under 100 people, and a few with hardly any at all.

The normal type of settlement, both in the upland and the lowland regions, was the nucleated settlement; variations from that norm are usually found to have some special explanation. A variation which was not uncommon in the highland zone was the township with a single nucleated settlement surrounded by small hamlets or single farms. The village of Gisburn in Lower Craven had around it at least nine dispersed farms within its township: the village itself may well have been settled at an early date, but there was room for people to come and settle beyond the edge of its fields, probably in the later medieval period. This pattern of settlement within a township reflects both availability of land and freedom to take advantage of it. It is much more unusual to find upland townships without any sign of a nucleated settlement at all: they occur only in remote areas that were once hunting-grounds, where there may have been no settlement at all before 1500 or even later (for example the townships known as Higher and Lower Bolland Forest). Even in forest areas the majority of townships have nucleated hamlets, some of which may even antedate the creation of the forest itself. There is evidence that settlement was still expanding in the uplands in the fifteenth and sixteenth centuries. It sometimes took the form of piecemeal enclosure or encroachment on waste land, without the permission of the lord. Landlords are found taking action against such squatters from time to time. In 1557, for instance, the Earl of Cumberland held an enquiry on his manor of Silsden (in Craven) which produced a long list of minor encroachments without licence over the previous ten years.[2] A more spectacular case of upland expansion of settlement, in which the initiative was taken by the lord himself,

---

[1] P.R.O.: SC 6/Hen VIII/4409; estimate based on the number of dwellings recorded in an apparently full minister's account.

[2] Y.A.S. Library, Leeds: DD 121/Bundle 31. For comparable instances in neighbouring Lancashire, see G. H. Tupling: *Economic History of Rossendale* (Chetham Soc. n.s. LXXXVI, Manchester, 1927).

occurred at Erringden (in Sowerbyshire). In 1449 Richard
Duke of York ordered that his park there, 3,000 acres
of very barren ground, be broken up and leased out in
enclosed parcels to tenants; as a result, by 1545 there were
said to be about fifty households there. The project can have
had only temporary success, however, for there are many
fewer houses than that in Erringden township now.[1] The
fact that such unpromising land was being settled in the
mid-fifteenth century could be taken as an indication that
the uplands of the Riding were approaching the maximum
density of population that could be supported by agriculture
alone. But by this time, as we shall see, agriculture was
ceasing to be the sole employment of the inhabitants of at
least some upland areas with the rise of cottage industry.

A second variation from the nucleated pattern of settlement was the deserted village: that is, a township which had
once had a village but no longer possessed one by the mid-
sixteenth century. Professor Beresford has explored the
reasons for this situation in a series of studies which combine
the disciplines of history, geography and archaeology.[2] By
supplementing his discoveries with data of my own, I have
been able to count thirty-one townships in the West
Riding where there were at least fifteen contributors to the
poll-tax of 1377, but which to-day have no nucleated village;
and at least another four townships where one out of two or
more original nucleated settlements became depopulated
after that date.[3] The majority of these townships were in
lowland areas; but two (Hammerton-in-Bolland and Skibeden) were upland townships. It is not always easy to ascertain
date of desertion or depopulation, but where documentation
is available it often supports Professor Beresford's thesis that

---

[1] For 1449, see Y.A.S. Library; DD 99/B 2/1–2; for 1545, P.R.O.: SC 11/991.
[2] M. W. Beresford: *The Lost Villages of England* (Lutterworth, 1957) and 'The
Lost Villages of Yorkshire', *Y.A.J.*, xxxvii (1951) and xxxviii (1952–5); the last
volume includes a detailed list of West Riding deserted villages (pp. 231–40).
[3] The 31 townships are: Allerton Mauleverer, Alwoodley, Bilham, Byram-cum-
Poole, Chevet, Frickley, Givendale, Grimston, Haldenby, Hammerton-in-Bolland,
Hangthwaite, Hazelwood, Kirkby Hall, Lotherton, Newby-and-Mulwith, Newton
Waleys (by Ledsham), Nunwick, Parlington, Great Ribston, Scawsby, Skibeden
(near Skipton), Stancil, Steeton-Ainsty, Stockeld, Hampole Stubbs, Thorpe
Stapleton, Toulston, Westwick, Wilstrop and Wrangbrook. The four other places
are Cridling, Gawthorpe (and its hamlets), Skelton, and Temple Newsam.

a great many cases of this kind belong to the century or so before 1520. At Cridling for example (to be distinguished from the neighbouring and still flourishing Cridling Stubbs) there were twenty-two dwellings as late as 1425, but they were all enclosed within Cridling Park sometime before the end of the fifteenth century by Henry Vavasour, the Crown's lessee in perpetuity.[1] At Steeton-in-Ainsty there were forty-five poll-tax contributors in 1377, but a mere four houses besides the Fairfax mansion in 1514.[2] Occasionally we have a dated licence to empark, as at Gawthorpe (in Harewood township) where Sir William Gascoigne's licence of 1480 probably explains the disappearance of that village and of several hamlets in the vicinity.[3]

Professor Beresford is probably right too in emphasizing the desire to convert arable land to grass as the principal factor in the desertion of villages in that period. At least seven of the parks shown on Saxton's map of the West Riding in 1577 were in places where there had once been a village: a park was both scenically attractive and economically profitable.[4] But there are some cases where the depopulation of a village in whole or part may have been due to pestilence, not necessarily in one of the great Black Death years but as a result of some purely local outbreak. The clearest instance in the West Riding occurs at Foulby and Wragby (now a single township) where as many as twenty-one cottages in the two villages were unoccupied and paid no rent in 1541, because of a recent pestilence there.[5] What chance has preserved in the records in this case could easily have happened unrecorded elsewhere. But whatever its immediate cause, the depopulation of so many villages, and the shrinkage of others, must have reflected a decline in the population of the affected township. The fact that there are many more townships where this happened in the lowlands

[1] P.R.O.: DL 42/106/f. 50 (survey of 1425) and DL 29/515/8293 (account of 1537).
[2] Inq. *post mortem* of 1514, P.R.O.: C 142/29/1.
[3] *Calendar of Patent Rolls, 1476–85*, pp. 203–4; Gascoigne was permitted to empark altogether 2,600 acres, including 1,200 acres of arable land.
[4] The seven parks were those of Allerton Mauleverer, Cridling, Gawthorpe, Ribston, Temple Newsam, Wilstrop and Wothersome; the last may have been depopulated before 1377.
[5] P.R.O.: SC 6/Hen VIII/4579.

than there are in the uplands could be interpreted to mean that in the fifteenth and early sixteenth centuries there was more growth of population in the western half of the Riding than in the east. There are other suggestions of a decline in population in the latter area. Snaith, on the fringes of Marshland, is a notable example: in 1540 as many as 380 acres of one-time demesne arable had reverted to waste for lack of tenants, whilst other parts of the demesne had been incorporated into Phippin Park.[1] In Marshland itself is found one of the more spectacular cases of village-desertion, though it cannot be very precisely dated: at Haldenby there were 117 tax-payers in 1379, and the place had been assessed at 38s. for the fifteenth of 1334; since then the village has completely disappeared.[2] Perhaps we have here the beginnings of a generalization: that population pressure was being reduced on the eastern part of the lowlands, where it had previously become too high, and was by the sixteenth century building up further west, in the uplands. But before we try to test that hypothesis, we must take a more detailed look at the economic activity of which the changing pattern of settlement was both the framework and the reflection.

III

Agriculture was the predominant economic activity throughout rural England in the sixteenth century, but the detailed character of agricultural production would vary from region to region, for local peculiarities would certainly have some effect on choice of crops and livestock. The physical environment may well have influenced peasant diets, and it is quite possible that the people of Craven ate proportionately more meat and cheese than those of the Vale of York, and rather less bread; in Marshland and Hatfield consumption of fish was probably higher than elsewhere. People would have long since learned to eat, if not to enjoy, those foodstuffs which it was easiest to produce locally. For the rural economy was still to a large extent based on subsistence, not at the family level but within each locality;

[1] P.R.O.: DL 29/550/8722.
[2] *Y.A.J.*: xxxviii, p. 237.

transport of food was possible, but not for all purposes or at all times. The use to which any acre was put depended not only on the nature of the land itself, or on the economic opportunities for the sale of its produce, but also on the social context within which it was cultivated. As Tawney remarked, it depended a good deal on the size of the farmer's holding and the extent to which he could sell what he did not need and buy what he did not grow.[1] Usually, the smaller a man's holding the higher the proportion of it he would devote to arable crops: only larger holdings were in a position to specialize fully in their choice of land-use. Flexibility also depended on the farmer's relations with his neighbours, for communal systems of cultivation made individual specialization more difficult than it was where the land was farmed in severalty.

These considerations lend some support to the idea that one can distinguish between two levels of agriculture in the sixteenth century: the level of the peasant small-holder and that of the larger holdings, many of which were demesnes belonging to large landowners but farmed out to substantial tenants. At the smallholding level there was far less regional diversity in agricultural production than the physical geography of the Riding would have permitted. Since peasants had to keep some land under crops, every area had its share of arable. Even in Craven, whose grasslands were of much higher quality than any arable there, it was not until the eighteenth century that farmers began to convert almost all of their land to meadow and pasture and to rely on grain brought in from elsewhere.[2] Conversely, in the low-lands—even in the rich arable country round Pontefract—some land had to be set aside for common pasture to ensure that there were draught animals available for ploughing as well as to provide milk and cheese. Only within this broad framework was any measure of variation possible, and unfortunately we do not know a great deal about it. Professor Hoskins, in his essays on the Leicestershire farmer, has made good use of probate inventories to learn something of

[1] R. H. Tawney: *The Agrarian Problem in the Sixteenth Century* (London, 1912), pp. 105–7.
[2] G. Rennie, *et al.*: *General View of the Agriculture of the West Riding* (1794).

the crops and livestock of ordinary tenants in this period.[1] But he had the advantage that he was dealing with a more homogeneous county than Yorkshire, and also that he was dealing with a long period. For the West Riding, there are only a few inventories relating to the period before about 1560, and they are scattered over widely differing types of country: there are not enough of them to produce coherent statistics. The only usable material we have of this kind relates to demesne farms and even that is incomplete.

Absence of evidence about crops grown by peasants makes it difficult to come to any conclusion on the question of the degree of flexibility enjoyed by individual farmers within the open field system in the sixteenth century. For it was on the peasant level of farming that communal arrangements may have operated against specialization by individuals. Unfortunately we know hardly anything about the way open fields were organized in the West Riding at this period, though we now know enough about the subject in general to beware of applying indiscriminately the generalizations drawn by H. L. Gray from his study of the Midlands or those drawn by the Orwins from their survey of Laxton.[2] Each district probably had its own peculiarities which only hard evidence from that district will enable us to specify. Nor can information gleaned from eighteenth-century and later documents be taken as applicable to the sixteenth century: the arrangement of strips in open fields, and the freedom of each tenant to use them as he would, appear to have changed considerably before the 'enclosure movement' finally brought most of these systems to an end.

What can be said with more confidence is that in some parts of the West Riding the trend towards enclosure of open fields was already under way by 1540; indeed, in a number of upland townships it had already gone so far that most of the arable was by that time enclosed. At Dent a survey made sometime in the reign of Henry VIII shows that most of the open field there was enclosed, and

---

[1] W. G. Hoskins: 'The Leicestershire Farmer in the sixteenth century' in his *Essays in Leicestershire History* (London, 1950).

[2] H. L. Gray: *English Field Systems* (Harvard 1915), esp. p. 63; C. S. and C. S. Orwin: *The Open Fields* (2nd edn., Oxford, 1954).

only a small amount remained open. At Hipperholme, near Halifax, a deed of 1522 recorded an exchange between two small freeholders of plots in a field called Northegge, which could well have been the preliminary to a private enclosure of consolidated strips.[1] Evidence of this kind proves beyond doubt that the lack of eighteenth- and nineteenth-century enclosure legislation relating to upland arable fields does not mean that such fields had never existed but only that they had been enclosed at an earlier date. References to land held in bovates (that is, open-field units of measurement) are found in Craven in several sixteenth-century estate records: at Hellifield and Eastby in 1537, and at Threshfield as late as 1570.[2] The earlier enclosure of upland fields appears to be confirmed by Professor Beresford's survey of glebe terriers: he found that, in the seventeenth century, the glebe was much more often enclosed in upland than in lowland areas.[3] The explanation for this earlier enclosure lies partly at least in the availability of wide pastures which meant that there was less need to use open arable for commoning livestock than in lowland areas. There was also plenty of land available for enclosure outside the common arable fields, and the habit of severalty farming may have taken root on the margin of cultivation and then spread to the core. However, all this should not be taken to mean that there was no piecemeal enclosure by tenants in lowland townships. Professor Beresford's glebe terriers (belonging mostly to the late seventeenth and eighteenth centuries) show that some glebes were farmed in severalty even in the lowland coal measures and the Vale of York. Occasionally we can observe enclosure going on in the sixteenth century: at Kippax between 1515 and 1519 seven tenants paid for licences to enclose small parcels amounting in all to six acres of arable and nine acres of meadow.[4] And when John Leland wandered through the southern part of Yorkshire around 1540 he found himself sometimes in 'champaine' country and

[1] P.R.O.: SC 12/19/7 (Dent), and *Yorkshire Deeds*, Y.A.S.R.S., lxxxiii, no. 371 (p. 126).
[2] P.R.O.: SC 6/Hen VIII/4356, 4254; and E 164/38/f. 80.
[3] M. W. Beresford: 'Glebe Terriers and the Open Fields in Yorkshire', *Y.A.J.*, xxxvii (1948–51), 325–68.
[4] P.R.O.: DL 29/515/8293.

sometimes going 'by much enclosed and meetly wooded ground'.[1] Nonetheless, open fields were the norm in lowland Yorkshire, and many of them were not broken up until after 1800.

Another communal element in peasant agriculture, besides common of pasture which was universal, was milling. Frequently it came under the prerogative of the manorial lord who exacted mulcture for the right to use his mill. Again there was a contrast between the highland and lowland zones. In the hill valleys, and as far down as Leeds and Wakefield, there were water mills to which men from the surrounding countryside had to bring their grain, and they were of no small value to the lords who owned them, as well as the millers who farmed them. To the south and east, where the land became flatter, windmills were more usual; but they for some reason did not yield anything like the high rents paid for watermills, and some were even in decay.[2]

The impression that in domanial agriculture choices were already being influenced by the market, and knowledge of the best economic use of land, can be supported by a certain amount of documentary evidence. Trade in agricultural produce cannot be studied systematically in any detail, but occasional clues to it can be found in the early Chancery Proceedings when specific contracts gave rise to litigation. The bailiff of the Abbot of Selby was sued by a Wakefield clothier or merchant in 1530 for failing to deliver a promised load of rye. In two other suits grain was being transported from Whitgift to Knottingley (both on the Aire) and from Barton-on-Humber (Lincolnshire) to Selby.[3] Very occasionally we get a glimpse of a producer for the market and his whole field of operations. When Thomas Tattersall, yeoman of Milnethorpe near Wakefield, was attainted for his part in the affair of 1541, a thorough inventory of his goods was made which also included information about his own debts and those owing to him. Several men in Wakefield, Thornes and Alverthorpe owed him money for oxen he had

[1] T. Brayshaw: 'The Yorkshire Portions of Leland's Itinerary' *Y.A.J.*, x (1889), 239–41.
[2] On watermills, cf. *infra*, p. 47; on windmills, see ministers' accounts, P.R.O.: DL 29/515/8293 and 549/8718.
[3] P.R.O.: C 1/606/71; C 1/635/37; C 1/1065/19.

sold them, for which they were paying in instalments; probably they were farmers and the oxen draught animals, which Tattersall seems to have reared for the market; similar enterprises no doubt catered for the demand for meat and leather in the towns.[1] The clothing area, the towns, and above all York, must have depended a great deal for their food and other needs on the agriculture of the surrounding country.

There is a certain amount of information about land-use on larger holdings or demesnes, and even the quantities of different crops which they grew. Most of it is contained in surveys and inventories made after the confiscation of land by the Crown: notably after the Dissolution of monastic houses, sometimes (as in Tattersall's case) after the attainder of a rebel. Table I gives some indication of the diversity of

TABLE I

Land Use on Some West Riding Demesnes, c. 1540.

Acres

Demesne	Arable	Meadow	Pasture	Total
Hampole Priory (1539)	337	24	271	632
Campsall (1537)	162	11	common only	173
Middleton (Wm. Legh, 1541)	102	13½	72½	188
Kirklees Priory (1539)	42	27	137	206
Haddockstones (Fountains Abb, 1540)	64	78	132	274
Bashall (N. Tempest, 1537)	c. 25	c. 30	c. 120	175
Airmyn (1542)	none	232	463	695
Roundhay: four tenants of Lord Darcy (1537)	none	none	1,060	1,060

	Wheat	Rye	Barley	Oats	Peas	Total
Hampole Priory (1536)	40	1	76	50	50	217
Middleton (1541)	13½	16¼	3	15	9	56¾
Kirklees Priory (1536)	3	7	—	10	—	20
Bashall (1537)	2½	—	2¾	20½	—	25¾

Sources: P.R.O.: SP 5/2/f. 185 (Hampole); DL 29/515/8293 (Campsall); E 315/171 (Middleton); E 315/401/195–7 and SP 5/2/ff. 191–2 (Kirklees); LR 2/254/ff. 247–55 (Bashall); E 318/290 (Airmyn); DL 43/11/16 (Roundhay); and Surtees Soc. xlii, p. 317 (Fountains: Haddockstones).

[1] P.R.O.: E 154/2/28. Chancery suits sometimes arose from the failure of butchers to pay for livestock, e.g. P.R.O.: C 1/329/9.

land use and crop production which these records reveal. If it can be called a pattern at all, the pattern is what we should expect from our knowledge of the physical environment: arable was most prominent in the rich central lowlands, much less so in the uplands, in the Ripon area (represented by Haddockstones), and in Marshland (e.g. Airmyn). As for crops, the largest arable demesne (Hampole) had the greatest diversity, though well paralleled by Middleton which is also situated in the best arable region. In the higher areas, wheat would grow less readily and there was a predominance of oats both at Kirklees and Bashall. If the table contains a surprise, it is at Roundhay which was a much less likely place for pasture than either Bashall or Airmyn. It had in fact once been a grange of Kirkstall Abbey and the monks used at least part of it for arable, for the 'ridge and furrow' of medieval ploughing can still be seen in the present Roundhay Park which belongs to Leeds Corporation. We do not know the date of the conversion to pasture, but clearly it was a deliberate act and was probably accompanied by the creation of the six large closes into which this land was divided by 1537.[1] Large farms were not always enclosed in the sixteenth century, though their strips may have been collected together in one part of each field. At Hampole, there were three large areas of arable, each between 110 and 120 acres in extent, and one of these was kept fallow, which explains why in 1536 only two-thirds of it was actually under crops. The same may have been true at Campsall; and at Middleton and Kirklees we can see that only half the arable was cropped in the years for which we have details. But fallowing need not mean that land was still open, for the resting of arable at intervals had more to do with availability of manure than with communal arrangements for cultivation. Thus at Kirklees the parcels have names which denote situations in a common field, such as Lyon-rode or Elleytree flatt, but the survey clearly designates them as closes and indeed some of the fields with names of this kind were now being used for pasture.

Thus far, the word 'enclosure' has been used without any hint of the controversy which surrounded it during the

[1] P.R.O.: DL 43/11/16.

reigns of Henry VIII and Edward VI. Enclosure itself was
a neutral thing; so too was the conversion of arable to
pasture. Both operations could take place on peasant land
or on the lord's acknowledged demesne without any dis-
turbance of other men's rights. Conflict was caused only
when changes were made, or attempted, involving the transfer of land from the small-holding sphere to the level of
domanial cultivation. For this was what happened whenever
a lord converted peasant arable to domanial pasture, or took
in large areas of common pasture for his own use.

In the fifteenth century, when population was lower than
it had once been, such transfers were easily accomplished.
Many peasant holdings had fallen vacant, and even where
peasants were evicted there was room for them to settle
elsewhere. Professor Beresford's thesis is that it was in these
conditions, accompanied by rising wool prices, that most of
the depopulation of medieval villages took place. It was not
until the early sixteenth century that the pressure on arable,
and likewise on common pastures, began to build up again
with a renewed growth of population. Only then did the
government intervene at all seriously, with Wolsey's statute
of 1515 and the county commissions appointed two years
later. By the time the net began to close, a new balance
between arable and pasture had already been struck in
regions such as the Yorkshire lowlands, and the returns
which the commissioners made provide only a marginal
picture of the transformation. The commissioners sat at
York Castle on the 3rd of October 1517 and heard twenty-
nine presentations for enclosure since 1489.[1] Eleven of
them involved only pasture and woodland and a twelfth
only three acres of arable, whilst one of the others was a
charge against the tenants of Aldborough that, as a body,
they had converted 180 acres of their arable to pasture. That
leaves us with sixteen cases, in which thirteen individual
land-owners were said to have enclosed and converted to
pasture just over 600 acres of arable and to have destroyed

[1] I. S. Leadam: 'The Inquisitions of 1517', *Trans. of Royal Hist. Soc.*, 2nd ser.,
vii (1893), 240–5, where the Yorkshire returns are printed, from B.M.: Lansdowne
MS L, no. 55. The serious limitations of the 1517 returns as a measure of enclosure
were discussed by E. Kerridge: 'The Returns of the Inquisition of Depopulation',
Eng. Hist. Rev., lxx (1955), 212–28.

twenty dwellings of husbandmen. They can be divided into four regional groups: half of them were in the vicinity of Leeds and Barwick-in-Elmet, the area where Lord Darcy had such extensive pastures at Roundhay, Temple Newsam and Rothwell; indeed Lord Darcy was the landlord in two of the presentations. Another five were in the lower Craven area, around Rimmington and Hammerton-in-Bolland, an area whose suitability for pastoral husbandry has already been emphasized more than once. Of the other three, two were not far from Wakefield, and one was far away from the rest at Thrybergh near Rotherham. In all these areas one can see good reasons why arable should be converted to pasture at this time, for Leeds, Wakefield and Rotherham were all prospering towns with an increasing need for meat and cheese. In the 1530s and 1540s we hear less of depopulation and more about pressure on common pastures. We shall have reason to look more closely at some of the conflicts (between landlord and tenant and between one landlord and another), which this pressure produced, when we come to discuss local politics in Chapter IV. It is enough at present to observe that these conflicts were not necessarily caused by a desire for more domanial pasture. In one case we are left in no doubt that the purpose for which a common was enclosed by the lord (the common was at Morley and Gildersome and the lord was Sir John Wentworth) was to plough it up to grow oats. The dispute was taken to court in 1543, and we may suppose that by then the demand for food in the nearby clothing district was great enough to warrant a reversal of the trend from arable to pasture.[1]

The theme of 'sheep eating men' is too well known to require emphasis here, and up to a point it provides an acceptable explanation for the creation of new pastures. But it is not the whole story. In a county which is famous amongst medieval economic historians for its monastic sheep flocks and the export of their wool, it is as well to bear in mind the importance of cattle both in the sixteenth century and before. A great many sheep were kept, but on some estates they were less numerous than cattle. That even goes for the Fountains Abbey estate, whose livestock were

[1] P.R.O.: DL 3/43/F.1.

counted in an inventory made sometime between 1516 and the dissolution and were found to include 2,356 cattle and only 1,326 sheep.[1] In the upper dales, there were areas largely devoted to cattle farming by such lords as the Archbishop of York, who had nine 'vaccariae' in Nidderdale in 1532, and the Earls of Northumberland who had what were termed 'loggia' in Langstrothdale Chase.[2]

IV

There were three areas of the West Riding where agriculture was supplemented as a source of income by industrial activity in the countryside. They were the woollen area between Wakefield, Leeds, Halifax and Bradford, where there was also some mining of coal and possibly of iron; secondly the cutlery district of Sheffield and Rotherham; and thirdly the lead-mining area on the moors between Ripon and Grassington. In addition, there were a few other towns which still had some textile crafts, notably Ripon; and throughout the Riding there were people engaged in such maintenance industries as building, woodwork and blacksmithery. In stone areas, and especially the magnesian limestone belt, we can add quarrying to the list. But not a great deal is known about these general activities; it is the rural industries which involved some measure of regional specialization that attract most attention. We can deal with them under the three heads of mining, metallurgy and textiles.

The location of mining was determined initially by the presence of minerals, and secondarily by the demand for metals and fuel. The most important mines in mid-sixteenth-century Yorkshire were those of lead, whose history has now been written by Dr. Rastrick and Mr. Jennings.[3] In Nidderdale and upper Wharfedale, the monasteries of Fountains, Byland and Bolton all had mineral rights over extensive tracts of land from the twelfth century onwards. Although there is little evidence about them in the Augmen-

[1] Printed (from the Vyner MSS) in Surtees Soc., xlii, pp. 294–5.
[2] P.R.O.: SC 6/Hen VIII/4409 and 4283.
[3] A. Rastrick and B. Jennings: *A History of Lead-Mines in the Pennines* (London 1965), esp. pp. 31–9 and 57–8; see also Maud Sellers: 'Medieval Mining and Smelting', *VCHY*, ii (1912).

tations accounts of these estates (made immediately after the
Dissolution), it would seem that they were still being worked
in the sixteenth century, mainly by lay farmers. For example
in 1554 there was a dispute between Avery or John Uvedale,
farmer of the former Byland Abbey mines in Nidderdale
since before the suppression, and Sir John York, purchaser
of the former monastic lands there.[1] Bolton Priory had similar rights in the lordship of Appletreewick, and in 1519 its
farmer of lead-mines there became embroiled in a dispute
with merchants at York. Farther up Wharfedale there is
evidence of fifteenth-century lead-mining at Grassington: a
document of 1484 relating to the dispute between Sir
Robert Plumpton and John Roecliffe indicates that before
being compelled by litigation to surrender the manor,
Plumpton had been mining lead there and probably also
smelting it.[2] The market for lead was not merely a local one.
A great deal of what was produced in Yorkshire found its
way to York, where the Fellowship of Merchants was trying
to secure a monopoly of all lead shipped out down the Ouse.
This brought it into conflict with both the men of Borough-
Bridge and those of Hull in the 1490s, and in 1502 we find
them complaining against the activity of the Abbot of
Fountains in buying and selling lead, which no spiritual man
ought to do. This trade in lead should be borne in mind when
we come (in Chapter VI) to the question of the sale of
monastic lead after the dissolution: that is, lead stripped
from the roofs of monastic buildings.

The iron ore deposits of the West Riding were more
widely distributed than those of lead but they were less
extensively mined: indeed less extensively in the sixteenth
century than had been the case in the thirteenth and fourteenth centuries. The monasteries had again played a leading
part in the mining and smelting of iron at that period. In
Nidderdale, Fountains and Byland Abbeys had the same
rights for iron as for lead; a little further to the south a
similar position was enjoyed by Bridlington Priory on the
edge of Knaresborough Forest. Fountains and Byland also
had mines and forges in the Huddersfield district, notably

[1] *Select Cases in the Court of Requests* (Selden Soc., xii, 1898), pp. 201–5.
[2] Skipton Castle MSS, Y.A.S. Library, Leeds: DD 121/112.

at Emley where the remains of 'bell-pits' can still be seen.[1] The monks of Rievaulx mined and smelted iron on their estate in Airedale, round Harden. There were also operations of this kind on the estates of the Percy, in the vicinity of Spofforth, and on those of de Lacy in the country round Leeds. But for some reason it had ceased to be profitable to exploit iron in the Riding by the sixteenth century; perhaps because new iron supplies of better quality or cheaper price were now available from elsewhere.

Coal-mining on the other hand continued to prosper. John Leland found at Rotherham that the people burnt 'much earth coal because it is plentifully found there and sold good cheap'.[2] The same was true of other parts of the coal measures, which as we have seen extended northwards to beyond Leeds. References to coal-pits are found in estate accounts from the thirteenth century onwards. In the 1540s some of them were leased at lower rents than formerly; but recovery came not long afterwards and is reflected by the increasing number of pits let out at higher rents from about 1575.[3] Since there was little demand for coal outside the locality where it was dug, the value of pits was geared very closely to levels of population, which in this area may not have quite recovered their thirteenth-century peak until the later part of Elizabeth's reign.

The main use of coal was for domestic fuel. Outside the coal measures country, that need had to be supplied by cutting down trees. There must have been a great deal more woodland in the lower-lying parts of the West Riding than survives to-day, although despite the existence of a number of very detailed timber surveys of the period, we have no means of estimating the overall extent of sixteenth-century woods. We can be equally sure in general, without being able to make precise measurement, that the amount of woodland was diminishing. We know for certain that in some cases purchasers of monastic property cut down timber in order to pay for the land they had just bought. We know

---

[1] D. A. Wray: *The Mining Industry in the Huddersfield District* (Huddersfield, 1929), and M. Sellers, as cited in note 3, p. 20.

[2] *Y.A.J.*, x (1889), 343–4.

[3] P.R.O.: DL 29/515/8292 and 520/8322.

too that in 1553 the citizens of York were sufficiently concerned about the disappearance of trees to instruct their members of Parliament to try to obtain an act forbidding the destruction of woods within a sixteen mile radius of the city. There must have been a good market for timber, which was used not just for fuel but also for building purposes both in houses and in ships. Nevertheless, concern about fuel bulked large in the thoughts of the York men, and they suggested that one factor in the drift of the textile industry away from the city to the Halifax–Wakefield–Leeds district was the presence of coal there, which meant abundant household fuel.[1]

Metallurgy was the speciality of the Don Valley towns, especially Rotherham, Sheffield, Hallam and Ecclesfield. The streams were used to drive cutlers' wheels, and in 1588 there were at least twenty of them on the estates of the Earls of Shrewsbury.[2] The Earls were prepared to encourage the industry and in 1565 granted the cutlers a series of ordinances which is sometimes referred to as their first charter. Unfortunately not a great deal is known about Hallamshire metallurgy at this period. There no doubt existed elaborate arrangements for the import of metal to the area, for its distribution amongst the various craftsmen and sale afterwards. But these activities have left no records, and we cannot tell how many people were involved, nor who made the most profit from them.

The source material is more helpful to the historian of the cloth industry, though here too there are many gaps in our knowledge which are never likely to be filled. The ground has been well covered by the work of Heaton,[3] and the fact is now well established that cloth manufacture grew up in the rural West Riding at the period when it began to decline in the city of York and other lowland towns: that is, the fifteenth century. The new pattern was beginning to establish itself by the period 1468–75, for which a number

---

[1] A. G. Dickens: 'Tudor York', *VCHY, City of York* (1961), p. 125. On the cutting down of monastic timber, cf. *infra*, p. 235.

[2] Sheffield City Library: ACMS, 117.

[3] H. Heaton: *The Yorkshire Woollen and Worsted Industries* (Oxford Historical and Literary Studies, x, 1920).

of aulnagers' accounts have survived. Despite the unreliability of this source, owing to the tendency for aulnagers to
repeat the figures of a previous year rather than make precise
returns for every account, it has some value as a record of the
relative importance of different aulnage centres at a particular
period. No more than this should be read into the figures of
Table II, and certainly no effort should be made to estimate
fluctuations of cloth production from year to year on the
basis of these accounts.[1]

TABLE II

*Numbers of Cloths recorded by Aulnage Centres at York and in
the West Riding, 1468–75.*[1]

Aulnage centre	1468–9 (46 weeks)	1473–5 (two years)	West Riding percentages 1468–9
Ripon	888	1,386½	33·5
Halifax	853	1,493½	32·0
Wakefield	231	160	8·75
Almondbury	160	427	6·0
Leeds	176¾	320	6·5
Bradford	88½	178½	3·5
Pontefract	106	214½	4·0
Barnsley	88½	142½	3·5
Doncaster	35½	35½	1·25
Selby	26½	19	1·0
WEST RIDING:	2,653¾	4,377	100·0
YORK CITY:	1,596	2,346½	—

The significance of this table is obvious enough. Moreover, the trend continued over the next century and more.
By 1502 cloth from Ripon, Knaresborough, Leeds, Bradford, Wakefield and Halifax was being marketed in York
itself. Gradually, Ripon and Knaresborough followed York
in losing their manufactures to the area further south. John
Leland's observation at Ripon that the tenters standing on
the south bank of the Skell denoted an industry which no
longer flourished, so that 'idleness is sore increased in the
town and cloth-making almost decayed', finds confirmation

---

[1] The figures in the table are based on Heaton, *op. cit.*, pp. 69–76. On the general
unreliability of the aulnage rolls, see E. M. Carus-Wilson: 'The Aulnage Accounts,
a Criticism', *Econ. Hist. Rev.*, ii (1929).

in an estate account of 1532 which says that several tenters were vacant for lack of tenants.[1] Another indication of the trend is the increase in the number of fulling mills in the area which prospered most, the Leeds–Wakefield–Halifax triangle. Leeds had only one fulling mill in 1425; by 1548 there were four, and by 1612 five.[2] About the middle of the sixteenth century there were over twenty-five fulling mills in three wapentakes of Agbrigg, Morley and Skyrack, ranging in rental value from a few shillings to over £3. This part of cloth production had probably been at one time a prerogative of the lord of the manor, like corn-grinding; but by now there was plenty of room for private enterprise. Fulling mills existed in other wapentakes (for example at Skipton and Giggleswick in Craven, and at Kimberworth near Rotherham), but they were smaller and less numerous. The effects of expansion in the Leeds–Halifax area were not felt only in York, Ripon and Selby, but also in other rural areas. At Knottingley and Hillam the fulling mills were no longer functioning at all in 1537, probably because there was no longer any reason to make cloth there.[3]

It is upon the Agbrigg–Morley–Skyrack district therefore that we must focus our attention. The most famous description of cloth manufacture there is contained in the preamble to the 'Halifax Act' of 1555 whose purpose was to permit in the vicinity of Halifax the activities of wool-dealers and other middlemen which had been generally forbidden by statute three years earlier. It was necessary because Halifax was an area where clothiers operated on a much smaller scale than in other counties, or even than in nearby Leeds. The act describes the town as 'planted in the great wastes and moors where the fertility of ground is not apt to bring forth any corn nor good grass but in rare places', and where the inhabitants 'altogether do live by cloth-making'. It asserts that within the past forty years the number of households there had risen by over 500, possibly an exaggeration but by no means impossible. These poor clothiers 'neither getteth corn nor [are] able to keep a horse

---

[1] *Y.A.J.*, x (1889), p. 332; and P.R.O.: SC 6/Hen VIII/4409.
[2] P.R.O.: DL 42/106, and Gascoigne Coll., Leeds City Library: GC/DL/9.
[3] P.R.O.: DL 29/515/8293.

to carry wool, nor yet to buy much wool at once, but have
ever used only to repair to the town of Halifax'. Their depen-
dence on middlemen was consequently inevitable.[1] Heaton
commented on the differences in organization and size of
enterprise between Halifax area and the country round
Leeds, where clothiers sometimes employed journeymen
and had larger quantities of stock in hand. A description of
requirements of cloth making, believed to date from about
1588, seems to contain part of the explanation: namely that
Leeds methods of production were different from those
followed round Halifax. For in the former place they made
broadcloths and in the latter kerseys.[2] It is a pity that we
cannot probe deeper and explain how this specialization
arose.

The number of people working at cloth production in the
West Riding at this time cannot be satisfactorily estimated.
Some in any case were not engaged in it full-time, having
parcels of land to cultivate as well. The only clue of any kind
is a list, drawn up sometime in the 1530s, of offenders against
the laws which prohibited 'flocking' of cloth. It is mutilated,
but the surviving parts contain 542 names of people described as 'clothier'. Over half belonged to the parishes of
Halifax, Heptonstall and Elland; the rest were scattered
amongst ten others, including Huddersfield, Almondbury,
Dewsbury, Wakefield, Leeds and Bradford.[3] Five hundred
and forty-two households would have meant something like
2,500 or more people; but this was probably only a fraction
of the total number who were in some way dependent on
cloth making for their livelihood. There were probably a
good many people who specialized in a particular branch of
the industry and who worked for others, being described
as 'weaver' or 'shearman' rather than 'clothier'. One such
man figures in Professor Dickens' study of early Yorkshire
protestantism: William Bull, a local man who lived at

[1] *Statutes*, iv, 2 & 3 Phil. and Mary, cap. 13, which is partly reproduced in R. H.
Tawney and E. Power: *Tudor Economic Documents* (London, 1924), i. 187. The
Act refers to the clothiers of the parish, not just the township, of Halifax.
[2] Historical MSS Comm.: *14th Report*, iv, pp. 572–3: a document in the Kenyon
MSS.
[3] P.R.O.: E 101/345/25. The list may possibly be related to the commission
appointed to deal with 'flocking' in Yorkshire in 1533, *L.P.*, VI, no. 1211.

Dewsbury in 1543 when he was called up before the
Archbishop of York to answer for his heretical opinions; but
who had learnt his craft of shearman as an apprentice far
away in Suffolk.[1]

The degree of regional specialization represented by the
cloth industry of Halifax, Wakefield and Leeds depended
of course on trade. The Chancery files referred to in connection with agricultural marketing sometimes also throw light
on trade in manufactured produce or in raw materials. One
case shows William Armitage of Almondbury buying wool
in Derbyshire; it is quite likely that much of the raw wool
used in the West Riding industry came from outside the
cloth area itself. In another case we find John Rokesby, a
Wakefield dyer, purchasing woad from merchants in Hull
and so running foul of Richard Pymond, a powerful
merchant of his own town who had formerly supplied him
and now sued for payment.[2] As for the sale of West Riding
cloth, we have already seen it being bought in York in 1502,
and probably much of what was made went to clothing the
townsmen of that and other northern centres. But there was
also some cloth exported from the port of Hull, and this in
all likelihood came from the West Riding. In the period
1530–45 Hull sent overseas between 475 and 1,025 cloths
a year; in an average year about 685.[3] These figures are
much lower than those recorded for several years around the
turn of the century, when 2,500 or more cloths would pass
through the port in a good year. Perhaps the decline was due
to the expansion of London, whose merchants were tending
to draw trade away from smaller places at this period, rather
than to any decline in the output of Yorkshire. Certainly by
the middle decades of the century we find Yorkshire clothiers
selling part of their produce in London. Some of them had
booths at St. Bartholomew's Fair; and in 1561–2 a list of
clothiers fined for selling defective cloths at Blackwell Hall
included five Yorkshiremen, all selling what the Londoners
called 'Penistone dozens'.[4] We cannot tell what proportion

[1] A. G. Dickens: *Lollards and Protestants in the Diocese of York* (Oxford, 1959), 48–9.
[2] P.R.O.: C 1/746/31, and C 1/708/38.
[3] Cf. *infra*, pp. 35–7 and Table IV.
[4] G. D. Ramsey: 'The Distribution of the Cloth Industry in 1561–2', *Eng. Hist. Rev.*, lvii (1942), 361–9.

of West Riding cloth was exported, whether through Hull or through London, but the wider the market for it the greater the region's sensitivity to fluctuations in the overall demand for English cloth.

It is much to be regretted that we cannot build up any coherent overall picture of trading activity within the Riding at this period. Private trading is hinted at by a very small number of lawsuits, but quite impossible to quantify. As for trading in markets, we have no records of what went on there, not even of disputes in courts of 'pie-powder'. All that can be said is that certain places had markets and that some trade took place under their aegis whilst other trade was carried on outside them. There were about thirty markets in the West Riding in this period and a slightly larger number of fairs: that is, about one for every twenty townships.[1] Many of them were of local importance only, though they would be visited by pedlars who travelled up and down the country. Others were large enough to attract purchasers form farther afield. Ripon's horsefair for example was known throughout England and was visited by such people as Sir Anthony Fitzherbert, itinerant justice and author of the *Book of Husbandry*.[2] Even more important were the markets and fairs of York, which had two markets a week and a fair every fortnight. Apart from these, the largest markets were presumably those of the cloth area (Wakefield, Halifax, Leeds), of the cutlery area (especially Rotherham), and of the chartered boroughs of Doncaster and Pontefract.

V

Let us return now to the suggestion that in the century before 1540 there was a more noticeable expansion of population in the upland than in the lowland zone. The evidence just considered, relating to various sectors of the economy of the Riding, does not provide any clear answer to the question—except that it shows industrial expansion in one part of the

[1] K. L. McKutcheon: *Yorkshire Fairs and Markets* (Thoresby Soc., xxxix, 1940), Appendix I.

[2] J. E. Thorold Rogers: *A History of Agriculture and Prices in England*, iv (London, 1882), p. 53.

upland zone. But it does enable us to interpret another category of evidence which we can use to measure very roughly the geographical distribution of wealth: namely the records of yields from taxation. Two sets of such figures have been analysed in Table III. Those for 1334 are derived from the tax-quotas fixed in that year for the townships of each wapentake, which were maintained as the basis for the 'fifteenths and tenths' granted by Parliament to the King over the next two centuries or so. Under the earlier Tudors this kind of taxation was supplemented, then superseded, by the subsidy, a tax levied on the value of men's lands or of their goods. The figures for 1543–7 are based on the recorded tax-yields arising from the subsidy statutes of 1543

TABLE III

Regional Pattern of Tax Yields in the West Riding, 1334 and 1543–7.

Wapentakes	Percentage of total area of W.R.	Fifteenth yield in 1334	Subsidy yield in 1543–7
Strafforth and Tickhill	16%	£156 (21·4%)	£898 (12·5%)
Staincross and Osgoldcross	11%	£155 (21·3%)	£910 (12·7%)
Agbrigg and Morley	18%	£81 (11·1%)	£2,437 (34·0%)
Skyrack	6%	£56 (7·8%)	£599 (8·3%)
Barkston and the Ainsty	8%	£122 (16·3%)	£663[a] (9·2%)
Claro, Ripon and Knaresborough	15%	£89[b] (12·3%)	£857 (11·8%)
Staincliffe and Ewcross	26%	£71 (9·7%)	£812 (11·2%)
WEST RIDING	100%	£730 (100%)	£7,176 (100%)

Notes: [a] This figure is for Barkston alone, since the figures for the Ainsty are inseparable from those for York at this date.
[b] This figure represents a fifteenth of the total valuation, although in fact part of the area (the liberty of Knaresborough) contributed a 'tenth'.

Sources: The figures for 1334 are from a book compiled in 1415, but recording quotas fixed in that year: P.R.O.: E 164/7/ff. 282–95. For the figures for 1543–7, I am indebted to Dr. R. S. Schofield, who abstracted them from P.R.O.: Enrolled Subsidy Accounts, E 359/38, 41–2, 44.

and 1545. The object of the analysis was to show what proportion of the total West Riding yields at these different dates came from each of its twelve wapentakes. (It was necessary in practice to present the results of the analysis in terms of seven areas, since some wapentakes could not be taken separately in both years. The seven divisions of the table are shown in Map II.)

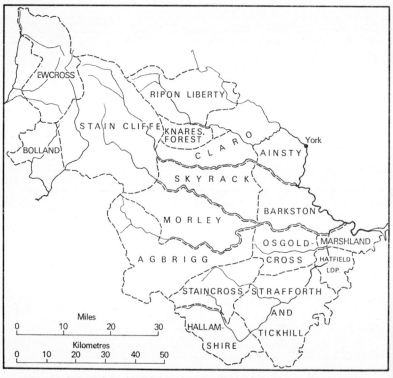

Map II. Administrative divisions and sub-divisions of the West Riding

The table also gives the percentage of the Riding's total area covered by each of the seven divisions. It is thus possible both to relate the proportions of the total tax-yields to the percentages of total area, and to observe how the pattern changed in the interval between 1334 and 1543–5. In the fourteenth century the tax-proportions followed the pattern one would expect, assuming that the lowlands were richer and more densely populated than the uplands. In Strafforth and Tickhill, in Osgoldcross and Staincross, and Barkston and the Ainsty, proportions of the tax-yield were much higher than proportions of total area; in Agbrigg and Morley, and in Staincliffe and Ewcross, proportions of total area were rather high, whilst in Skyrack and in Claro the two proportions were roughly even. But when one looks at the figures for the sixteenth century one finds that things have changed: the whole pattern has been disrupted by the remarkable position now occupied by Agbrigg and Morley, which contributed over a third of the total tax-yield, although it amounted to less than a fifth of the total area of the Riding. This change was accompanied by an equally striking decline in the proportions contributed by Osgoldcross and Staincross and by Strafforth and Tickhill. The other divisions made roughly the same contributions as before, with a slight rise in two cases: Skyrack and Stain-cliffe–Ewcross. The figure for Barkston cannot be compared with that for Barkston and the Ainsty in 1334, but it seems unlikely that there was a very serious fall in its proportion.

The shift in the distribution of wealth which these comparisons denote cannot be doubted. Nor is it very difficult to explain, for the interval between the two dates saw the growth of the cloth industry, in Agbrigg and Morley wapentakes, and to a more limited extent in Skyrack. There must indeed have been an increase in both wealth and population there, as the authors of the Halifax Act described. The other upland areas also held their own, which could mean that they experienced an increase in population without necessarily any increase in wealth per head. The most difficult feature to explain is the contrast between Barkston and the Ainsty on the one hand, and the more southerly lowland areas on the other. For it was the latter which experienced a serious decline in prosperity, which was most strongly marked of all in the wapentake of Osgoldcross. That division amounted to a mere 6·5 per cent of the West Riding's acreage, yet in 1334 it contributed 16 per cent of the 'fifteenth'. The two most important places in Osgoldcross were Pontefract and Snaith; whilst the former shows no obvious signs of decline at this period, we

4

have already seen that at Snaith there was a marked con-
traction of the acreage under arable cultivation, for want of
tenants. The value of the market and tolls of Snaith also
declined: they had been farmed out for £16 in 1420, but in
1540 they brought in a mere £1. 6s. 8d.[1] One possible interpretation, though we should need more evidence to be
certain of it, is that in this south-east corner of the Riding
the pressure of population became too great in the fourteenth
century, and that in the fifteenth century there was a
tendency to move away from the area. We need not suppose
that utter disaster struck Osgoldcross and that it was the
scene of widespread famine and disease; it simply ceased to
be the focus of economic development and trade. It may have
shared this fate with parts of nearby Lincolnshire, where
similar evidence has been found of abandonment and decay.

The situation in Barkston and the Ainsty was probably
less unhappy, perhaps because the population density of the
fourteenth century was less great in relation to the quality of
the soil. An important factor in the economy of this region
was its proximity to York. Dr. J. N. Bartlett's analysis of
the economy of York in the later middle ages led him to
conclude that the city's prosperity reached a peak soon after
1400, and that there followed a decline during the next 100
years or more.[2] Professor Dickens confirmed the impression
that the decline continued into the sixteenth century,
although he also pointed out that whilst weaving and
spinning suffered seriously from the competition of the
West Riding clothiers, other crafts such as garment-making
and tanning were expanding.[3] It may well have been the
mercantile element which suffered most seriously at this
period, and it was they who were no doubt behind the city's
loud lamentations that its prosperity was waning. They
probably lost ground not only because of what was happening in York itself but also because of Hull's loss of trade to
London, already alluded to above. Nonetheless, York still
had a sizeable population; Professor Dickens places it at

[1] P.R.O.: DL 29/550/8722.
[2] J. N. Bartlett: 'The Expansion and Decline of York in the Later Middle Ages',
Econ. Hist. Rev. 2nd ser. xii (1960).
[3] A. G. Dickens: 'Tudor York' in VCHY, City of York, p. 127.

over 10,000 in 1549. These people still had to be fed, and as far as Barkston and the Ainsty were concerned this would mean a continuing demand for agricultural produce.

VI

Long-term change has for long been a concern of economic historians, but the short-term fluctuations which are so important in an agrarian society have only much more recently received the attention of writers on sixteenth-century England. It is not at all easy to reconstruct changes from year to year, either for the country as a whole or for a single county. There are four elements of the economy which must be taken into account: first, demographic statistics and particularly the numbers of births and deaths; second, the effects of weather upon harvests and food prices; third, the volume of trade and especially the level of demand for exported produce; and lastly, the volume and flow of currency which was closely related to the distribution of income. In the demographic field Dr. Laslett has set forth the hypothesis that pre-industrial England had a cycle of population change which, though the long-term trend was one of gradual increase, would mean that growth was punctuated by periodic crises when mortality temporarily exceeded fertility.[1] The primary cause of these crises is thought to have been the weather: if there were two or three bad harvests running, the price of bread would be driven up and widespread disease and famine would follow. In areas of rural industry this pattern might sometimes be complicated by changes in the demand for cloth.

Fluctuations in the price of bread and in the volume of exports have been the subject of a number of recent books and articles, and enough calculations have been made for us to try to gauge some of the fluctuations which affected the West Riding in the time of Henry VIII. Table IV represents an attempt to bring some of this information together, to see if any significant pattern emerges; it covers the period 1515–53, in order to include several years on either side of the period which is our main concern. The information about

---

[1] P. Laslett: 'Did the Peasants really Starve?' *The Listener*, 1 March 1962.

TABLE IV

Fluctuations in Prices, Trade and Mortality in England and in the West Riding, 1515–53.

Year[a]	Harvest in south	Price index (1451–75 = 100)	Cloths exported: (i) London ('000s)	Cloths exported: (ii) Hull ('00s)	Morley[b] vital statistics	References to disease
1515–16	Ave.	110	—	—	—	—
1516–17	Good	111	—	—	—	Ewcross wapentake
1517–18	Good	116	—	—	—	—
1518–19	Good	129	65	13·5	—	—
1519–20	Defic.	137	67	9·8	—	—
1520–1	Dearth	167	54	10·4	—	—
1521–2	Bad	160	50	2·9	—	—
1522–3	Good	136	57	4·1	—	—
1523–4	Good	133	69	10·2	—	—
1524–5	Good	129	79	11·4	—	—
1525–6	Good	133	70	6·5	—	—
1526–7	Good	147	71	12·3	—	—
1527–8	Dearth	179	81	14·2	—	—
1528–9	Bad	159	75	12·3	—	—
1529–30	Defic.	169	71	10·6	—	—
1530–1	Good	154	65	4·8	—	—
1531–2	Ave.	179	62	5·5	—	—
1532–3	Ave.	169	83	4·8	—	—
1533–4	Ave.	145	89	8·7	—	—
1534–5	Good	131	78	4·9	—	—
1535–6	Bad	164	91	8·1	—	—
1536–7	Ave.	155	86	8·2	—	—
1537–8	Abund.	138	85	7·1	—	—
1538–9	Abund.	147	97	6·2	—	—
1539–40	Abund.	158	100	6·9	—	—
1540–1	Good	165	110	6·7	+ 215	—
1541–2	Good	172	97	8·2	+ 265	Foulby, Wragby
1542–3	Good	171	71	6·7	+ 95	—
1543–4	Ave.	178	119	10·2	+ 156	—
1544–5	Ave.	190	—	—	+ 124	—
1545–6	Bad	248	(118)[c]	—	+ 53	—
1546–7	Abund.	231	(118)	—	+ 106	—
1547–8	Abund.	193	—	—	+ 138	—
1548–9	Abund.	214	—	—	+ 239	—
1549–50	Defic.	262	—	—	+ 238	—
1550–1	Bad	285	132	—	+ 152	York
1551–2	Bad	276	112	—	+ 163	Halifax, York
1552–3	Good	259	85	—	+ 267	—

Notes: [a] Harvest information relates to the first year given. The cloth export figures are for years from Michaelmas to Michaelmas. The Morley vital statistics relate to years from March to March.
  [b] Excess of births over deaths recorded in parish registers.
  [c] Average for the years 1545–7.
The sources are cited in the text.

harvests and prices (the latter not merely of food) has been taken from studies by Professor Hoskins and by Professor Phelps Brown and Miss Hopkins.[1] Unfortunately it relates entirely to the southern counties; so far it has not proved possible to produce comparable figures using materials drawn solely from northern England, but as we shall see the Hull customs accounts may occasionally help us to discover differences of harvest quality between the North and the South. The next two columns of the table are derived from the compilation by Professor Carus-Wilson and Miss Coleman of cloth exports recorded in the customs accounts for various ports.[2] These figures may not be a wholly accurate representation of the volume of trade, but they deserve, nonetheless, to be given consideration. Finally the table includes figures for the excess of births over deaths in Morley wapentake, as estimated from the parish registers of Halifax Parish by Mr. M. Drake.[3] That author has made a full study of the registers of the wapentakes of Morley and Agbrigg, and in the second half of the sixteenth century he found clear evidence of demographic crises in the years 1557–8, 1587–8 and 1596–8. It is most unfortunate that this kind of analysis is possible only on the basis of parish registers, which were not effectively instituted in England before 1538 and often survive only from an even later date. Nevertheless, as we shall see, such evidence as there is fits in very well with Dr. Laslett's hypothesis; and in all likelihood the same sort of pattern existed before 1540.

Professor Hoskins' assessment of the quality of southern harvests shows three series of years when harvests were persistently inadequate: 1519–21, 1527–30 and 1549–51; there were also isolated bad years in 1535 and 1545. Since we know nothing about grain storage in this period, we cannot tell at what point the shortage of bread became acute,

[1] W. G. Hoskins: 'Harvest Fluctuations and English Economic History 1480–1619', *Agric. Hist. Rev.*, xii (1964), 28–46; and E. H. Phelps Brown and S. V. Hopkins: 'Seven Centuries of the Price of Consumables compared with Builders' Wage-Rates', *Economica*, n.s. xxiii (1963).
[2] E. M. Carus-Wilson and Olive Coleman: *England's Export Trade 1275–1547* (Oxford, 1963), pp. 114–19.
[3] M. Drake: 'An Elementary Exercise in Parish Register Demography', *Econ. Hist. Rev.*, 2nd ser., xiv (1961–2), 427–45.

but after two bad harvests the scarcity must have become very apparent. We do, however, know a little about the way in which grain was moved about the country, or even imported from abroad, thanks to the work of N. S. B. Gras.[1] He has published, amongst a wealth of statistics, series of figures showing the import and export of corn in the northern ports of Hull and Newcastle, which we can use to test whether there was any difference between the northern and the southern harvest. Customs records exist for these ports only in certain years, so the figures cannot be meaningfully tabulated; but it seems very likely that the situation recorded in the years 1521–2, 1531–2, and 1540–1, when there were neither imports nor exports of corn at Hull, was the more normal state of affairs. Corn would be moved only for special reasons. In several cases the customs evidence ties in very neatly with Professor Hoskins' results. In 1519, 1,450 quarters of corn were imported into Hull (and none exported), suggesting that Yorkshire fared even worse than the south in that year; again in 1529–30 Newcastle drew on supplies of corn from outside to the extent of 885 quarters. In the 1540s, there are signs of greater divergence between north and south. The import of 5,385 quarters into Newcastle in the two years 1543–5 was probably connected with the war against Scotland, though it may signify that owing to shortage of grain in the north itself the army had to depend to a greater extent than usual on supplies from further afield. But this can hardly be the explanation for the import of 2,648 quarters of corn into Hull in 1541–2, when the harvest elsewhere seems to have been good. The possibility that this import had some connection with the royal visit to the north in 1541 cannot be dismissed; but a bad northern harvest seems the likeliest explanation. And indeed the mortality evidence of 1541–2 also points towards a serious food shortage. We have already seen that the villages of Foulby and Wragby were decimated by plague at this time and may have experienced a permanent shrinkage of population as a result. And in Morley wapentake (that is, Halifax Parish) the year which began in March 1542 saw

[1] N. S. B. Gras: *The Evolution of the English Corn Market* (Harvard, 1926), pp. 274–5, p. 277, p. 287, p. 291.

a sudden drop in the excess of baptisms over burials. A similar fall coincided with the bad harvest and steep price rise of 1545–6; and another fall occurred in 1550–1. Moreover in the latter year and the following one we have reports of plague at York and in Halifax itself. So far as it goes, this evidence seems to confirm Dr. Laslett's general theory.

The fluctuations in cloth exports are at first sight less easily interpreted. Mr. Drake's theory that demand for cloth affected mortality in the West Riding relates chiefly to home demand, which was closely geared to harvest experience and prices. External demand may, of course, have been influenced by Continental harvest conditions, but was also bound up with prices and finance. Thus Professor Fisher attributed the sudden slump in London's cloth exports to Antwerp in the years 1551–3, to the effect on exchange rates and international prices of Henry VIII's depreciation of currency.[1] Table IV, however, suggests another possible correlation: between harvests and food prices on one hand, and productivity in the textile industry on the other. It shows four periods when cloth exports seem to have dropped suddenly from one year to the next: 1519–21, 1529–31 (more noticeable at Hull than London), 1541–3, and 1550–2. Each of these falls happened shortly after a serious food crisis, which on three occasions was general, and on one occasion was limited to the north. Might it not be that one of the consequences of food shortage was a reduction in cloth *output*, which would inevitably mean that less was available for export and possibly also that the price of cloth was increased? The canvas of the West Riding is too small to test this hypothesis, and it must wait further research.

The fourth element in short-term economic change, the volume and flow of currency, does not lend itself to representation in hard figures: it is quite out of the question to compile statistics for the total amount of money in circulation at different dates, in an area as small as the West Riding. Polydore Vergil attributed opposition to taxation in

---

[1] F. J. Fisher: 'Commercial Trends and Policy in Sixteenth-Century England', *Econ. Hist. Rev.*, x (1939–40), 95–117.

Staincliffe wapentake in 1513 to the scarcity of money there, but whilst this can be taken as a possible sign that Craven had a less ample coinage than most parts of England, the observation is not necessarily applicable to the West Riding as a whole.[1] The evidence concerning trade presented earlier implies that money was an essential feature of the economy, and there are other documentary references to coinage. One unhappy man, probably from the Wakefield area, was in 1534 languishing in York Castle charged with making his own gold coins.[2] Less melodramatic information is supplied by the inventories of people who had saved money in the form of coin or plate. Thomas Tattersall of Milnthorpe, whose cattle-dealing was cited earlier, left behind him in 1541 a silver salter and cover, three goblets, three 'massors', a taster and twenty-five spoons. A more spectacular example of hoarding comes from Halifax, where the vicar, Dr. Robert Haldsworth, kept a pot of gold coins under his stair worth about £800: a fact which came to light in 1536 when the vicarage was occupied by rebels and the pot was found, and alleged to be treasure trove, to the vicar's discomfiture.[3] Another aspect of the flow of money was credit, whose importance for peasant farmers was frequently asserted by R. H. Tawney. It too enters the records only when something went wrong and litigation arose. For example in 1543 Thomas Smith, a chantry-priest of Aldborough, lent the sum of £3. 1s. 4d. to William Storrey, a Boroughbridge yeoman; he had still not repaid it when the priest died, and had to be sued for it by his executors.[4] Despite the canon laws against usury, priests were probably a not infrequent source of credit for ordinary men. Canon Purvis in his burrowings amongst the consistory court records at York found a case of 1455 where Nicholas Ledys, parson of York Minster, was hauled up on a charge of usury, for lending money to two men of the city who bought and sold oak trees.[5] Credit was probably a much more important factor in the flow of money than is reflected

---

[1] Cf. *infra*, p. 199, note 1.
[2] Referred to in a Star Chamber suit, Y.A.S.R.S. xli, pp. 189–92.
[3] *L.P.*, XII (ii), 316, 339, 369.
[4] P.R.O.: C 1/1143/22.
[5] J. S. Purvis: *A Medieval Act Book* (n.d.), p. 54.

by the tiny number of documentary references, and the rare cases which concern ordinary people are therefore more interesting than the borrowing of substantial landowners, who would have both a greater need for cash and at the same time land to mortgage in order to obtain it. We shall meet with the latter kind of transaction again in Chapter VI.

The volume and flow of money was likely to have effects of the greatest importance on both prices and the level of employment. It is well known that increases in the quantity of money flowing through Europe in the sixteenth century were a major cause of inflation. What is less often noticed is that a reduction in the supply of coin would, in conditions such as those of sixteenth-century Yorkshire, have the effect of reducing the level of employment. If there was plenty of money, and if it was in the hands of people willing to spend it, there would be a continuing demand for goods of all kinds. But if the supply of cash was for any reason reduced, demand for goods would decline and those who produced for the market would begin to suffer a loss of income. We have here an explanation for one of the greatest economic fears expressed by Yorkshiremen of Henry VIII's time: the fear that the Dissolution of the monasteries and the confiscation of their lands would diminish the level of expenditure of goods and services within the county, because large sums would now be paid in rent to the King in London. Robert Aske was amongst those who argued thus, at the time of the Pilgrimage of Grace in 1536. One of his reasons for demanding restoration of the monasteries was the hard economic fact that without them 'there should be no money or treasure in those parts, neither the tenant to have to pay his rents nor the lord to have money to do the king's service withal. For so much as in those parts was neither the presence of his Grace, execution of his laws, nor yet but little recourse of merchandise'.[1] This was said when only a few of the smaller monasteries were being dissolved; but Aske may have already envisaged the wider measure of dissolution that was later to follow. The complaint probably became even louder, though the Commons were subsequently too cowed to rebel, when those further suppressions

[1] Aske's confession, April 1537, printed in *Eng. Hist. Rev.*, v (1890), 336.

actually took place. Five years later, in May 1541, Ambassador Chapuys reported to the Queen of Hungary regarding the King's projected visit to Yorkshire: 'it appears that the chief grievance of which the people in the north complain is that there is no currency among them in consequence of the king having seized the rentals not only of the abbeys and monasteries in those provinces but likewise those of the principal lords in the land, like Northumberland and various others, by which means all the money which circulated in the northern counties now comes to this city of London'.[1] A like observation was being made as late as 1549, when Sir Thomas Smith wrote his *Discourse of the Common Weal*.[2] He added the further comment that when confiscated lands came up for purchase, yet more money was transferred from the counties to London by those who were prosperous enough to buy them.

The monasteries of the West Riding had constituted an important source of demand for goods, as well as employing a certain amount of labour and making frequent doles of alms to the poor; they may also have been money-lenders, though we have no definite evidence of that. The first dissolution statute, passed in 1536, laid down that laymen who received leases or grants of monastic sites must 'keep or cause to be kept an honest continual household on the same site or precinct and to occupy yearly as much of the same demesnes in ploughing and tillage of husbandry' as had been usual before the suppression.[3] But if this demonstrates the Government's awareness of the problem, it does not mean that it was solved. There may have been some attempt to enforce the statute, but West Riding evidence suggests that it was ineffective. In any case, farmers and purchasers of monastic demesnes only seldom acquired the whole estate of the same house, and often they were not rich enough to maintain the same scale of expenditure as the monastic households. In this respect, Aske's fears would seem to have been fulfilled. As for monastic charity,

---

[1] *Calendar of State Papers, Spanish*, IV (i), no. 163; cf. *infra*, p. 210.
[2] *A Discourse of the Common Weal of this Realm of England*, ed. E. Lamond London, 1893), p. 85; a work previously attributed to John Hales.
[3] *Statutes*, iii, 27 Hen. VIII, cap. 28.

Professor Jordan is convinced that the disappearance of the monasteries was followed by a crisis of poverty in Yorkshire during the years after 1540.[1] Although his argument may be oversimplified, it was sadly ironic that the event which reduced the level of expenditure, and therefore of income, at one and the same time removed one of the greatest bulwarks against destitution.

The evidence does not, however, all point in one direction. Three factors at least, all operating during the 1540s, must have mitigated the effects of the suppression on the supply of money. First, we have seen that some men had hoarded up plate and coin before 1536, and it is possible that some of this idle money was brought out into the open during the period of greatest scarcity, even if much of it went to purchase land at the court of Augmentations in London. Secondly, we must not forget that the King confiscated lands and sold them again largely because he needed money, and having collected his rents he must have immediately spent them on political adventures. These included the war against Scotland, which called forth both men and supplies from many parts of England, including Yorkshire. Some of the money that was once spent by monks now found its way into the pockets of soldiers returning from the Borders, or into those of farmers who supplied grain or cattle to the army. The third factor was the inflation which took place during the 1540s, and which meant that even in good years agricultural and other prices were higher than they had been in the early years of the reign. The trend is indicated clearly by Table IV. It is very likely that a consequence of this inflation was a subtle but cumulative redistribution of income between those who cultivated the land and sold produce, and those who drew rents from it. For whilst prices rose from one decade to the next, bringing an immediate increase in income to the farmer, rents could not always be raised so quickly, and could often only be raised at all by using the device of higher entry fines at each change of tenant. This transfer of income probably operated as much on royal as on private estates, and meant that more of the

[1] W. K. Jordan: *The Charities of Rural England 1480–1660* (London, 1961), p. 227.

income generated by land was available for local expenditure, and less was taken to London by the King's officials, or saved in coffers by large landowners. And small men would, moreover, spend their income on better food and more clothes, better houses and more rooms, rather than on luxuries manufactured in London or imported from abroad. This factor, like so much else in the West Riding economy around 1540, is impossible to measure. But in time it alone would serve to reverse the effects of the dissolution on the flow of money.

II

LORDSHIP, PROPERTY AND LANDED INCOME ON THE EVE OF THE REFORMATION

I

THE diversity of patterns of control over the land in different kinds of agrarian society cannot be explained in any facile way, for example as the result of environmental differences or of contrasting types of economy. It has roots deep in the past, and it is only by exploring the past that we can hope to understand the peculiarities of a particular region at a given date. The kind of control over land most familiar to modern minds is one in which estates, of varying sizes, are owned by individuals, family trusts, or corporations, each estate yielding a money income to its owner. Such a situation existed in England by the second half of the seventeenth century, when John Locke wrote his classic defence of property as a natural right. By then a man was readily understood to be either the owner of his land or a tenant, either its occupier or a landlord. But not all societies have been dominated by those concepts, and even in the England of Henry VIII they were still not clearly established as the only way of thinking about men's relationship to the land. The pattern of that time was still in transition, from a state of affairs which had once been quite different. If we go back to the twelfth century we find a pattern whose dominant concepts were not ownership and income, rents and profits, but rather lordship, tenure, and service. The whole land of England was then divided into units of lordship in each of which a feudal lord exercised rights to services, renders in kind, and some revenues in money, over people who were to some extent his subjects, not just his tenants. The lordship, much larger than a manor or village, was the most fundamental element in the control over land in medieval Yorkshire. It can be distinguished from the estate

(a unit of ownership) by the fact that it involved rights of
jurisdiction over people as well as rights over the land itself.

In its medieval form the lordship, sometimes called an
honour or barony, sometimes a soke or liberty, comprised a
focal township (often with a castle), surrounded by a number
of lesser towns or villages (or manors) which were in some
way or other its dependencies. The structure is well illustrated by the Honour of Knaresborough, sometimes known
as the Soke and Forest, sometimes as the Liberty of Knaresborough, which belonged in the sixteenth century to the
Crown. Its administrative centre was the town of that name,
with a castle whose ruins still dominate the place, and with
its honorial court and the office of the receiver of revenues.
The Soke of Knaresborough (which included what had
once been the lordship of Aldborough) covered seventeen
townships.[1] Of these, five were kept 'in hand' by the lord,
which meant that their customary tenants paid their dues
directly to the chief lord of the whole Honour, and owed suit
to his local courts and mills. The other twelve townships
for the most part belonged to 'mesne lords', holding manors
from the chief lord by military tenure or in socage: in these
cases the dues and suit of court of the customary tenants
were owed to the mesne lord. By the sixteenth century there
were considerable differences of social status between these
mesne lords: some were peers or knights, whilst others were
merely small gentlemen with no importance outside their
own district. As for the Forest of Knaresborough, it too
included seventeen townships or villages, of which all but
two were kept in hand by the chief lord; the two exceptions
were both held by religious houses. The Forest townships
were all relatively thinly populated, a reflection of the fact
that they were situated in an area whose natural poverty
made it a suitable choice for a hunting-ground of the
medieval lord. In the sixteenth century the area included

---

[1] The description which follows is based on estate records of the 1530s: P.R.O.:
DL 29/475/7693 etc. and 485/7835 etc. The term 'soke' is a pre-Norman word for
an extensive territorial lordship, defined in terms of the lord's right to hold his
court. For a description of a comparable medieval lordship in Lancashire, at an
earlier period, see R. B. Smith: *Blackburnshire: a Study in Early Lancashire History*
(Occasional Papers in English Local History no. 15, Leicester University Press,
1961).

three large parks, Bilton, Haya and Haveragh, and the last of these had a hunting-lodge whose vestiges are still known as 'John o' Gaunt's Castle'. Not all the fifty or so lordships of the medieval West Riding had all the features of Knaresborough; but all had an administrative centre and a number of dependencies. Moreover, it was very often the centres of lordships which were still the most important towns in the sixteenth century. Some of the medieval lordships had by that time become fragmented almost beyond recognition, but in the majority of cases the basic structure was still apparent in the time of Henry VIII. (They are listed, together with the principal monastic estates, in Appendix II.)

Lordship implies obligations, and it was the obligations of the twelfth century that developed into the land revenues of the sixteenth. Within the medieval lordship there were two levels of obligation: that of the mesne lords towards the chief lord, and that of the manorial tenants towards either the chief lord himself (if they lived in a manor or village kept in hand) or a mesne lord. Many mesne lords had once held their manors by military service but by 1500 this had long since ceased to be demanded, and if such men served in the army under the command of the chief lord it was according to the terms of a specific contract or indenture. In some cases they paid small sums of annual rent to the chief lord, but very often their position was symbolized by a small token of no financial value. Likewise the chief lord's jurisdiction over the mesne lords was far less important in the sixteenth century than it had been three or four centuries before. One element of tenure by military service, however, survived, and was even strengthened in Tudor Yorkshire: that of the lord's right to wardship and marriage, which arose when the heir to a tenancy in fee proved to be a minor or an unmarried girl and therefore technically unable to satisfy the conditions of military tenure. Henry VII and his son made increasing use of this right to wardship, and in 1540 a special court of wards was established at Westminster to administer the temporary confiscation of wards' lands and the sale of wardships.[1] Great care was taken

---

[1] H. E. Bell: *Introduction to the Court of Wards and Liveries* (Cambridge, 1953) and Joel Hurstfield: *The Queen's Wards* (London, 1958).

during these reigns to ensure that the Crown did not lose track of its rights in this sphere. The county escheator made an inquisition *post mortem* into the lands of any deceased landlord who might conceivably have held some of his land in fee from the King: a circumstance which might arise either if the man had been a tenant in chief of the Crown (holding perhaps a large lordship in this way) or if he had held some land as a mesne lord from one of the lordships whose chief lord happened to be the King. It was not only the Crown which benefited from this antiquated obligation of the tenant in fee: any lord who had within his lordship mesne lords holding their manors by military tenure could impose the rules of wardship. Equally, of course, any lord except the King himself was liable to suffer wardship since all lordships were held ultimately of the Crown. Nevertheless the land law was highly complex and many people in this position took advantage of the loophole which allowed them to enfeoff their land for the 'use' of their heirs (or even of someone else) so that the tenure in fee was vested in a trust which never died and could never be liable to wardship. This led Henry VIII in 1536 to enact the Statute of Uses, and in 1540 the Statute of Wills, both of which restricted the possibilities for evading royal wardship in this way.[1]

Most of the revenues of a sixteenth-century landlord had developed out of the ancient obligations of the peasantry: that is, of the small free tenants, the 'customers' and 'bondsmen' of the thirteenth century, whose descendants were the freeholders, copyholders, leaseholders and tenants-at-will of the Tudor period. The obligations of a West Riding bondsman are well illustrated by the example of Stephen Tuglad, who in about 1300 was tenant of a toft and two bovates of land in the Archbishop of York's lordship of Otley.[2] He owed a fixed annual rent of 6s. 8d., and in addition four hens a year, valued at 4d. if the lord preferred money. His obligation to service consisted of one day's ploughing and two days' reaping, whose cash value was put

---

[1] *Statutes*, iii, 27 Hen. VIII, cap. 10; 32 Hen. VIII, cap. 1.
[2] Y.A.S. Library, Leeds: MD/130.

at 5*d*. He could be tallaged at will by the lord. For permission to keep his pigs in the lord's wood he must pay pannage. For the use of the lord's mill to grind his corn (and he was forbidden to take it elsewhere), he had to pay mulcture. His personal freedom to move from his land was limited, and he must pay merchet or leyerwite for the marriage or misconduct of his daughters. Probably about one fifth of Tuglad's value to his lord therefore consisted of services, renders in kind, and dues arising from special obligations or on specific occasions. His labour services were by no means heavy by comparison with peasants on some estates in the Midlands and South at the same period; but they were not unusually light for Yorkshire. In his survey of the different forms of rent in thirteenth-century England, Kosminsky found on a sample group of estates in Yorkshire that only 8 per cent of the total rent due was accounted for by services, compared with 23 per cent on a sample of estates in the south Midlands.[1] He also found that produce-rent (renders in kind) represented a significant proportion of total rent in Yorkshire estates: 18 per cent compared with a negligible proportion in the south Midlands. Mr. T. A. M. Bishop confirms this impression with his observation that in the whole of Yorkshire he knew of only one place where week-work rather than boon-work (a small number of ploughings and reapings per year) was demanded by the medieval lord; it was in fact Tanshelf, next to Pontefract, which was one of the most important medieval centres in the Riding.[2] Another feature of Tuglad's burden which calls for brief comment is his obligation to mulcture. In many parts of the North, where corn mills were worked by water, medieval lords drew a substantial income from this source, and this continued to be true in the sixteenth century. In the lordships of the Duchy of Lancaster, there were mills at

[1] E. A. Kosminsky: *Studies in the Agrarian History of England in the Thirteenth Century* (London, 1956), pp. 194–5. The figures were based on analyses of 21 inquisitions *post mortem* for estates in Yorkshire, and 4 for estates in Bedfordshire, Buckinghamshire, Berkshire, Oxfordshire and Warwickshire. Inquisitions *post mortem* contained more details of tenants and their obligations in the thirteenth and fourteenth centuries than was the case in the sixteenth century.

[2] T. A. M. Bishop: 'The Norman Settlement of Yorkshire' in *Studies in Medieval History presented to F. M. Powicke* (Oxford, 1948), pp. 13–14.

Boroughbridge, Knaresborough, Castleford, Knottingley, Rothwell and Leeds, each of which was farmed out at an annual rent of between £12 and £25 a year; they probably drew mulcture from very wide areas, perhaps even from the manors of mesne lords.[1] In the areas where milling was done by wind-power, on the other hand, mulcture does not seem to have been very important, to judge from the very much smaller value of windmills. Finally mention should be made of the obligation of suit to the lord's court, which is not specifically stated in Tuglad's case but which must surely have applied to him as to all other customary tenants or bondsmen. In most manors the lord's court was probably the only one with jurisdiction over customary tenures, even when the expansion of royal justice deprived manorial and village courts of their jurisdiction over petty crime. The receipts from such courts were another item in the lord's income, in the sixteenth century as earlier, although it will not be possible to bring them into the statistical reckoning in the present chapter.

There is no way of telling what proportion of Stephen Tuglad's obligations were fulfilled in cash, and what proportion in produce or services: even his annual rent, though recorded as a sum of money, may have actually been paid in grain. Estate accounts of the sixteenth century will occasionally refer to renders in kind and to commuted services. But by then it seems likely that the monetary element in rent was predominant, and the custom of the manor had certainly hardened by then, often in the tenant's favour. The situation was nearer to the modern one in which a tenant pays a given sum of money, on entry and then annually, for a holding whose terms of tenure are stated in a specific contract; but the latter was still far from the established norm, as we shall see. As money became more important it also became usual for the lord of a great lordship like Knaresborough to draw most of his revenues from the townships kept 'in hand', and from the pastures of his parks and forests. Gradually too, this financial revenue began to replace older rights of lordship as the basis of local power. The change which came over the pattern of territorial

[1] P.R.O.: DL 29/475/7697 and 515/8293.

control between 1300 and 1700 may be characterized as the
decline of the 'feudal' power of chief lords and the disappearance, under the impact of monetary relationships, of the
distinction between chief lords and mesne lords: both
categories were submerged in that of landowner. But this
transition was not a sudden one, and it was not completed in
the time of Henry VIII; the traditional superiority of the
chief lord over the mesne lords died hard, especially where
the lordship had at its centre a powerful castle. The idea that
property and income counted for more than rights of lordship was only finally established by the cataclysm of civil
war in the seventeenth century, and the extinction of the
castle as a form of local defence. Even then, it should be
remembered that the effects of money were felt much earlier
at the level of relations between chief lords and mesne lords
(or, let us say, between noblemen and gentry) than at the
level of relations between a landlord and his smallholding
tenants. It must not be supposed that the development of
money income killed the idea of patronage: it merely
changed some of its forms.

It is sometimes said that 'feudalism' lasted longer in the
northern counties than in the Midlands and the South.
What this implies is that the power of lordship remained
stronger in the North in the sixteenth century, and that the
transition from 'lordship' to 'ownership' took place either
later or less rapidly there than in southern England. The
contrast should not be exaggerated, for the process was
not rapid in any part of England. Moreover, there were
contrasts within the north country itself, and the experience
of the West Riding perhaps had more in common with that
of Midland counties than with that of Northumberland and
Cumberland, or even of the North Riding of Yorkshire.
When speaking of sixteenth-century England it might be
wiser to concentrate on the details of local differences
between counties, than to attempt broad distinctions between 'North' and 'South' on the basis of too little local
enquiry. Some of the differences which have often in the
past been attributed to different rates of economic and social
development might be more satisfactorily explained in
terms of differences in the ancient patterns of lordship of

individual counties, which existed long before trade and money began to dominate the economic life of any part of England.

II

The framework of lordship was the product of long centuries of growth and change, and apparent 'revolutions' in its structure conceal an element of continuity which, if there were space for a full enquiry, might take us back beyond Domesday Book to the time when 'iron age' chieftains were building such ancient forts as those at Wincobank (near Sheffield) and Almondbury, or that on Ingleborough Hill.[1] A detailed study of earlier periods is not possible here, but one thing is clear: before we can begin to analyse the pattern of landed property and the distribution of income, we must first try to reconstruct the medieval pattern of territorial lordship in the West Riding. It is not without significance that the main outlines of this palimpsest can be reconstructed almost entirely from sixteenth-century records: ministers' accounts, surveys of large estates, and inquisitions *post mortem*. Some features however can be understood only by reference to earlier sources.

About fifty medieval lordships in the West Riding can be identified from the estate records of the fifteenth and sixteenth centuries. Not every village in the Riding can be assigned to a medieval lordship: some places always occupied a special position outside the system, whilst in other cases the lordship pattern had become so fragmented by the sixteenth century that it cannot be reconstructed. The list in Appendix II covers over 450 of the 600 or so townships of the West Riding, a large enough proportion to demonstrate that the lordship was the normal unit of control over the land. It was not, however, the only type of large territorial division found in the Riding. There were also administrative divisions, known as wapentakes, whose creation was of considerable antiquity. The wapentake was the equivalent of the 'hundred' in southern England and its name indicates that it existed (if it was not created) at the

[1] E. S. Armitage and D. H. Montgomerie: 'Ancient Earthworks' in *V.C.H.Y.*, ii (1912), 1–72.

period when Yorkshire was ruled by Scandinavian con-
querors. Moreover, the wapentakes survived as administrative divisions when the lordships were breaking up, and in
the sixteenth century they were the units used for the
assessment and collection of taxes and for the holding of
musters. Their judicial importance did not survive: although
they were named after the places where in pre-Norman times
wapentake courts had been held, the jurisdiction of their
courts was undermined by the reorganization of the lordships under Norman rule after 1069, and its only vestige
was the item of 'wapentake fine' which appeared on the
accounts of either the Sheriff of Yorkshire or the lords of
certain lordships. It was presumably collected from the
inhabitants along with other ancient dues, but the sums
were small compared with those paid in rent and even for
commuted services.[1]

Although some lordships had dependencies in more than
one wapentake, the pattern of lordships was not entirely
unrelated to the boundaries of wapentakes. If one looks at
the geographical relationship between the two types of unit
it is possible to see a number of wapentake boundaries
which appear to be more significant than the others, and to
divide the Riding into four major areas. In analysing the
pattern of lordship summarized in Appendix II and shown
in Map III, it will be convenient to take these four areas
in turn.

I. *Strafforth and Tickhill*

Tickhill was a liberty within the wapentake of Strafforth,
and between them the two areas covered a large part of the
southern half of the Riding. The principal centres here were
Doncaster, Tickhill, Conisbrough and Sheffield. Doncaster,
which originated as the Romano-British *Danum*, became a
medieval borough and with a charter of full incorporation
paid a fee-farm rent directly to the King. Already by 1066 it
seems to have been overtaken in importance by Conisbrough,

[1] The wapentake fines for the whole of Osgoldcross and Staincross wapentakes in
1537 amounted to £25; the total value of rents and farms from all townships in
those wapentakes must have been over £2,750 to judge from the calculations on
which Table VI were based. P.R.O.: DL 29/515/8293.

which was in the hands of Earl Harold on the eve
of the Battle of Hastings and which after 1066 acquired an
imposing Norman castle.[1] But from the twelfth century,
Tickhill increasingly took over the dominant position and
the amount of land dependent on Conisbrough declined; by
the sixteenth century only the lordship of Hatfield was still
attached to Conisbrough, apart from the villages in the
immediate vicinity of the town itself. Tickhill was a post-
Conquest creation, which took over as its dependency an
older lordship centred on Laughton-en-le-Morthen. It was
granted a Liberty, and by the fourteenth century a great
many towns or manors owed suit to its court which had
formerly been attached to Conisbrough. Tickhill also had a
number of dependencies in north Nottinghamshire, a
reminder that even county boundaries did not always coin-
cide with the limits of lordships. By 1500, Conisbrough and
Hatfield were part of the Duchy of York lands, in Crown
hands from 1461, whilst Tickhill belonged to the Crown
Duchy of Lancaster.

A third lordship was territorially intertwined with those
of Tickhill and Conisbrough, that of Maltby and Kimberworth; at one time the property of the Duke of Clarence,
it was in the hands of the Clifford family in the time of
Henry VIII, and was given by the first Earl of Cumberland
to his son, Lord Clifford before he succeeded to the Earldom. The small outlying lordship of Bawtry, in some way
related to Maltby, also belonged to the Clifford. It was out
of the lordship of Maltby that there had been created, by a
series of grants sometime after 1147, the central estate of the
Abbey of Roche. The only other major monastic estate in
the area was the lordship of Rotherham, which belonged to
Rufford Priory. Lying away to the west, and hardly over-
lapping with any other lordship, was the Lordship of Sheffield, frequently referred to as Hallamshire.[2] Its compactness
was of long standing, for it had been held by Earl Waltheof

---

[1] The Domesday Survey for Yorkshire is printed in *V.C.H.Y.*, ii (1912), 133-327.
[2] The term 'shire' is often applied in the north country to areas smaller than the
medieval (or modern) counties: for example Hallamshire, Sowerbyshire, Kirkbyshire, Burghshire, Cravenshire (in the West Riding); Richmondshire and Allerton-
shire (in the North Riding); and Blackburnshire (in Lancashire). Cf. J. E. A.
Jolliffe: 'Northumbrian Institutions', *Eng. Hist. Rev.*, XLI (1926), 1-42.

in 1066; its lord in the sixteenth century was Talbot, Earl
of Shrewsbury, and it had a castle at Sheffield.

II. *The Central Wapentakes*

The six wapentakes of Osgoldcross, Staincross, Agbrigg,
Morley, Skyrack and Barkston were too closely bound up
with one another in the pattern of lordships to be treated
here as anything but a single whole. In every one of them
there were villages, manors, or whole lordships owing some
kind of obligation to the Honour of Pontefract. Indeed
Pontefract might almost be called the medieval capital of
this central area of the Riding. The town itself with its imposing castle was established by the Norman family of de
Lacy, but the neighbouring town of Tanshelf had had a wide
soke dependent upon it before 1066; and not far away was
the town of Castleford which had defended the principal
Roman crossing of the Aire and had had a Romano-British
fort called *Lagentium*. All three places lie near to the point
where the boundaries of five wapentakes intersect.

The Honour of Pontefract was both very extensive and
very complicated in structure, features which stem from the
circumstances of its creation around 1086 by a series of
grants from the King to Ilbert de Lacy. These circumstances
have recently been studied in some detail by Dr. Wightman
in his work on the de Lacy family and its whole patrimony.[1]
As it appears in the late medieval and sixteenth-century
documents (when it was a part of the Duchy of Lancaster),
the Honour of Pontefract may be described as consisting of
five main parts.

(i) The core of the Honour was the eastern half of the
wapentake of Osgoldcross, around the town of Pontefract itself. Eleven villages in that area were kept in
hand by the chief lord (that is, the Duchy), whilst most
of the others were held by mesne lords, as were a
number of villages on the eastern edge of the wapentake
of Agbrigg and on the southern fringes of the wapentake of Barkston.

(ii) In the wapentake of Staincross, although no villages

[1] W. E. Wightman: *The Lacy Family in England and Normandy 1066–1194*
(Oxford, 1966).

were any longer kept in hand, all the townships were in some way dependent on Pontefract. One group of about ten townships was a little apart in belonging to the lordship of Brierley (a possession of the Stanley family): but Brierley itself was a dependency of Pontefract. It is possible that Barnsley had once been the centre of some kind of subsidiary lordship, but by this time it was in the hands of Pontefract Priory; we must return in a moment to the monastic estates of the area.

(iii) The lordship of Almondbury, almost cut off from the rest of the Pontefract dependencies by the intervening soke of Wakefield, was virtually a separate honour, with its own castle and control of a large tract of land above Huddersfield; it was not, however, a very densely populated area until the advent of the cottage woollen industry.

(iv) The lordship of Rothwell (which was partly kept in hand) was the most important of the dependencies of Pontefract in Morley wapentake, and the townships or manors of that wapentake which owed suit to Pontefract may originally have had some connection with Rothwell. On the other hand Morley may once have been a centre of some importance: its position in the sixteenth century is now somewhat obscure.

(v) Finally, the lands which had before 1066 been dependent on Kippax, in the wapentake of Skyrack (with some outlying dependencies possibly in Barkston), represent one of the most complicated parts of the Honour of Pontefract. Kippax itself was much less important in the sixteenth century than it had been in the eleventh; Barwick-in-Elmet on the other hand retained some of its ancient importance, as well as the vestiges of two small castles. There had once been some kind of link between Barwick and the townships around Barkston, and even in the sixteenth-century estate accounts we find tenants in Saxton, Barkston and Towton paying small sums of money for the commutation of boon-works formerly due to the lord of Barwick. On the west, an outlying member of this complex was the manor of Leeds, which for economic reasons was a very much more important place in the sixteenth century than it had been at the time of Domesday Book. Barwick, Leeds and several other places were kept in hand in the sixteenth century.

In the areas of the Honour so far described, there were four monastic foundations with extensive estates. The Priory of St. John at Pontefract and that of Monk Bretton were both Cluniac houses founded by the lords of Pontefract: the former had estates round Monkhill and Ledston (once a dependency of Kippax); and both had estates in and around Barnsley. The Priory of St. Oswald at Nostell had its most important estates in its own vicinity and around Castleford. Lastly, the Cistercian Abbey of Kirkstall had an extensive estate centred upon Headingley which should perhaps be regarded as a lordship in its own right since the Abbot collected 'wapentake fine' there.[1]

Besides the Honour of Pontefract and the subsidiary lordships which accounted with it in the sixteenth century, there were two other Duchy of Lancaster lordships in these central wapentakes of the Riding. The eastern half of the Wapentake of Osgoldcross included the lordship or soke of Snaith where two villages were kept in hand. And the western part of Morley Wapentake was taken up by the lordship of Bradford, which extended from the town of that name into the upper part of Bradford-dale to include the country round Stanbury and Haworth. Both these lordships were attached for accounting purposes to the Honour of Tickhill in the sixteenth century. But the connection was not one of long standing, and both had probably been associated with Pontefract at an earlier period: the townships which geographically appear as the dependencies of these lordships in fact owed suit of court to Pontefract even in the sixteenth century.

The second most important focal point in this central area of the West Riding was Wakefield, which had never had any association with Pontefract so far as is known. The Soke of Wakefield had belonged to King Edward (the Confessor) before 1066 and at that period had dominated

[1] P.R.O.: SC 6/Hen VIII/4590.

the wapentake of Agbrigg. Like Conisbrough, however, it suffered some truncation as a result of William I's reorganization of the Riding after the Norman Conquest: it lost some of its dependencies to Pontefract. Nevertheless in the sixteenth century the lordship of Wakefield, with an important castle at Sandal, still included seven townships in hand and six or more held by mesne lords. Closely attached to it from very early times was the lordship of Sowerby, sometimes known as Sowerbyshire, which included five townships in hand and extended into upper Calderdale. Like the lordship of Almondbury, Sowerbyshire was very sparsely populated until the rise of the textile industry from about 1400. A further small lordship should be noted in this area, that of Halifax; it originally had links with Wakefield, but not a great deal is known about it, because at an early date it was granted to the priory of Lewes in Sussex and no detailed records of it exist.

The relationship between Wakefield and Pontefract in the pattern of territorial control was almost as complex as that between Conisbrough and Tickhill further south. It was made more complicated by the dispute about the lordship of Elland which had arisen by the end of the fifteenth century and which caused some inconclusive litigation in the time of Henry VIII.[1] The Savile family of Thornhill held the manor of that name and also the lordship of Elland as mesne lord, from the Honour of Pontefract. But they claimed also to have jurisdiction over six other townships which according to the lord of Wakefield (in fact the King) were part of the latter lordship. It may be that the sixteenth-century dispute derived originally from some special position once enjoyed by Elland that had been allowed to lapse.

It remains to describe briefly the lordships in Osgoldcross, Barkston and Skyrack wapentakes which lay outside both the Honour of Pontefract and the Lordship of Wakefield. In Osgoldcross, the area known as Marshland lay mostly within the liberty of Airmyn, which belonged to St. Mary's Abbey at York; the precise nature of the liberty

---

[1] e.g. Star Chamber case brought by tenants of several townships against Savile, sometime in the period 1529–32; Y.A.S.R.S., li, pp. 138–40. Cf. *Select Cases in the Court of Requests* (Selden Soc., xii, 1898), pp. 1–3.

is not clear. A little further north there was another monastic estate of some importance, that of Selby Abbey, which had been created by a grant out of the barony of Sherburn and had been expanded by grants from the Barkston section of the Honour of Pontefract. Sherburn Barony was one of the two lordships of the Archbishop of York in this area; it too seems to have suffered truncation when the Honour of Pontefract was created, for in 1066 it still dominated almost the whole wapentake of Barkston. In the later medieval period the Archbishop had a castle within the barony, at Cawood, and also for a time used a hunting-lodge in Rest Park. His other lordship was Otley, which occupied the whole of the western part of Skyrack wapentake as well as having two dependencies across the river in Claro. It may possibly have been the successor-lordship to Ilkley, the Roman *Olicana*, which had certainly declined in importance by the medieval period.

Finally, three other lordships may be mentioned briefly to complete this survey of the central wapentakes. Bardsey (with Collingham) lay to the north of Barwick-in-Elmet and it too may at one time have had dependencies in both Skyrack and Barkston wapentakes. But by the sixteenth century possession of it had been divided amongst six noble families; its central part was held together only by the fact that at some time before the division it had been granted in perpetual farm to the Abbey of Kirkstall which kept it till the Dissolution. Further up the valley (still to the south of the Wharfe) was the lordship of Harewood, held in chief of the Crown and not dependent on any other lordship or Honour. By the sixteenth century it was divided between two families of substantial gentry: Ryther and Redmayne. The third lordship was that of Bingley: it seems to have been a liberty, lying outside any of the surrounding wapentakes, and it is highly unfortunate that we know little about it beyond the fact that in the sixteenth century it was in possession of the Astley family, whose principal estates were in Staffordshire.[1]

To sum up, the central area of the Riding is notable for its extensive royal lordships (both Pontefract and Wakefield being in Crown hands by 1500) and for its important Church

[1] T. D. Whitaker: *History of Craven* (3rd edn. London, 1878), p. 190.

estates. The distribution of these Church estates was, however, rather uneven, and one area (the wapentakes of Agbrigg and Morley) had very little ecclesiastical property within its bounds. The possible significance of this fact will become apparent in due course.

III. *Claro and the Ainsty*

Once across the Wharfe we are beyond the country dominated by Pontefract. Its place is taken by Knaresborough, which had been the local capital since the building of its castle in Norman times. Earlier the principal centre in Claro had been Aldborough, the *Isurium Brigantum* of the Romans, whose lordship was sometimes called Burghshire. Before 1066 there appear to have been two separate lordships or sokes of Aldborough and Knaresborough, but already by that time they were both in the hands of one lord: King Edward (the Confessor), which explains why they were the only part of the West Riding to be regarded as 'ancient demesne of the Crown' in the fourteenth century and later.[1] The internal structure of these lordships (or rather, the Honour of Knaresborough by the sixteenth century) has already been described above. After 1399, as a member of the Duchy of Lancaster, the Honour was once again a royal possession.

In the area between the boundary of Knaresborough and the river Wharfe, which included the Ainsty, there were two lordships of the Percy Earls of Northumberland: Spofforth and Tadcaster. The barony of Spofforth occupied the western portion of this area, having three dependencies on the north side of middle Wharfedale, separated from one another by dependencies of the lordship of Otley. Spofforth itself had a late medieval castle and was for a time one of the Percy residences in Yorkshire. Tadcaster, the Romano-British *Calcaria*, was still a town of some importance in the medieval period, but the lordship was declining in importance by the sixteenth century. The sixth Earl of Northumberland granted Healaugh, one of its most important members, to Sir Thomas Wharton, who after about 1540

---

[1] The question of 'ancient demesne' will be discussed in Chapter III, *infra*, pp. 115-16.

became a leading figure in this area. Healaugh also had a priory, a Percy foundation, with a small estate in the vicinity, but it was not on the same scale as the large monastic estates associated with other lordships. In the remainder of the area between the Nidd and the Wharfe the medieval lordship pattern had all but disintegrated by the sixteenth century. Only the vestiges can be traced of the fee which had been granted to Osbern de Arches shortly after the Norman Conquest. Its centre may have been Thorp Arch, which belonged to Gascoigne of Gawthorpe in the sixteenth century and which had around it seven manors only nominally dependent on it. But Thorp Arch itself was held (as were four other manors in this area) from the Earl of Derby's Honour of Thirsk, in the North Riding.[1] It would take a good deal of painstaking research into documents of the period between Domesday Book and 1500 to work out precisely what changes lay behind this complicated situation. As for Church estates in this area, there were several valuable monastic manors, but only one compact estate: that of the preceptory of Ribston, belonging to the Knights Hospitallers.

To the north of the Honour of Knaresborough there were two more centres of ancient lordships: Ripon and Kirkby Malzeard. The Liberty of Ripon had been granted to the Archbishop of York in the seventh century and was the oldest lordship in the whole Riding. It included the town of Ripon, within which there was a small area around the collegiate church where the Archbishop had very considerable powers; the rest of the Liberty comprised six villages kept in hand, and ten dependent manors held by mesne lords. Kirkby Malzeard, a lordship of the Earl of Derby, sometimes known as Kirkbyshire, included a number of townships to the north of Ripon and in Nidderdale; but it had no great castle and was not of the first importance. In between these two lordships was a monastic enclave, the central estate of Fountains Abbey whose monks had been invited here by the Archbishop of York and had received a grant out of the Liberty of Ripon.

[1] The connection is indicated by an inquisition *post mortem*, P.R.O.: C 142/181/70.

IV. *Craven and Ewcross*

The wapentake of Staincliffe (that is, Craven) was
dominated by two large medieval estates: the Clifford
family's Honour of Skipton and the Percy Fee of Gisburn
and Settle. The former was the more important by the early
sixteenth century, and before 1536 they were in fact united
in Clifford possession as a result of the marriage between
the first Earl of Cumberland and Margery Percy, daughter
of the fifth Earl of Northumberland.[1] Skipton, though it
may have been a place of some antiquity, does not emerge in
the documents as an important centre before the twelfth
century. Its Honour was situated mostly in Airedale, with
some land centred on Barden in Wharfedale. The lordship
of Carleton was probably associated with it in some way
at a very early period, but for some reason we find it coming
(back?) into the hands of the Clifford in 1540 as a result of
royal grant. Another estate which was originally associated
with the Honour of Skipton was that of the Priory of Bolton
Canons; it was a Clifford foundation, and when the King
dissolved it a large part of its land was sold back to the same
family. The Percy Fee was administratively centred upon
Settle by the sixteenth century, and occupied the central area
of Upper Ribblesdale together with an outlying forest area
in Langstrothdale. But there is reason to suppose that its
original centre had been Gisburn, before that lordship was
granted to the Percy foundation of Salley Abbey. Salley had
a substantial estate in the southern half of the Percy fee by
1500. A third monastic estate in Craven should be noticed:
the lordship of Malham, where Fountains Abbey had a
number of townships with some of the richest upland graz-
ing in the county.

The Duchy of Lancaster appears again in Craven as the
holder of two minor lordships, both of them bordering on
the more important Duchy Honour of Clitheroe, in Lancashire. Bolland Forest, with its centre at Slaidburn, was
administratively attached to that Honour; it was made up
entirely of a forest area. Barnoldswick lordship may have
had some ancient connection with Bradford, for like the

[1] A. G. Dickens (ed.): *Clifford Letters of the Sixteenth Century*, Surtees Soc.,
clxxii (1962), p. 23.

latter place it was attached for accounting purposes to the Honour of Tickhill in the sixteenth century. Kirkstall Abbey had originally been founded at Barnoldswick and continued to maintain an estate there after its move to Airedale.

The wapentake of Ewcross was not only the most remote part of the West Riding, but also the last to be 'annexed' to it: it was added to Yorkshire only in the time of Henry I, having previously been associated with Lonsdale. Even in the sixteenth century, much of the area looked towards Lancashire or Westmorland as frequently as towards York. The two most important lordships were Burton-in-Lonsdale and Dent: Burton, whose dependencies included the forest or chase of Ingleborough, was part of the extensive north-western estates of the Earl of Derby, whose most important possessions were in South Lancashire; Dent belonged to the Parr family, whose principal northern seat was at Kendal in Westmorland. There was also a large monastic estate in the wapentake, belonging to the Lancashire abbey of Furness.

III

Within this framework of territorial lordship, whose significance was declining but by no means dead, we may now begin to consider the pattern of property distribution (in what might be called Locke's sense of the word), and to see it in proper perspective. If we wish to examine the distribution of financial revenues from land in a typical year (let us say 1535), we must concentrate our attention on the estates of individuals or of families: an estate may be defined in this context as all the land belonging to a particular owner, regardless of geographical location. Ownership may for the moment be taken to mean possession according to one of the free tenures recognized in common law, and to exclude land held on lease or according to the custom of the manor. It is possible to distinguish four principal categories of estate owners in the West Riding in 1535: the Church, the Crown, the nobility and the gentry.

'The Church' cannot be regarded as a single owner, for it embraced a great variety of property-owning institutions, ranging from wealthy monasteries to small chantries. Church property, moreover, did not consist only of estates,

but was of two kinds: spiritual and temporal. Only about
55 per cent of ecclesiastical income in the Riding in 1535
was drawn from temporalities.[1] The most important
elements in spiritual income were the glebes and tithes
attached to vicarages and rectories, which very often were
appropriated to monasteries. The temporal estates included
those which have already been mentioned in the survey of
ancient lordships, but also a great many smaller possessions
granted to the Church at various dates when particular
individuals had the inclination to do so. The largest single
ecclesiastical owner in the Riding was the Archbishop
of York, who was lord of three of the oldest lordships,
Sherburn, Otley and Ripon. He had no spiritual possessions
there, before 1545, when the King forced on him an
exchange of temporal for spiritual properties.[2] The spiritualia of York Minster belonged not to the Archbishop but
to the Dean and Chapter, who had their own estate administration. There were about fifty houses of religious orders
with some property in the West Riding, half of them being
situated within its bounds and the others outside it. But the
twelve houses whose large estates are noted in the list of lordships (Appendix II) had over three-quarters of the total
gross temporal income of religious orders in the whole Riding.
The larger monasteries usually had estates made up mostly
of whole manors, having been founded at an early date when
the laity was most generous towards religion. The smaller,
later foundations had more piecemeal possessions, the smallest of all being those of the chantries. Some chantries only
had pensions from larger institutions, but 190 of them in the
Riding had their own lands, and an average annual income
of about £4 each.[3] The colleges and hospitals, though their
estates were larger than those of chantries, also tended to
have estates made up of small parcels of land rather than
whole manors.

The estates of the Crown can also be better understood if
one considers the way in which they had come into royal

[1] Calculated from the figures used for Table V, *infra*, p. 73.
[2] *L.P.* XX (i) 465 (39).
[3] The information concerning income from chantries has been taken mainly from
the *Valor Ecclesiasticus*, v; but see also clerical subsidy assessment for Deanery of
Boroughbridge, 1523: P.R.O.: E 36/149.

possession. Although some of them (Knaresborough, Wakefield and Sowerby) had belonged to Edward the Confessor before 1066, none had been continuously in Crown hands since the Conquest. All had belonged to non-royal noble houses, and in two cases had become Crown lands only when the latter seized the throne. This explains the lack of uniformity in Crown estate administration. A large part of the West Riding estates belonged to the Duchy of Lancaster, whose estate administration had been kept completely separate from that of the existing royal patrimony when the Duke of Lancaster seized the throne in 1399. Thanks to the work of Sir Robert Somerville a great deal is now known about the details of that administration throughout the period down to 1603.[1] When the Duke of York seized the throne in his turn in 1461, his estates were also added to the Crown possessions (including Wakefield, Sowerby, Conisbrough and Hatfield); this merger was more complete, since they were incorporated into the large estate which by 1535 was administered by the General Surveyors.[2] So too were the borough of Doncaster, held of the King in fee farm, and the manor of Kettlewell which was the sole West Riding dependency of the lordship of Middleham (in the North Riding). We shall see in Chapter VI how the confiscation of the monastic and rebel estates under Henry VIII after 1536 led to the creation of a much more complicated system of royal estate administration. But before that time the Crown estates were organized in much the same way as those of a large noble family, though on a grander scale.

Of the noble families who had estates in the West Riding, five were lords of one or more of the territorial lordships analysed earlier, and a sixth had an important estate that had previously belonged to the Knights Templar. The principal rising family amongst the West Riding nobility at this period was that of Clifford, whose inheritance here comprised the Honour of Skipton and the Lordship of Maltby. It was only in 1525 that Henry Lord Clifford was made first Earl

[1] R. Somerville: *The Duchy of Lancaster*, i (London, 1953).
[2] B. P. Wolffe: 'Royal Estates under the Yorkists', *Eng. Hist. Rev.*, lxxi, (1956); and F. C. Dietz: *English Government Finance 1485–1558*. (Univ. of Illinois, 1920).

6

of Cumberland. By the time he died in 1542 he had added
to this patrimony the lordship of Carleton (in Craven) and
the Percy fee in Craven, and had purchased from the King the
main part of the Bolton Priory estate: he left to his son
the largest private lay estate in the Riding.[1] By contrast the
Percy estates here were declining. The Craven fee was
signed away by the marriage agreement between the fifth
Earl of Northumberland and the Cliffords, whilst the sixth
Earl virtually gave away to members of his household three
of the most valuable manors in the lordships of Tadcaster
and Spofforth. In 1536, when he died, the remainder of the
sixth Earl's estate passed to the Crown under his will.[2]

Two other Earls had West Riding lordships in 1535.
Talbot, Earl of Shrewsbury, had the lordship of Hallamshire, with a castle at Sheffield which he still used as a
residence; in 1537 he extended this South Yorkshire estate
by acquiring the ex-monastic manor of Rotherham. And
Stanley, Earl of Derby, had the lordships of Kirkby Malzeard and Burton-in-Lonsdale; but neither included much
land kept in hand, and neither had any lordly residence by
this period. Derby's main estates were in Lancashire and he
was not much interested in the West Riding: Kirkby
Malzeard was in fact part of the Countess of Derby's dower
lands in the 1530s. The fifth of the nobles mentioned above
as owners of lordships in the Riding was another Stanley,
Lord Mounteagle, whose estates included the lordship of
Brierley and some land in Dent and Sedbergh. But for much
of Henry VIII's reign the Mounteagle estate was in wardship, and part of the Brierley income belonged to Sir Arthur
Darcy.[3] The latter was the sixth lord mentioned, with
residences and valuable manors at Temple Newsam and
Temple Hirst; he also had the manor of Silkstone, in Staincross wapentake. But his position in the Riding was not
based only on his ownership of these places: he was also
steward of Pontefract, and the power which that office

---

[1] On the Clifford estates see R. T. Spence: *The Cliffords, Earls of Cumberland,
1579–1646: their Fortunes*. (Unpublished thesis, Ph.D. London, 1959), introductory
chapters.

[2] J. M. W. Bean: *The Estates of the Percy Family 1416–1537* (Oxford, 1958),
pp. 151–4.

[3] By grant of 1524, *L.P.* IV, no. 1298.

brought him is a reflection of the continuing importance of some ancient lordships. There were another eight noblemen with small properties here in 1535, but none of them had more than £50 a year from than West Riding.[1]

We come now to the fourth category, whose description by the term 'gentry' calls for some comment; perhaps it would be better to say 'gentry and other lay landowners'. Somewhat later in the sixteenth century Sir Thomas Smith defined the category of 'gentleman' in such a way as to include anyone able to bear 'the porte and countenance of a gentleman', a definition not easily applicable in the compilation of statistics of estate-ownership. The King's heralds were rather more rigorous, drawing a sharp (if not easily definable) distinction between families which were entitled to bear arms and those which were not. But to apply that criterion would involve a great deal of heraldic research, for which the material is far less complete in this period than in the reign of Elizabeth I.[2] In common parlance the term is usually used by writers on the sixteenth century to cover all people with the titles 'knight', 'esquire' and 'gentleman'; but that too is a rather vague criterion, and one cannot be sure that these titles were correctly used in every document available to us. The distinction between the nobility and commoners is far easier to apply than any distinction between different kinds of commoner. For the purposes of a survey of property therefore, it seems better to adopt a measurable economic criterion, and to count as 'gentry' all those who, below the rank of nobility, had freehold estates of a given value per year, regardless of whether they or their descendants were entitled to bear arms. The distinction between the minor squire and the prosperous yeoman was not economically a sharp one, and any figure chosen to define the category is bound to be arbitrary. The figure I have chosen is £10 a year, for whilst some yeomen rose above that annual

[1] They were: Lord Roos (£50), the Earl of Westmorland (£26), the Earl of Rutland (£13), the Countess of Salisbury (£13), Lord Dacre of the South (£22), Lord Scrope (£15), Lord Beaumont (£28), and Lord Powys (£12): P.R.O.: C 142/198/47, C 142/88/68; SC 6/Hen VIII/4590, 5728, 6135; and C 142/88/30.
[2] Tonge's visitation of 1530 exists, but it includes far fewer families than the visitations of 1563-4 or of 1584-5. *Heraldic Visitation of the Northern Counties in 1530*, Surtees Soc., xli (1863).

income (from freehold lands) few gentlemen if any were below it. Even if the procedure leads to the inclusion of some people who were not strictly speaking 'gentle', at least we know who does and does not belong to the category economically.

Altogether the category included about 350 families, many of whom were resident in the Riding although some merely owned land there. (The £10 a year by which the category is defined refers to the total income from land of a given family or individual, not just to the value of land situated within the Riding; but in the calculation of income distribution within the Riding, only land actually situated there will be counted.) It would be a serious mistake to think of each of these 'gentry' estates as a compact unit, whether large or small. Such estates had been built up piecemeal over many generations, with frequent partitions and changes of ownership consequent upon family accidents: failure of male heirs, marriage of an heiress, the need to provide dowers when daughters married, and so on; not to mention outright sales of land which were becoming increasingly common by the sixteenth century. Something of the complexity of family estate history will become apparent when we discuss the role of the gentry and the nobility in the development of the land market, in Chapter VI.

This said, it can be observed that many of the 'gentry' owners fit into the pattern as mesne lords of manors dependent on honours, baronies, etc. Only in two cases, those of Gascoigne and Savile (by far the wealthiest gentry families resident in the Riding), do we find commoners as chief lords of lordships, and in neither case was the lordship an important one.[1] As mesne lords, holding manors (or even smaller units) from an honour or barony by military tenures, the gentry were liable to wardship; and since the King himself was chief lord of so many parts of the West Riding this meant that royal wardship was an important institution there in the sixteenth century. In addition, we find gentry land-

[1] Sir William Gascoigne was lord of Thorp Arch, which as we saw earlier (*supra*, p. 59) had ceased to be a coherent entity by this time; Sir Henry Savile was lord of Elland, but his claim that it was independent of that of Wakefield was never established (*supra*, p. 56).

owners in two other roles in the great lordships; those of
the estate official (steward, bailiff, etc.) and the farmer of
demesnes, parks, fisheries, etc. The more lowly estate
officials, such as the manorial bailiff or the clerk of the
manor-court, were usually yeomen or very minor gentlemen;
but on the estates of the Crown, the nobility, and the great
ecclesiastical landlords, there was need also for stewards,
receivers, and even constables of castles. It was in the latter
capacity that the Crown and the Church often employed
substantial gentry or even noblemen. As far as the King
was concerned, important estate offices were a significant
element in royal patronage at the local level.

Thus in 1535 (and for many years previously) Thomas
Lord Darcy was steward and constable of Pontefract and
Knaresborough; in 1537 he was replaced by Sir Henry
Savile at the one place and by the Earl of Cumberland at the
other.[1] The Steward of Wakefield before 1537 (and also
constable of Sandal Castle) was Sir Richard Tempest of
Bolling; despite the latter's fall from grace as a result of the
commotions of 1536, he was in time succeeded in those
offices by his younger son Sir John Tempest. These were
men of substance, and their substance (or at least their
influence) was enhanced by their positions in Crown estate
service. The principal ecclesiastical landowners also employed gentlemen and occasionally noblemen in like
capacity, as we can see from the *Valor Ecclesiasticus* of 1535.
Lord Darcy was steward of three large monasteries: Fountains Abbey, Pontefract Priory and Selby Abbey; his son
Sir George Darcy was steward of several important monastic
manors, for example at Barnsley (for Pontefract Priory) and
at Garforth and Deighton (for Saint Mary's Abbey at
York). Sir George Lawson, who was for some time receiver-
general of the Duchy of York lands in the West Riding,
was bailiff of Saint Mary's Abbey's manor of Poppleton.
Lesser offices had lesser men as incumbents. All in all the
monasteries of the Riding probably spent about 3 per cent of

---

[1] The principal officers of the Duchy of Lancaster estates are listed by R. Somerville (as cited in n. 1, *supra*, p. 63) pp. 514, 522–5, 528–9, etc.; those of other royal
estates are frequently recorded on the patent roll, covered for this period by *Letters
and Papers*; for the Tempests see *L.P.* III (ii), no. 1451 (20) and XVIII (i), no. 981
(11).

their gross income on the stipends of lay estate officials.[1] It is unfortunate that all our evidence of this practice comes from a date as late as 1535 (that is, the *Valor*), for it is possible that monastic landlords took to this practice only quite late, in the hope of securing lay support at a time when they were beginning to fear suppression. In any case, of course, it is very likely that noblemen and knights employed as stewards on Crown and Church estates would have lesser men to deputise for them in the actual performance of their duties.

Estate administration was perhaps already a highly skilled profession by this time. One type of office was even held formally by men whose qualification was professional skill rather than their prominence in West Riding society: namely the receivers of revenue. One such was John Byrnand (Brennand), probably of Knaresborough, who was receiver of the Honours of Knaresborough and Pontefract. Whilst his appointment may well have been due to some connection with the steward, Lord Darcy, he does not appear to have been a landowner of any substance in his own right; and he held the position from 1526 till 1545, despite the fall of Darcy in the interval, which suggests that his work was entirely of administrative and not at all of political significance.[2] Some interesting examples of the profession of estate official will be found in the Court of Augmentations, founded in 1536, where many holders of important posts were lawyers, like Leonard Beckwith, or specialists in accountancy like James Rokeby.[3] For men of their stamp, service to the Crown was a preliminary to the acquisition of estates of their own, not vice versa.

The estate official would receive a fee for his office, which was regarded as a part of his perpetual income and might be included in his assessment for subsidy payments. An office therefore represented an income as well as possibly a source of influence, and we must take this factor into account when we come to look at the distribution of landed revenues. More directly economic in character were the farms or leases

---

[1] *Valor Ecclesiasticus* (Record Comm. 1825), v, *passim*.

[2] R. Somerville, *op. cit.*, p. 516. Possibly he was the son of Robert Burnand, who died in 1508 leaving a son (John) aged sixteen, and lands in Knaresborough and the vicinity worth just over £13; P.R.O.: E 150/219/18.

[3] The careers of these men will be discussed in Chapter VI, *infra*, pp. 224 ff.

of domanial property, which might sometimes be acquired by people with no other source of income, but which very often went to people who also had freehold estates of their own. Unfortunately the available records do not tell us to what extent possession of a lease of this kind enabled a land-owner to add to his income. But the extent of the practice can be very roughly measured. A sample analysis of 102 properties on a number of large estates, some lay and some ecclesiastical, which were leased for annual rents of between £3 and £30 at some time in the period 1535–40, showed that almost a quarter of them were farmed by men who also had a substantial amount of freehold property.[1] There were some gentry who specialized in farming properties of this kind, especially pastures. Sir John Nevill of Chevet for example secured leases of the herbage or agistment of two royal parks: Phippin Park (near Snaith) in 1518, and Wake-field Old Park in 1525; he subsequently obtained appoint-ments to offices in the parks of Wakefield lordship which brought him an income of £11 in fees. It is impossible to know whether he kept these parks in his own hands, or sublet his farm at a profit, but he must surely have made a worth-while profit on the leases for himself.[2] Similarly gentlemen and nobles might become farmers of the spiritual properties which had been appropriated to monasteries; it was not unusual for a landowner to have the farm of the tithes in an area where he was also the landlord. In such cases his tenants would find themselves paying both their temporal and their spiritual dues to the same man.

IV

Having established our four categories of recipients of income from land, we come now to the problem of measuring the income itself. In principle the most satisfactory method

[1] P.R.O.: estate records of the Crown (DL 29/515/8293, 475/7701 and 550/8722; SC 6/Hen VIII/4090, 4125); of the Archbishop of York (SC 6/Hen VIII/4409 and SC 12/17/58); of Thomas Lord Darcy (SC 6/Hen VIII/4306); and of the following monasteries: Kirkstall (SC 6/Hen VIII/4590), Monk Bretton (ibid. 4539), Roche (ibid. 4534), Pontefract (ibid. 4584), Selby (ibid. 4606), Nostell (ibid. 4579), Bolton (ibid. 4542), Fountains (ibid. 4452), Knaresborough (ibid. 7304), Healaugh (ibid. 4471), Bridlington (ibid. 4430), St. Mary's York (ibid. 4595); and of Ribston Preceptory (ibid. 4458).

[2] L.P. IV (i), no. 1533; P.R.O.: DL 29/550/8722 and SC 6/Hen VIII/4125.

of measuring the distribution of landed property is in monetary terms; measurement by acreages, or by counting manors, is much too crude. Tawney's attempt to measure changes in property distribution by counting manors was a not unreasonable response to the otherwise insoluble problem of gauging the flow of manorial property in the land market, over a long period of time in which property values were continually changing; but for a static survey of land ownership at a single date, the method is neither appropriate nor necessary. Although the measurement of money income from land in the sixteenth century is no easy task, the defeatism which has prevailed amongst researchers on the subject is not entirely justified, at least for the first half of the century. Of course it is not possible to trace every penny of income from every acre of utilized land in the Riding to its recipients, be they great landlords, peasant cultivators, or merely agricultural labourers. The only kinds of land income that can be quantified from documentary sources are those from freehold estates and from the spiritual possessions of the Church. But within this limited sphere the sources can be made to yield some very interesting information. What I propose to attempt is to measure the proportions in which these two kinds of income were distributed amongst the four categories of owner: the Church, the Crown, the nobility and the 'gentry'.

It happens that for the years shortly before and after 1535 there exists a remarkable array of land-records relating to property in the West Riding. For the Crown estates, for the estates confiscated by the Crown from the Church between 1536 and 1540, and for certain noble and 'gentry' estates, there are series of ministers' accounts and sometimes also estate surveys. Additional information about Church wealth is available in the *Valor Ecclesiasticus* made in 1535. The 'gentry' estates for which there are no private estate records can be covered to a considerable extent by using the escheators' inquisitions *post mortem* and the feodaries' surveys made in connection with royal claims to wardship in Henry VIII's reign; for the escheator was ordered to enquire not only in cases where there was likelihood of an actual wardship, but wherever there was need to keep trace of potential royal rights. Both the reliability of these records and the extent to which they cover the land of all owners have been called in question by previous writers; in particular there has been a reluctance to accept wardship records at their face value. But it should be remembered that we are dealing here with the period before the great inflation became rampant. In the century or so after 1540, the steep rise in land values was not matched by any improvement in the methods of valuation by royal officials, and this means that for the later part of the sixteenth century wardship records, and even rentals and surveys, do not give a very accurate picture of the actual income received from estates. An important reason for this is that the increased income of landlords did not take the form of straightforward increases in annual rents; it more often took the form of higher entry fines (the sums paid by tenants on entry into a lease or customary holding), and consequently it came in as a series of intermittent lump-sum payments. Estate administrators, and certainly royal officials, failed to develop any technique for representing entry fines as annual income, at least before the seventeenth century, and they therefore continued to record only annual rental values in their surveys and inquisitions. As a result the figures recorded for annual values of land became increasingly notional as the sixteenth century drew to its close, and historians are right to mistrust them. But in the 1530s, although entry fines were sometimes levied, they represented a much smaller proportion of estate income: rental values still had real significance, and officials seem usually to have made some attempt to ensure that estimates of annual rental values were reasonable, if not totally accurate. Estate accounts, which record the actual receipt of annual rents, are also more easily used in the period before entry fines became so important. Some of the problems involved in assessing the reliability of the land records will be discussed more fully in Appendix I, where I have attempted to justify my willingness to rely on them to give at least reasonable minimum estimates of income from freehold land.

As for the extent to which all the land of the West Riding is covered by the sources, we may be fairly confident that

the estates of the Church, the Crown and the nobility are
covered almost in their entirety, and moreover are covered
by estate records for the most part. The 'gentry' estates
are less often covered by accounts and surveys, and we have
to rely very largely on the wardship records. Not every
estate can be covered, and some gaps have proved impossible
to fill; but nevertheless the number of inquisitions and
feodaries' surveys is great enough to convince me that a
very large proportion of the lands of the 'gentry' can be
included in a survey. It is a disadvantage of wardship
records, however, that they must be drawn from a much
wider range of dates than estate records, since they were
made every generation rather than every year. Some estates
can be covered only by using inquisitions *post mortem* as far
apart in date as 1510 and 1558. This raises two difficulties.
Changes in land values over a long interval cannot be allowed
for in any systematic way, although for the reasons already
mentioned changes would be less marked in the first than in
the second half of the century; and it might well be that
annual values recorded in the 1550s are a more reliable
indication of the actual values of twenty years previously
than of current values when the record was made. But a
more serious difficulty arises from the frequency with which
land passed from one family to another, through family
settlement as much as by sale and purchase. The greater the
range of dates in the records used, the more danger there is
of counting the same manor or parcel of land twice owing to
a change of ownership in the interval. In order to avoid this
risk of double-counting I adopted the procedure of placing
all the information about landed income, from whatever
source, on cards relating to individual townships. In this
way I was able to see whether any land appeared twice,
without the necessity of long and complicated research into
the manorial history of every township. (This is the point at
which, had they been compiled, the *Victoria County History*
volumes for the West Riding would have been most useful.)
I was also able to discover what gaps still remained in the
survey of income, when all the sources had been examined.
This procedure made it possible, by adding together the
results from different groups of townships, to discover the

distribution of freehold income not only in the West Riding as a whole but also in its various regions. The results of this township-by-township survey are summarized in Tables V and VI.

In Table V, temporal freehold income has been estimated in two ways. In the first column, headed 'temporal freehold

TABLE V

Distribution of Freehold and Spiritual Income from West Riding Land c. 1535.

(a) *Detailed Analysis.*

Owners	Spiritual income	Temporal freehold income	'Corrected' temporal income
Church:			
Archbishop and Minster of York	£80	£670	£670
Religious Houses	£2,044	£4,785	£4,640
Colleges and Chantries	£669	£1,016	£1,000
Vicarages, Rectories, Prebends of York	£2,240	—	—
Crown:			
Duchy of Lancaster	—	£1,549	£1,400
Other estates	—	£798	£680
Nobility:			
Earl of Cumberland	—	£612	£585
Earl of Shrewsbury	—	£367	£350
Earl of Northumberland	—	£340	£325
Thomas Lord Darcy	—	£440	£420
Other Nobles	—	£331	£315
Gentry (i.e. other lay landowners)	—	£10,616	£12,740

(b) *Summary of Analysis.*

	Spiritual income	Temporal freehold income:	
		'Gross'	'Corrected'
CHURCH	£5,033	£6,471 (30·1%)	£6,310 (27·3%)
CROWN	—	£2,347 (10·9%)	£2,080 (9·0%)
NOBILITY	—	£2,090 (9·7%)	£1,995 (8·6%)
GENTRY	—	£10,616 (49·3%)	£12,740 (55·1%)
TOTAL	£5,033	£21,524 (100%)	£23,125 (100%)

Note: The sources on which these calculations have been based are discussed in Appendix II.

income', I have entered the actual figures produced by my township calculations. These are interesting enough in themselves, and the reader may prefer to take them more seriously than the 'corrected' figures in the other column. Some attempt at correction nevertheless seemed desirable for two reasons. First, the undervaluation of the wardship records and the existence of gaps in the survey are both factors affecting the fourth category of owners, the 'gentry', rather than the other three categories: this means that in the township calculation the income of the fourth category is under-estimated: £10,616 must be seen as a minimum figure. Second, there is an important difference between figures for annual value derived from estate accounts and surveys, and those derived from wardship records. The latter are clearly stated to be, in the words of the inquisition *post mortem*, values *ultra reprisis*: that is, 'beyond all expenses', or 'net' values. On the other hand figures derived from estate records, especially on large estates, can only be entered on the township cards as 'gross' income. It is possible to deduct from them small local expenses, but not the fees of estate officers and other expenses which were deducted after the money had been collected by the receiver of the honour or barony; it is quite impossible to assign these latter expenses to individual townships. Since it is the first three categories for which we have information from estate records, once again it is the fourth category whose income is comparatively underestimated. Indeed it is a double fault, since the 'gentry' were very often the recipients of the fees which could not be deducted from the income of the Church, Crown and nobility. The following 'corrections' have there-fore been attempted. From the incomes of the first three categories, deductions have been made to allow for fees: in the case of Crown income, this could be done from the accounts, and the sums deducted are those actually paid to officers whose duties were wholly or mainly in the West Riding; for the other two categories a rough estimate was made, and figures for monastic income were reduced by 3 per cent, for college income by 1 per cent and for noble income by 5 per cent. It was less easy to decide by how much 'gentry' income ought to be increased, and the decision to raise it by 20 per cent was in the end quite arbitrary. What the figures in the 'corrected' column in fact represent is a situation in which the defects of the actual calculation have been reversed: £12,740 thus represents probably the maximum figure for 'gentry' income in 1535, and the two columns therefore give us the range of possibilities.

So far as I know this is the first attempt at a statistical representation of the distribution of money income from land throughout an English county at this period. How far the results can be called typical of the England of Henry VIII is a question which must await further research on other counties. The West Riding figures do not however give cause for surprise, except perhaps to those who have assumed that before 1536 almost all the land in England was owned by the Church, the Crown and the great noble houses. It is true that the great medieval lordships were mostly in the hands of those three categories of owner, but the ancient lordship was ceasing to be the most important

TABLE VI

Distribution of Temporal Freehold Income, by Wapentakes,
c. 1535.

Wapentake	Church (temporal)	Crown	Nobility	Gentry, etc.	Total
Strafforth and Tickhill	£564 (18·3%)	£412 (13·4%)	£465 (15·1%)	£1,632 (53·2%)	£3,073
Osgoldcross and Staincross	£872 (26·8%)	£418 (12·9%)	£117 (3·5%)	£1,857 (56·8%)	£3,264
Agbrigg and Morley	£326 (9·8%)	£663 (20·0%)	£89 (2·7%)	£2,234 (67·5%)	£3,312
Skyrack	£518 (25·2%)	£240 (11·2%)	£331 (16·1%)	£975 (47·5%)	£2,064
Barkston and Ainsty	£1,130 (41·2%)	—	£122 (4·3%)	£1,484 (54·5%)	£2,736
Claro, Ripon, Knaresborough	£1,395 (44·0%)	£374 (11·8%)	£138 (4·4%)	£1,267 (39·8%)	£3,174
Staincliffe and Ewcross	£863 (27·9%)	£240 (7·7%)	£828 (26·7%)	£1,167 (37·7%)	£3,098
Whole Riding	£5,668 (27·4%)	£2,347 (11·3%)	£2,090 (10·1%)	£10,616 (51·2%)	£20,721

(Percentages read across.)
Sources: as for Table V.

form of control over the land. Financial income from land was much more evenly distributed: in the West Riding the 'gentry' already had at least half the total revenue from temporal freehold estates, and even if spiritual income is included in a single calculation, the share of the 'gentry' would still be about 40 per cent. And even the 'corrected' figures do not allow for the income that some members of the 'gentry' received in profits from their leases of demesnes, parks, etc. on larger estates. This, moreover, was before the Dissolution, that is before the 'rise of the gentry' had even begun.

The figures for the distribution of income in seven regional divisions of the Riding are given in Table VI, unfortunately without any 'correction' being possible. Also, Chantry lands are mostly omitted here, since their precise location is often unclear. The contrasts are quite striking. The Crown's share of income was highest in the regions where the principal royal lordships lay: in Strafforth and Tickhill, those of Tickhill, Conisbrough and Hatfield; in Osgoldcross and Staincross those of Pontefract and Snaith; in Agbrigg and Morley, those of Wakefield and Sowerby, of Bradford and part of the Honour of Pontefract; in Skyrack too, dependencies of Pontefract, including Barwick and Leeds; and in Claro the Honour of Knaresborough. The high proportion of royal income in Agbrigg and Morley is especially remarkable. The Church's proportion of income in different regions also follows the pattern one would expect from the geographical distribution of its major estates, which was determined largely by the accident of lay generosity towards monasteries in the eleventh and especially the twelfth centuries. In Claro and Ripon, the proportion was high for two reasons: because of the Archbishop of York's lordship of Ripon, and because of the large estate of Fountains Abbey. In Barkston and the Ainsty, the Archbishop's barony of Sherburn was an important factor; another was the presence of a good many monastic manors, especially those of Selby Abbey in southern Barkston. These were the areas where the Church had an especially high proportion of landed income. By contrast it had a very small proportion in the wapentakes of

Agbrigg and Morley, for there were no important monasteries in that area. Interestingly enough, the twelfth-
century lord of Wakefield and Sowerby lordships had been
the Earl de Warenne whose estates lay mainly in the South,
and the only large grant of land to a monastery in Agbrigg
and Morley was that of Halifax to the Priory of Lewes in
Sussex (where de Warenne had a major castle).

The position of the nobility is notable in three areas: in
Strafforth and Tickhill, where the Earl of Shrewsbury had
the lordship of Hallamshire (Sheffield); in Skyrack, where
one finds the rich pastures of Thomas Lord Darcy; and in
Staincliffe wapentake, where the Earls of Cumberland and
Northumberland both had important fiefs. But it is the
figures relating to the gentry that are the most noticeable
of all. In Agbrigg and Morley they had a proportion as high
as 67 per cent, whereas in Claro, Ripon, Knaresborough
and also in Staincliffe and Ewcross, it was under 40 per
cent. One possible explanation for these figures is that they
reflect the nature of the source material: that in the former
area there were important royal lordships and therefore a
larger number of inquisitions *post mortem* was made than in
the other two areas where the principal lordships (except for
Knaresborough) belonged to the Church or to the nobility.
But I am reluctant to accept this as the whole explanation.
The detailed township figures, and other local information,
do not suggest that a seriously large number of gentry
families have been left out of consideration in the northern
and western parts of the Riding, with the possible exception
of Ewcross wapentake. Moreover, when we come to look at
the pattern of social structure revealed in the subsidy rolls,
we shall find that there are other reasons for accepting the
impression that the gentry did in fact own a high proportion
of the land in Agbrigg and Morley and also in Staincross
wapentakes. It must be borne in mind that the present
analysis of income distribution is not the equivalent of a
survey of social structure, even in relation to the landowning
classes. We are dealing here with the land of the West
Riding, regardless of whether its owners actually lived there:
consideration of the incomes of West Riding *inhabitants*
must be postponed until the next chapter.

There is one adjustment which ought if possible to be made to the figures given in Table V in order to make it a more accurate picture of the effective distribution of annual income about 1535. Mention has already been made of the right to wardship enjoyed by the chief lord of an honour or lordship over his tenants in fee. The effect of this right was that in any one year there were likely to be a small number of estates (usually gentry estates but sometimes those of noblemen) whose owner was a minor or an unmarried woman, and which were consequently in the hands of either the Crown or of someone who had bought the wardship from the King. The Crown had two kinds of income from the right of wardship: intermittent income from the sale of the persons of wards (and in some cases also an annuity amounting to the income from the ward's lands) and annual income from those wards' lands which had not been sold or granted in this way. The former income was probably the more important, but it cannot be translated into an annual estimate. The annual income from temporarily confiscated lands on the other hand can be estimated. The earliest feodary's account giving details of this Crown income from wards' lands belongs to the year 1540–1, immediately after the creation of the Court of Wards.[1] In that year the Court drew about £230 from wards' lands in the West Riding, and this does not seem to have been untypical of the 1540s. The figure around 1535 may have been lower. Before the Statutes of Uses in 1536 and of Wills in 1540, it was usual for the greater part of an estate to be assigned either to the widow's jointure or to the performance of the deceased man's will: only a small part, if anything, 'descended with the ward'. The statutes of 1536 and 1540 were intended to ensure that where wardship arose the Crown was not deprived of its rights in this way: after 1540 the King could by law claim one third of a ward's estate, after jointure had been allowed for. But even if, in 1535, the Crown had an income of as much as £230 from wardship lands in the West Riding, that would not make a very great difference to the pattern of distribution indicated by the Tables. That sum would represent no more than 2 per cent

[1] P.R.O.: Wards 8/1/ff. 36, 47, 51, 64, 91, 95, 97, 113, 127.

of £12,706, which was the total combined income of nobility and gentry resulting from the initial calculation; and an even smaller proportion of the combined noble and gentry income in the 'corrected' figures. If any serious distortion of the pattern of income distribution was caused by the system of wardship it was due to the sale and purchase of wardships; although this factor cannot be represented as an annual figure, it does represent a significant channel through which landed income from time to time passed from gentry and noble families into the coffers of the King.

V

It was mentioned earlier that during the century after 1540 landlords came to rely more and more on raising the entry fines payable by customary and leasehold tenants in order to make their income keep pace with the continuous rise in prices. Although this practice did not reach its height until after the middle of the century, it does appear in the land records of Henry VIII's time and it cannot be entirely ignored in the present context. Again we are dealing with something which cannot be quantified as annual income. Concerning customary fines some of the most interesting information relates to the wapentakes of Staincliffe and Ewcross. On some manors there, fines (or 'gressums') were levied with unusual frequency, and not just on the occasion of the death of a tenant. On the Mounteagle manors of Longacre and Sedbergh for example, a record of 1523 says that at the former place the tenants paid their 'gressums' every seven years, whilst at Sedbergh it was every three years. In a case like this it is possible to represent the fines as a sort of annual tax, amounting to between half and a third of the annual rent of the same tenants.[1] The only other place where a similar practice is found is Barnoldswick: in 1558 a series of new leases on the Duchy of Lancaster's estate there provided for 'gressums' of about one year's rent to be paid every ten years.[2] More typical perhaps was the custom found on the Clifford estates in Craven, including some of those which had once belonged to the Percy fee. In the early

[1] P.R.O.: SC 6/Hen VIII/6301.
[2] P.R.O.: DL 29/552/8739.

1540s a number of tenants of the Clifford entered into tenancies by warranty, which was stated to be for 'life and life'
and meant that a change of tenant was deemed to occur
on the death of either the tenant or the lord. Fines were
presumably payable on both occasions, but all we know are
the sums paid for the warrants themselves. On the manors of
Skipton, Settle and Giggleswick they mostly amounted to
between two and three-and-a-half years' rent.[1] For the Percy
lands in both Craven and Claro, Dr. Bean collected what
material he could find relating to entry fines before 1536.
In 1498, when the fifth Earl of Northumberland entered
into his inheritance, his tenants of Spofforth paid fines
amounting to something like a quarter or a third of a year's
rent. In 1525 the accounts for the whole Percy estates in
Yorkshire show that £52 was received in entry fines from
tenants whose total annual rental was £724: again the
fines were probably less than a full year's rent.[2] Random
evidence such as this cannot be used as the basis of generalization, but there may be some small significance in the fact
that these Percy figures indicate a rather lower level of fines
in 1498 and 1525 than that suggested by the Clifford
warrants of the 1540s.

There is another set of information concerning fines in
the records of the Duchy of Lancaster, and it has special
interest because some of it relates to the question whether
fines could be increased indefinitely by landlords, or whether
there were limits fixed by the custom of the manor. In 1559
an enquiry into the customs of Knaresborough and Aldborough revealed that on entry to a copyhold, whether
through death and inheritance or as a result of purchase, a
tenant must pay 6s. 8d. for an oxgang or bovate, or else
6d. or 12d. per acre. This was virtually one year's rent. But
since these sums were specifically stated in the manorial
customs they were fixed, and the Duchy could not follow the
example of Craven landlords and increase them from year to
year.[3] Similar evidence exists at Almondbury, where a

---

[1] Skipton Castle MSS, Y.A.S. Library, Leeds: DD 121/Bundles 29 and 31. At
Giggleswick, for example, fines totalling £48. 5s. were received for warrants whose
annual rental was £19. 19s. 9½d.
[2] J. M. W. Bean, op. cit., pp. 51–63.
[3] P.R.O.: DL 44/13.

survey of 1584 established that fines were fixed at one year's rent on death or alienation, or at half a year's rent if someone acquired a reversionary interest in a copyhold tenancy.[1] In the lordship of Wakefield the custom of fixed fines was called into question in 1608 by James I's officials and Miss M. J. Ellis has examined the results of this belated endeavour to increase royal revenues.[2] Up till then it would seem that the Crown was lenient towards its tenants in the West Riding in the matter of fines, although one should bear in mind Dr. Kerridge's observation that in Wiltshire Queen Elizabeth's I's stewards may well have taken the opportunity to line their own pockets from illicit entry fines taken on their own initiative.[3] Two cases in Yorkshire seem to indicate a similar practice there, even as early as the reign of Henry VIII. In 1529 John Frobisher, farmer of the Duchy of Lancaster manor of Altofts, was taken to court by an anonymous informer for taking 'gressums' there contrary to both the custom of the manor and the terms of his lease.[4] In about 1536 a more distinguished informer, Sir Henry Savile, accused his rival Sir Richard Tempest of misusing his farm of the bailiwick and courts of Wakefield lordship to obtain entry fines on new assarts of land; but in this case he may have done no more than he was entitled to do.[5]

One reason for the increasing tendency to let land on lease, instead of according to custom (or by copy of court roll), may have been the desire to escape inflexible rules about entry fines. The tendency itself is beyond question. On the Percy estates in the Riding before 1536 there were very few leaseholders; but by 1570 when Humberstone made a full survey of the same manors there were hardly any tenants at will (or by custom) on the manors of Spofforth and Tadcaster.[6] The Archbishop of York granted a number of leases in his lordship of Ripon in 1532, and in this case

[1] Spencer-Stanhope MSS, Cartwright Hall, Bradford: MS. no. 1331.
[2] M. J. Ellis: 'A Study in the Manorial History of Halifax Parish in the sixteenth and early seventeenth centuries', *Y.A.J.*, xl (1960–1) 259–61.
[3] E. Kerridge: 'The Movement of Rent, 1540–1640', *Econ. Hist. Rev.*, 2nd ser., vi (1954), 30–2.
[4] P.R.O.: DL 1/22/R10.
[5] Y.A.S.R.S., xlv, pp. 46–8; li, pp. 28–30.
[6] P.R.O.: SC 6/Hen VIII/4283; E 164/37/ff. 208–25.

we have details of the fines, which were almost exactly one year's rent in each case.[1] A sample survey of 195 leases on the West Riding estates of eight monasteries, still in force at the time of the dissolution, showed that as many as 62 had been granted before 1530. Nostell Priory had begun to introduce this form of tenure in place of customary tenure (and not just for farms or demesnes) before 1520; Roche Abbey was another house which was using the method increasingly during the 1520s. From about 1530 the lease became increasingly popular amongst monastic landlords.[2]

We must not, however, take it for granted that the only motive for converting tenures from copyhold (or from tenure at will) to leasehold was that of the landlord. It is possible that on the side of the tenants there was preference for a form of tenure that would give security for a fixed period, regardless of the accidents of death and inheritance fines. Another factor may also have come into play on the monastic estates, after the first dissolutions of 1536. In the sample of 195 monastic leases just noticed, as many as 81 dated from the years 1537–9. Could this mean that the monasteries were willing to exchange the future benefits of ownership (which they would themselves lose if the houses were dissolved) for immediate financial gain in the form of entry fines, or even simply for good will in the locality of their estates? There is nothing to show whether fines were levied on these late leases, but the inclusion in the dissolution statute of 1539 of a clause to the effect that purchasers of monastic property could rescind leases granted within a year prior to the suppression suggests that the tenants under such leases gained unfairly by them. We know that the Earl of Cumberland successfully challenged the validity of certain leases made by the Prior of Bolton to tenants on land later bought by the Earl.[3] Lest this should leave the reader with the impression that monastic landlords were in

[1] P.R.O.: SC 6/Hen VIII/4409.
[2] The eight monasteries were: Bolton Priory (P.R.O., E 303/15–50), Healaugh Priory (ibid. 292–314), Kirkstall Abbey (ibid. 325–420 and SC 6/Hen VIII/4590), Monk Bretton Priory (E 303/480–699), Nostell Priory (ibid. 608–780), Pontefract Priory (ibid. 768–867), Roche Abbey (SC 6/Hen VIII 4534), and Rufford Priory Notts. (SC 6/Hen VIII/2827).
[3] P.R.O.: E 315/108/ff. 103–4.

a general way more lenient than their lay counterparts, it is worth noticing that when the Pilgrimage of Grace began in 1536 one of the grievances of the commons was that certain monastic landlords had taken unreasonable fines on customary holdings in Kirkbyshire and Nidderdale. The Church was sometimes, it would seem, a harder landlord than the Crown.[1]

Whatever the defects of this discussion of income from freehold and spiritual 'property', we are on much firmer ground in that sphere than when we come to other kinds of income from land. Concerning the profits of agriculture taken by the tenants who paid the landlords' rents, we have hardly any documentary evidence at all. Indeed there is less material about actual agricultural operations and finance in the early sixteenth century than we have for the thirteenth century, when some of the great lords and monasteries kept their demesnes 'in hand' and kept records of the yield and sale of grain and the wages paid to their labourers. By 1535 such demesnes were more usually farmed out to smaller men, who had no need to keep records of their activity and possibly could not even write; it is not until the late sixteenth century that we begin to find farm-records kept by yeomen. Nor do subsidy records help us very much here, for as we shall see Tudor subsidies were more often assessed on a man's moveable goods than on his income from land, especially when he had no freehold land of his own.

There is, however, one calculation that can be made, as a means to guessing the total agricultural income of the Riding. It is not one upon which great reliance should be placed, but it might enable us to place the information about total freehold income into better perspective. Its starting-point is the fact that practically all farmers had to pay a tenth of their produce to the clergy as tithes. These were collected in the fields either by the clergy themselves or by their servants, or in some cases by their farmers; and the collection was presumably as regular as the harvest itself. Since the tithes were sometimes farmed out by the ecclesiastical institutions to which they belonged, and since the farmer presumably made a profit (at least in good years), we

[1] M. H. and R. Dodds: *The Pilgrimage of Grace* (Cambridge, 1915) i, pp. 369 ff.

cannot obtain a precise figure for their monetary value in any one year simply by taking the sum received by the Church as spiritual income. In any case, part of the £5,133 drawn by the Church in 1535 from its spiritualities came from other sources than tithes: from oblations, church pennies, and the like.

Nevertheless the figure of £5,133 is not totally irrelevant, and we might be able to make use of it if we could assume that the profits of farmers and the non-tithe sources of income cancelled one another out. If this assumption is made, we can make the basis of our calculation the supposition (it is no more) that in an average year in the 1530s the tithes of the West Riding were worth somewhere around £5,000. If the tithe was in actual fact a tenth of the total produce (another assumption which cannot be tested), this would mean the total value of agricultural production in the Riding was £50,000 a year. Now we know that the total of freehold and spiritual income in 1535 was probably in the region of £28,000; possibly, with the growing income from entry fines it was nearer to £30,000. If these two estimates are placed side by side, we find that over half the agricultural income of the Riding was drawn by the landowning sections of society. The rest, about £20,000 perhaps, was shared by the rest of the rural population of the Riding.

III

THE SOCIAL STRUCTURE AND THE
SUBSIDY ROLLS OF 1545–6

I

ONLY a small number of the inhabitants of the West Riding belonged to land owning families, and a study of their fortunes is no substitute for an analysis of the structure of the whole society. The latter task, which we must now attempt, demands a quite different approach from that adopted in Chapter II. There the appropriate units of study were lordships and estates, or quantities of revenue derived from them; here we must be concerned with people. Not all those who owned land in the Riding actually lived there; but here we must deal exclusively with the resident population. When landowners are referred to they will be those who lived in the Riding; and in economic terms we shall be interested in their whole incomes, even if some of their land-revenue came from outside the West Riding. The statistics to be presented in his chapter therefore will not be strictly comparable to those of Chapter II, although we shall find that the pattern of landownership was an important factor in the social structure of different areas of the Riding. The natural unit for the study of social structure is the household. It should not be confused with the family, even in the sense of nuclear family. Some households included not only blood relatives of two or more generations, but also servants and even clients and hangers-on. A noble household was always quite large: Lord Darcy's in 1521 numbered eighty people, including not only menial servants but also sons of gentlemen or yeomen who performed services in return for being trained in the arts of sixteenth-century living.[1] Gentry households probably included a similar element, but on a smaller scale. Even the substantial yeoman or farmer would have a servant or two, and probably most of the secular clergy

[1] *L.P.* III (i), no. 1330.

would have a housekeeper of some sort. In towns, merchants and craftsmen might have an apprentice or journeyman living in. But the great majority of peasant households were probably limited to members of the family, and the relatively small number of very large households probably does not affect the demographers' assumption that the average size of a household was four or five persons.[1] It is unfortunately not possible to classify households according to size, though if that information were available it might be a good indicator of wealth and status. The three criteria most usually applied in social structure are those of status (in a formal sense), of occupation, and of income or wealth.

Distinctions of status certainly existed in sixteenth-century England. Apart from the distinction between laity and clergy, there was within each of those categories an acknowledged hierarchy of status and precedence. In the case of the laity it was indicated in some detail by the statutes of apparel which were still being passed, and being revised, not merely reiterated in old forms, by the Parliaments of Henry VIII. The statute of 1533 for example laid down the following categories of people and specified the kinds of apparel which were forbidden to all people below each rank:[2] the King and his family came first; then Dukes and Marquesses; Viscounts and Barons; Knights of the Garter; Knights, Barons' sons, and people with lands and fees worth at least £200 a year; men with lands of over £100 a year; heirs of Knights, and men with £40 a year; gentlemen with £20 a year; men with over £5 a year; yeomen and servants with a freehold income of £2 a year; husbandmen; and finally labourers or servants in husbandry, journeymen in handicrafts, etc., who took wages for their work. As an illustration, one may cite the fact that the wearing of sable fur and various other kinds of material was limited to people

---

[1] J. Krause: 'The Medieval Household, Large or Small?', *Econ. Hist. Rev.*, 2nd ser., ix (1956), 420–32. Mr. Laslett found that at Clayworth (Nottinghamshire) in 1676 many households had only three people, and the average size was 4·09; P. Laslett, *et al.*: *An Introduction to English Historical Demography* (London, 1966), p. 199.

[2] *Statutes*, iii, 24 Hen VIII, cap. 13. Cf. Sir Wm. Holdsworth: *History of English Law*, ii (4th edn., 1936), p. 465; and iv (2nd edn., 1937), pp. 405–6; and also F. E. Baldwin: *Sumptuary Legislation and Personal Regulation in England* (Baltimore, 1926).

who were Barons or of higher rank. Again, it was forbidden
to anyone below the category of men with £5 a year in lands
and fees to wear most kinds of foreign-made cloth, any kind
of silk, and any cloth at all costing more than 6s. 8d. a yard.
Special privileges were allowed to clergy, to holders of
certain royal offices, to mayors and aldermen, to graduates
of universities, and so on. But the fact that such regulations
were deemed necessary at all suggests that these distinctions
were breaking down in practice, and the preamble of the
statute virtually admits as much. Moreover the use of
figures for annual income to define some of the categories is
an indication that title alone was no longer an adequate
criterion of status. Thus whilst the distinctions made in the
sumptuary laws were not without significance, they hardly
amounted to a rigid caste system of the Hindu kind, and it
would be quite impossible to use them as a means to classify
every household in the West Riding, or even a meaningful
sample. There may be some point in treating the clergy
and the laity separately, and in distinguishing between the
nobility and commoners; but our most important need is for
criteria that will enable us to distinguish between different
categories of lay commoners, and for that purpose the terms
of the statutes of apparel are not suitable. A more realistic
approach, though not, alas, one which can be applied statistically to the population of the Riding, might be to combine
certain very obvious distinctions of status with some equally
obvious distinctions of occupation or function. By doing
that it is possible to identify seven broad social categories
in the West Riding in the time of Henry VIII.

(i) *Nobility and Gentry:* These are the lay landowners whom
we have covered in a different way in Chapter II. Of the
noble families who owned land in the West Riding in 1535
only three had residences there; four if one counts Percy,
but the sixth Earl seems seldom to have gone to Spofforth.
By the end of the reign there were still about three or four
noble residents in the Riding, but not the same families as
ten years before, owing to the changes consequent upon the
Pilgrimage of Grace and the Crown's acquisition of the
Percy inheritance. The vast majority of the lay landowners

who lived in the Riding therefore, at least two hundred of the three hundred and more who owned land there, were of gentry status; a few whom we have counted as 'gentry' because they had lands worth over £10 a year, would probably be more accurately described as substantial yeomen.[1] Roughly a score of West Riding men in 1535 were knights; many more used the title 'esquire', whilst the majority were mere 'gentlemen'. The range of incomes was considerable, with an upper limit well above £200. In 1535 (and also in 1546) the two richest families were those of Sir Henry Savile and Sir William Gascoigne: in the subsidy roll of the latter year they were assessed on lands worth £400 and £533 a year respectively.[2] Other heads of West Riding gentry families with over £200 a year on that assessment were Sir William Malleverer of Wothersome, Sir William Middleton of Middleton and Stockeld, and Sir George Darcy of Aston (who had lost his father's lands by attainder but had built up an estate of his own by marriage and purchases). But that makes only five families in this high category of tax assessment in 1546, from which we may perhaps conclude that on the whole the knights and prominent esquires of the West Riding were less wealthy than men of similar status in Southern England.

(ii) *Clergy:* The diversity of institutions and people embraced by the word 'Church' has already been remarked upon: it included men as different in status and wealth as the Archbishop of York or the Abbot of Selby and ordinary parish rectors, vicars and chantry-priests. Some of the individuals who entered the Church were related to important gentry and noble families; others were of peasant or artisan origins. Altogether there were probably about 900 people in the West Riding who should be counted as clergy on the eve of the Henrician reformation. Of these only about 500 to 550 remained at the end of the reign, and by 1553 only 250.[3] If the West Riding had a population of around 100,000, there must have been one cleric for every 110 laymen in

---

[1] The problem of defining 'gentry' economically was discussed in Chapter II, *supra*, pp. 65–6.
[2] P.R.O.: E 179/207/196 and 194.
[3] Cf. Table VII, *infra*, p. 93.

1535, but only one for every four hundred souls twenty years later. In the 1540s there was thus a sizeable group of ex-clergy: men who had been forced to leave the monasteries and resume some kind of secular existence.

(iii) *Professional Men:* One aspect of the social transformation of the two centuries between 1500 and 1700 was the tendency for certain occupations to become professions for which special training was required. By the beginning of the eighteenth century they included the Church, the Law, the Army, and perhaps also medicine, as well as teaching. This trend had not gone so far in the time of Henry VIII, but it had certainly begun to apply to the Church (already counted as a separate category) and to the Law. There were perhaps ten or a dozen men living in the West Riding in the 1530s and 1540s who had undergone the full rigours of a legal training in the Inns of Court. There must have been many more who knew something of the law and practised it at a local level. Successful lawyers, who rose to be judges for example, could become very rich and might join the ranks of the higher gentry: prominent Riding families whose fortunes had derived from success in legal practice during the fifteenth century included Fairfax, Vavasour and Gascoigne.[1] Others were much poorer, or else depended on the fees which their expertise could earn them, rather than on property of their own: Thomas Grice, a Wakefield lawyer who was in the service of Lord Darcy and also served on many commissions of the peace, and who died in 1546, left lands valued at only £8 a year; but in 1545 he had been assessed for the subsidy on lands and fees together worth £33 a year.[2] Other recipients of fees on large estates may also have been professional men, in the field of estate administration; but there no formalized training such as that given by the Inns of Court was involved, and the opportunities for economic gain were (monastic lands apart) much smaller than in the case of the Law. As for medicine and school-teaching, the latter was probably carried on mainly

---

[1] On the position of common lawyers generally, see E. W. Ives: 'The Reputation of the Common Lawyers in English Society, 1450–1550', *Univ. of Birmingham Hist. Journal,* vii (1959–60), 130–161.
[2] P.R.O.: C 142/74/48; E 179/207/186.

by clergy down to the dissolution of the Chantries after 1547, whilst the former would probably be a specialist activity only for people employed in great households, as Mr. Wendy was employed by the sixth Earl of Northumberland.[1]

(iv) *Peasantry:* This was undoubtedly the largest class in the West Riding down to the eighteenth, or even the nineteenth century. There seems to be no way of applying to sixteenth-century England the classification sometimes made in modern agrarian societies, into 'rich', 'middle' and 'poor' peasants, which depends on the question whether a family has more land than it can cultivate without hired labour, just enough land, or too little land to live without going to work on others' land. But certainly there were differences of wealth between the various peasant families of a sixteenth-century village, with substantial yeomen at one end of the scale and mere cottagers at the other. We must postpone until later in the chapter the discussion of problems which arise when one tries to measure those differences statistically.

(v) *Craftsmen and manufacturers:* In all areas of the Riding, if not in every village, there would be blacksmiths, masons, carpenters, cobblers, and so on: essential craftsmen providing goods for the local community. In certain districts, where there was rural industry, the number of families engaged in manufacture would be much greater. In both cases it is probable that some of the people involved combined their craft or industry with agriculture. But the number of households which derived all or part of their income from these activities cannot be counted, and individual craftsmen come into the records of the period only rarely. Nor is there any means of knowing whether, in general, these people were better or worse off economically than those who lived entirely from farming.

(vi) *Merchants and traders:* It is likewise impossible to count the number of people occupied in some kind of

---

[1] J. M. W. Bean: *The Estates of the Percy Family 1416–1537* (Oxford, 1958), p. 146.

commercial activity, who ranged from wholesale merchants in towns like Wakefield and Leeds, to small shopkeepers and rural pedlars. A few such people can be identified, as we shall see, but as a group they are not easy to study statistically. Some of them, especially in the clothing district, became comparatively rich and were able to buy land; but even the larger wholesalers operated on a very small scale compared with the London merchants of the day. The majority of the people in the category were probably no better off than the peasantry.

(vii) *Servants:* Finally we must note in passing the not inconsiderable number of people employed as servants in the households of landowners, clergy, professional men and the better-off yeomen and merchants. So far as is known there was no household slavery in England by this period, although the laws of villeinage had been allowed to lapse rather than been repealed. How far household servants took advantage of their freedom to move from one employment to another is impossible to say, though one may guess that it happened less frequently in rural areas than in the towns. This group indeed is one whose presence in the Riding cannot be doubted, but it seldom appears in the documents and we can say little about its members as individuals.

This brief survey of functional or occupational groups suggests two important conclusions. First, the barriers to social mobility were not institutionalized, so that individual families could move from one group to another by taking up a new occupation; over time, a family might acquire a new status as well. Secondly, within each group there was considerable diversity of income and wealth. Even if we were able to place every family or household in the Riding into the appropriate category, according to occupation, we should still need to enquire separately into the pattern of income distribution. As it is, the sources that bear most significantly on the question of social structure relate to wealth rather than to occupation. Only when we have examined them in some detail will we be able to see occupational differences in terms of income and prosperity.

II

The most important sources relating to personal wealth in early Tudor England, indeed the only ones that can be used statistically, are the subsidy rolls. Laymen and clergy were taxed separately, which means that we have two separate sets of records, and since those which survive relate to different years it will be most convenient to deal first with the clergy and then with the laity.

The most complete assessment of clerical taxable wealth in the West Riding in a single year is contained in the *Valor Ecclesiasticus* of 1535, supplemented where necessary by the *Liber Valorum* of the same year. For the part of the West Riding which lay within the Archdeaconry of Richmond the records of 1535 are best seen in relation to the surviving portions of an earlier assessment, that for Wolsey's clerical subsidy of 1523.[1] To these sources must be added, for information about numbers of monks, canons and nuns in the various religious houses, the records made at the time of the Dissolution. The available information about the social structure of the Church in the West Riding about 1535 is summarized in Table VII. Altogether there were at least 347 regular clergy; another 110 or so people in the colleges, hospitals and preceptories of the Order of St. John; and 439 secular clergy, not counting the Archbishop of York who had his principal Diocesan residence at Bishopthorpe in the Ainsty. This makes a total of nearly 900 clergy. The wealth of the Church was not however uniformly distributed amongst them, as the table also indicates. Monks were a good deal richer than nuns; and, with the exception of St. Robert's at Knaresborough, the friars were much poorer than either, at least in terms of property. These averages, however, conceal uneven distribution of wealth within the religious orders. The thirty-two monks of Fountains Abbey had a net income per head of £30 a year (or more, if the *Valor* figure is an undervaluation), whereas the average income per head of the brethren of Roche Abbey was only £13 a year.[2] In practice no doubt the head of the house

---

[1] See note accompanying Table VII.

[2] D. Knowles and R. N. Hadcock: *Medieval Religious Houses in England and Wales* (London, 1953), pp. 108, 114.

would have much more than the average share of the income, and individual monks much less; in theory, of course, none of them was permitted any personal wealth at all. There were contrasts too between rich and poor amongst the secular clergy. Some vicars had under £5 a year, and a number of rectors had less than £10. At the other end of the scale were the dozen or so livings worth over £30 a year, including three worth over £50. Two of the latter were rectories: at

TABLE VII

The Clergy of the West Riding in 1535.

	Number of people	Approximate annual income per head in group
Religious Orders:		
Monks and Canons in eleven monasteries:	213	£20. 0s.
Nuns in seven nunneries:	90	£3. 10s.
Friars of Knaresborough:	10	£8. 0s.
Friars of four other houses:	34	£0. 10s.
Other Houses:		
St. John's preceptories:	10?	?
Colleges, hospitals:	100?	?
Secular Clergy:		
Rectors:	62	£20
Vicars:	108	£9
Chantry-priests:	269	£4

Note: The information here about religious orders is drawn from the more detailed figures given in Appendix III.

That for the secular clergy, colleges, hospitals, etc. is taken from the *Valor Ecclesiasticus*, passim.

Sources: Valor Ecclesiasticus (Record Comm., 1825), v, 1–79, 143–6 and 249–60; this incorporates the *Liber Valorum*. The information for 1535 was supplemented, for the Deaneries of Boroughbridge and Kirkby Lonsdale, by reference to the assessments of 1523: P.R.O.: E 36/149. The information for the religious orders is taken from the more detailed figures in Appendix III, *infra*, pp. 288 ff.

Spofforth Alan Perse (Percy?) drew £73, and at Darfield Henry Jackson had £53 despite the fact that half the rectory was impropriated.[1] The richest living of all in the Riding was the vicarage of Halifax, whose incumbent from before 1525 till his death in 1556 was the notorious Dr. Robert Haldsworth. We shall meet him again in connection with the Pilgrimage of Grace and a dispute over a hoard of gold found in his house; with an annual income of £84 from his

[1] *Valor Ecclesiasticus*, v, pp. 34, 55.

benefice he was on the same level as a substantial squire.[1]
This was an age when parsons were something more than
'passing rich on forty pounds a year'.

In the five years after the making of the *Valor Ecclesiasticus*
about 350 of the people counted in Table VII ceased to be
clergy, as a result of the policy of dissolving the religious
orders. The disappearance of a small number of chantries in
the Riding during the second half of Henry VIII's reign
meant another slight reduction in the number of clergy by
1546.[2] Then under Edward VI most of the chantries and
colleges were dissolved, leaving probably fewer than 240
clergy in the West Riding by the time of his death in 1553.
With a small number of exceptions, the deprived clerics
were not removed from the scene entirely but continued to
live in the county as laymen. Some were old and did not long
survive their expulsion from their houses; but in 1546 there
may still have been as many as 100 ex-religious in the
Riding, and some are clearly identifiable in the lay subsidy
rolls of that year, in receipt of pensions on which they paid
tax. Others had doubtless merged with the lay population as
yeomen or craftsmen. A few former monks, the 'quondam'
heads of houses, were granted pensions on a grander scale
and were able to end their days as country gentlemen.
William Browne of Monk Bretton retired on £40 a year,
and Marmaduke Bradley, the last Abbot of Fountains, got
£100 a year as pension. These sums, and indeed clerical
income generally, can be compared with the incomes of
some of the laymen in the tax records of 1546. The Prioress
of Hampole on the other hand got only £10 a year, and the
Prioress of Arthington a mere £2.[3]

III

The lay subsidy rolls are much more difficult to use than
the records of clerical taxation. But thanks to the work of

---

[1] Ibid., p. 70, Dr. Haldsworth will reappear in Chapter V, *infra*, p. 189.

[2] For example at Halifax, the chantry survey of 1546 shows that the Frith Chantry
had had no priest since 1539, the lands being occupied by one Edmund Ackroid;
Yorkshire Chantry Certificates, ii, Surtees Soc., cxii, (1893), p. 296. The commissions sent out to survey the chantries in 1546 were instructed to cover all lands that
had belonged to chantries at any time since 1536, suggesting that private disendow-
ment was becoming widespread by this time.

[3] *L.P.*, XIII (ii), no. 888; XIV (ii), nos. 587–8, 641.

Dr. R. S. Schofield a great deal is now known about the
complicated administrative system which produced them,
and with that knowledge at our disposal we can hope to get
the best out of these rolls whilst at the same time avoiding
some of the dangers of trying to stretch their meaning too
far.[1]

Unlike the 'fifteenth and tenth' of 1334 the subsidies
granted by Parliament to Henry VIII were not assessed on
the wealth of whole communities, but on the value of the
lands or goods of the more prosperous householders in each
place. A distinction was made between the nobility and the
rest of the population: the noblemen had the privilege of
being assessed before the Lord Chancellor at Westminster;
whereas commoners, regardless of status, were assessed by
the county or hundred (or wapentake) commissioners in the
district where they normally lived. Since there were only
three or four noblemen who could be called West Riding
residents at any one date in this period, we can ignore the
separate noble records for the purposes of a general survey.
The assessments were made according to specific regulations laid down in the statute granting the particular subsidy. These were very elaborate and the details changed
from time to time, but in general they called for two principal
kinds of assessment. One of these comprised the annual
value of a man's lands, fees, annuities and other regular
yearly income; the other the capital value of all his moveable
possessions, including money (with account taken of any
debts owed to him, or owed by him, at the time of assessment). The statute of 1523 provided for a third kind of
assessment, on day wages amounting to over £1 a single
year, but that experiment was not repeated. If all these
assessments had survived for every individual who paid tax
in any given year we should have a truly remarkable set of
records. But each person was taxed only once, either on his
annual income from lands and fees or on the value of his
goods, and consequently the subsidy commissioners needed
only to report to Westminster the assessment actually to be
used to determine the tax payable. Any initial notes they
had taken to decide which category of assessment was

[1] For a discussion of the subsidy rolls, see Appendix I, *infra*, pp. 264–6.

8

appropriate in each case were destroyed. The subsidy rolls which survive therefore consist of lists of names together with an assessment of either the land income or the value of goods beside each name. It is because the records were constituted in this way that they are so difficult to use, and at the same time so rewarding if used carefully.

The subsidy rolls hitherto most frequently used by historians writing on sixteenth-century social structure belong to the series made in 1524 which survives intact for a remarkably large area of England.[1] But for the reasons to be discussed in Appendix I, I have preferred to take the rolls of 1545–6 as the basis of the present analysis. For the West Riding they seem to be more detailed, if not more accurate, than those of 1524; and they have the added advantage of being closer in date to the other major sources studied here. The series of rolls made in 1546 is virtually complete for all parts of the Riding. It was made in accordance with the regulations set forth in the subsidy act of 1545, which granted a tax to be assessed on all laymen with lands worth £1 a year or more, or who had at least £5 worth of moveable goods. The rolls of 1545 survive less completely, but where they exist they form a valuable supplement to those of the following year, for the statute of 1543 under which they were compiled laid down as minimum qualifications for contribution in that year the possession of lands worth £1 a year or goods worth £1. The difference was significant: whereas only 4,361 inhabitants of the Riding were assessed in 1546, it would seem that nearly 15,000 were included on the rolls of 1545.[2]

The first stage in analysing the lay subsidy rolls of 1545–6 is to decide upon a set of useful categories and to count the numbers of people assessed in each category. The units of assessment were presumably households: occasionally two people in a single household may both have had to contribute at the same time, but this seems to have been

---

[1] Cf. W. G. Hoskins: 'English Provincial Towns of the early Sixteenth Century', *Trans. of Royal Hist. Soc.*, 5th ser., vi (1956), 2–3; and J. Cornwall: 'The Early Tudor Gentry' *Econ. Hist. Rev.*, 2nd ser., xvii (1965), 465 ff.

[2] P.R.O.: E 179/207, *passim*.

very unusual. The rolls of 1546 enable us to classify all the
contributors of that year, in every township of the Riding.
Two kinds of distinction are possible: between assessment
on lands and assessment on goods, and (within each of these
groups) between assessments of different amounts. A simple
analysis of the 1546 rolls in these terms is contained in
Table VIII, together with a note of the rate payable that
year by people in each category. Using the 1545 records,
which are fullest in relation to the lower categories of
assessment, it is possible to estimate fairly reliably that there
were another 10,000 people in the Riding with goods worth
£1, who paid tax in that year but were not liable for assessment in 1546. Neither this figure, nor those in the table,
should cause any surprise: there was, as one would expect,
a social pyramid with a large amount of wealth in the hands

TABLE VIII

*The Pattern of Lay Subsidy Assessments in the West Riding
in 1546.*

Category of assessment		Number of taxpayers	Proportion of total number (%)	Rate of tax payable
Lands:	over £100	16	0·3	2*s.* per £
	£40–£99	41	0·9	2*s.* per £
	£20–£39	77	1·7	2*s.* per £
	£10–£19	98	2·1	2*s.* per £
	£5–£9	173	3·7	2*s.* per £
	£1–£4	1,358	29·4	2*s.* per £
Fees only:	£1–£9	53	1·1	2*s.* per £
Goods:	over £50	12	0·3	16*d.* per £
	£20–£49	188	4·1	16*d.* per £
	£10–£19	470	10·1	12*d.* per £
	£5–£9	2,145	46·3	8*d.* per £
Lands and Fees: Total		1,816	39·2	—
Goods: Total		2,815	60·8	—
Grand Total:		4,631	100	—

Sources: Subsidy Rolls, P.R.O.: E 179/207/184, 185, 188, 190–1, 195–6, 198, and 217/110. The roll for
   Skyrack wapentake is printed in Thoresby Soc. Publications, ix (1899), 153–60. For rates payable, see
   Statutes, iii, 37 Hen VIII, cap. 25.

of a small number of the richer people. The subsidy rolls confirm the impression, generally held, that there was a gradation of incomes and wealth in society, rather than a sharp distinction between a few very rich and a mass of very poor people. A 'middle class' (if one dare call it that) already existed, though not of course in the Victorian sense of the term.

IV

The second stage of the analysis is more complicated. We must now try to discover what these various categories of tax assessment signified in terms of social structure: that is, of occupation and status. To begin with, what did it mean if a man was taxed on his goods rather than on lands? Certainly those who were taxed on land income cannot be regarded as possessing no goods; but equally one cannot infer that a man whose goods were assessed had no land. The terms of the statute simply laid down that each person should be taxed in whichever way would yield the highest actual payment to the Crown, given the value of his lands and goods and the rate of payment laid down by the same statute. Thus a man who had land worth £10 a year and also goods worth £25 was liable in 1546 to have to pay 20s. if he was taxed on his lands, but 33s. 4d. on his goods: so he was entered in the subsidy rolls as having goods worth £25, and it was on them that he made his contribution. There may have been a general tendency for the subsidy commissioners to assume that if a man had lands he would be better taxed on them (land, after all, being more difficult to hide than goods); but if they did their job thoroughly they might well discover the sort of situation just described. In short, we have no evidence to show that the distinction between assessment on lands and assessment on goods was anything but artificial. We cannot say that those taxed on land were landowners and those taxed on goods were not. Nor can we take it for granted that where men were taxed on goods the value on which they were assessed was a direct indication of social position. There is no indication of the nature of the goods valued, so that in some cases men with £25 worth of 'goods' might be clothiers or merchants with large stocks on their hands, whilst in other cases they might be successful farmers who had saved a quantity of plate. One would expect, in any event, that an older man would have a more valuable stock of goods than a younger man in a similar social position, if only because he had had longer to establish himself and to save. Finally, where goods are concerned, one has to bear in mind the likelihood of concealment. Two people in the same social and economic position might be assessed differently for no other reason than that one successfully concealed some of his possessions, whilst the other did not. Since the subsidy rolls on their own do not permit easy generalizations, we must try to identify some of the individual tax-payers by looking at other records, in particular at estate accounts and surveys.

Historians of medieval England, concerned with periods before 1300, have had to rely almost entirely on estate records for information about social structure; and the questions they have found least difficult to answer have been ones relating to sizes of holding, forms of tenure, and the obligations of the peasantry. Even Kosminsky, whose perspective was wider than that of most earlier writers on the subject, found himself devoting most space to questions of that kind, and ran into difficulties when he came to ask about peasant income and standards of living.[1] Tawney, following in the footsteps of Vinogradoff, devoted a good part of his study of the agrarian problem to an analysis of estate records of the sixteenth century, and produced figures classifying tenants on a large number of manors according to their sizes of holding and terms of tenure.[2] He satisfied himself that practically everywhere the regular patterns of the twelfth and thirteenth centuries that had been traced by Vinogradoff and Maitland had broken down by the sixteenth, though he found considerable differences of structure between estates in different parts of England. But Kosminsky found that the regular patterns only ever

[1] E. A. Kosminksy: *Studies in the Agrarian History of England in the Thirteenth Century* (Oxford, 1956), Ch. iv.
[2] R. H. Tawney: *The Agrarian Problem in the Sixteenth Century* (London, 1912), Ch. i.

existed on a certain type of large ecclesiastical estate, and that already in Edward I's time there was much variety in the pattern of peasant holdings on smaller estates. Another conclusion which Tawney reached was that by the sixteenth century types of tenure amongst smallholders probably mattered less for social differentiation than the custom governing customary tenures of all kinds. His observations on these points are no less valid now than when they were first made. He failed however to take into account the important factor of sub-tenancy. The landlord who had a survey or rental made for his estate was interested only in the amounts of land held, and the dues owed, by his direct tenants. But many of those direct tenants sub-let their land to others, and there may even have been under-tenants of under-tenants. The landlord's record was thus very far from being the equivalent of a full picture of the social structure of his estate. One is reminded of the Irish landlord in the mid-nineteenth century whose conscience was pricked by the disastrous famine of 1846: he sought help from the Society of Friends to have food distributed to his tenants, imagining that there were about sixty of them; but it turned out that because of sub-letting there were six hundred![1] Such an extreme situation is unlikely to have existed anywhere in sixteenth-century Yorkshire; but subtenancy certainly existed and for that reason we cannot use estate records on their own as a guide to rural social structure.

I propose here to use estate records as a means of expanding the information contained in the tax records: we may begin with an experimental comparison between a subsidy assessment and an estate survey relating to a single township. It must be a township where all or most of the land belonged to a single owner, and where a survey was made at a date not too far removed from that of the subsidy rolls. These conditions are both fulfilled at Selby, where it is possible to compare a full subsidy roll for 1545 with the virtually complete survey of tenants, holdings and rents, contained in the first augmentations account made after the suppression of Selby Abbey for the year ending at Michaelmas 1540. The main outlines of the assessment are shown in Table IX,

[1] Cecil Woodham-Smith: *The Reason Why* (Penguin Books, 1958), p. 116.

TABLE IX

Subsidy Assessments at Selby in 1545.

Category of assessment	Total number of people assessed	Number of people assessed who also appear in the account of 1540
Lands: £20–£39	2	2
£10–£19	—	—
£5–£9	1	—
£1–£4	5	2
Fees: £1–£5	8	6
Goods: £10–£19	9	8
£5–£9	20	11
£1–£4	68	31
Total:	113	60

Sources: P.R.O.: E 179/207/181, and SC 6/Hen VIII/4606.

using the same categories of assessment as those used for the whole Riding in Table VIII above. The first remarkable result to emerge from the comparison is the discovery (indicated in the same table) that not many more than half of the 113 contributors to the tax at Selby in 1545 are named in the account of five years earlier. Three possible explanations can be adduced. First, there may have been some changes of surname in the interval, either because of marriage or for some other reason. Second, there were sure to be some changes in the occupation of houses and holdings as a result of death and inheritance, and perhaps also of sales of holdings and even migrations into and out of the town. But third, and probably most important, there must have been some tenants whose circumstances changed little between 1540 and 1545, but who were simply never the direct tenants of the abbot, or later of the King. As inhabitants they would be taxed, if wealthy enough; but as subtenants the chief landlord had no interest in them.

Conversely let us take the 236 names which occur in the account: only sixty of them appear also in the subsidy roll, leaving 176 who were tenants of the Abbey at its dissolution but who were not taxed in 1545. Again the possibility of changes in name, and the likelihood of some changes of

TABLE X

Selby: A Cross-section of Society, as Reflected in the Subsidy Roll of 1545 and the Augmentations Account of 1540.

Name and other information	Assessment in 1545: Land	Fees	Goods	Held from Selby Abbey in 1540:	Rents paid in 1540: Free	Cust.
Robert Walker, auditor and clerk of courts to Selby Abbey (at fee of £19)	—	£27 (and land)	—	In Selby: 4 mess, 4 cots, 3 tofts, 5 closes. Other land in Brayton, T. Willoughby, Hambleton, Carleton; and some tithes in Barlow and Carleton	7s.	£2. 5s. 9d. / £6. 0s. 8d.
John Beverley, farmer of mills in 1540	£24	—	—	All Selby mills; 5 tofts, 6 closes; 31 acres	—	£11. 2s. 0d.
Oswald Sysson, farmer of Abbey site after the Dissolution, under Leonard Beckwith	—	—	—	Site and demesnes; no details	(not known)	
Thomas Stringer, who owned Selby's two ships in 1544	—	—	£15	3 mess; 1 cot; 1 barn; 1 toft; 1 bovate; 6 closes	2s.	£1. 17s.
John Pereson	—	—	£10	1 mess; 1 cot; 1 close	3d.	3s. 6d.
Richard Heirbread	—	—	£7	2 mess; 2 cots; 1 toft; 1 selion; 3 closes	1s. 5d.	£1. 10s. 4d.
Agnes Cutler	£2	—	£4	2 mess; 1 bovate; 2 tofts; 6 closes	2s. 8d.	£1. 1s. 9d.
Thomas Shepperd	—	—	—	1 toft, built on; 1 other parcel	2s.	—
Robert Burley, gentleman	—	£4	—	1 cottage	—	2s. 6d.
Thomas Rayner	—	£1	—	1 cottage	—	2s. 6d.
Thomas Watson	—	—	£3	1 messuage and some other land	—	2s. 4d.
Thomas Dixon	—	—	£1	1 messuage; 1 bovate; 1 close	—	12s. 0d.

Sources: as for Table IX, supra, p. 101.

tenancy, must be kept in mind. But two other explanations arise. Some of the 176 tenants absent from the tax roll probably did not live in Selby, and would be assessed for the subsidy elsewhere. Others, though direct tenants of the Abbot of the Crown, were probably not sufficiently prosperous to be called upon to pay tax, even with minimum qualifications as low as those of 1545. There may well have been others in this position whose names do not appear in either record: undertenants with too few goods to be assessed. It appears from this same account that there were 220 dwelling-sites in Selby in 1540, and even allowing for the fact that a few would be unoccupied, this seems very strong evidence that whilst there were 113 householders in the town who had to contribute to the 1545 subsidy, there must have been a hundred or so more who were too poor to pay.

So much for the overall comparison between the two types of record at Selby. Table X explores another aspect of the comparison. A sample of twelve people are listed about whom there is information in both documents. It shows, without further ado, that no systematic statistical correlation can be attempted between the amount of tax a man paid and either the size of his holding, the type of tenure, or even the amount he paid in rent. But it illustrates very well the contrast which is known to have existed in most towns and villages between the local aristocracy and the middling and poorer folk. It points to a technique which can be adopted more widely than the few ideal townships where an overall comparison can be made: that of taking each category of tax-payer in turn and trying to identify in the estate records and other sources a sample number of individuals. How many Oswald Syssons can we find in this way, or how many Thomas Watsons?

Leaving aside for the present the categories of people taxed on lands worth over £10 a year, and also those assessed on annual fees, we can divide the rest into four broad groups: those with goods worth over £50; those with goods worth between £10 and £50; those with goods worth under £10; and those assessed on lands valued at £5 or less per annum.

(1) *Goods worth over £50.* This was a small group, number-ing only twelve in the whole Riding in 1546. One of them we know was a landowner, Sir Francis Hastings who had been assessed on lands worth £40 in 1545 but was for some reason taxed on goods valued at £133 the following year. Three others lived in rural areas and were almost certainly landowners or large farmers. One of them can be identified: Joan Nelson of Monk Fryston, probably the widow of the William Nelson who had formed part of Selby Abbey's demesne lands there in 1540.[1] Of the other eight, six lived in the towns of Rotherham, Wakefield and Halifax, and half of them can be positively identified as merchants. They are typified by Richard Pymond of Wakefield whose goods were assessed at £80; we know that by this time he also owned some land, but probably not enough to equal the tax of £5. 5s. payable on his goods in 1546.

(2) *Goods worth £10–£50:* Of the 650 householders who fell within this category, eighty-six were in the five market towns of Rotherham, Pontefract, Wakefield, Leeds and Ripon, which suggests that one element in the group consisted of successful merchants and tradespeople. The fact that another sixty-five of these householders lived in six townships round Halifax and Sowerby seems to confirm (what one would expect) that successful clothiers also rose into this group. Unfortunately we have no list of West Riding clothiers nearer in date to 1546 than that which appears to have been made in connection with the flocking dispute of 1533; the interval is too great for us to expect much from a comparison, but at least three men named in the 1533 list are known to have been taxed on goods worth £10 or £20 in the later year, one at Warley and two at Bradford.[2] The great majority of these 650 people however (at least 400) lived in rural areas and away from the clothing districts. Some of them can be identified in estate records as farmers of demesnes, and seven examples are listed in Table XI; these were indeed men like Oswald Sysson of Selby. They were not gentlemen, but they were more than mere peasants;

[1] P.R.O.: SC 6/Hen VIII/4606.
[2] P.R.O.: E 101/345/25.

at the same time, since they did not always have any freehold land of their own, they do not fall within the normal definition of the yeoman. In general we can probably conclude that the majority of people in this group of taxpayers were substantial farmers, though not necessarily leaseholders as opposed to copyholders or small freeholders.

TABLE XI

Substantial Farmers in the Subsidy Rolls and in Estate Records.

Name	Assessment 1546 (goods of:)	Details of farm, and landlord	Annual rent
Richard Riddiall	£30	Blind Hardwick Grange, under indenture from Nostell Priory, jointly with Thomas Riddiall, by 1541	£12
Robert Midgeley	£20	Moor Grange, held from Kirkstall Abbey, 1540	£6. 13s. 4d.
Percivall Wilkinson	£20	Bardsey Grange, held of Kirkstall as last	£8. 7s. 8d.
Brian Bewley	£18	1 tenement and 180 acres: part of Pontefract Priory demesne at Ledston, with tithe of grain and hay on same land, held by lease of Priory, 1540	£12
Robert Lund	£13	St. Mary's Abbey (York) demesnes at Reedness, held at will from the Abbey at Dissolution	£7
William Adam	£12	Duchy of Lancaster demesnes at Owston: i.e. 184 acres, and pasture rights in park, under lease of 1526 for 33 years. (He was also reeve there by 1537)	£12
Lawrence Baynes	£10	Lord Darcy's new park at Roundhay, under lease of 1535 for 40 years; and Kirkstall Abbey's grange at Coldcotes (nr. Seacroft), by 1540	£20 £5. 16s. 1d.

Sources: P.R.O.: SC 6/Hen VIII/4579, 4590, 4584, 4595, 4306; and DL 29/515/8293.

(3) *Goods worth £1–£10.* This group was the most numerous of all: only 2,145 people (with goods of between £5 and £10) came within the scope of the 1546 subsidy, but the previous year about 12,000 or 13,000 had contributed within this category. Some can be identified, as at Selby; but it

is not possible to make any statistical correlations with size of holdings, for the reasons already stated. All one can say is that these were the more prosperous of the 'ordinary people' of the Riding; mostly they were peasants.

(4) *Lands worth £5–£10 a year:* The 173 people in this category were for the most part substantial yeomen; a few may have been people whose actual income was a little over £10 but who were under-assessed. Some people in this category can be traced both in the subsidy records and in the inquisitions *post mortem.* William Rayner for example, taxed on lands worth £6 at Liversedge, was probably the son and heir named in the inquisition of 1535 which valued his father's lands at £9 a year. The discrepancy may have arisen from inadequate assessment, or it may have been due to some family arrangement which temporarily reduced the younger man's income. The same possibilities exist in relation to the inquisition on the lands of William Killing-beck of Chapel Allerton, who was assessed on lands worth £6. 13s. 4d. in 1545, but whose lands were valued by the escheator at £12 after his death in 1547.[1] It may be significant that the majority of surviving inquisitions *post mortem* concerning men of this kind come from the 'central wapentakes' of the Riding; one reason was probably that the King, as chief lord of Wakefield and Pontefract, had more interest in wardship rights over small men in that area than elsewhere; but also they seem to have represented a somewhat higher proportion of all taxpayers in that area than elsewhere.

(5) *Lands worth under £5 a year:* This, the last category, is also the most enigmatic, for two reasons: first, because it is not easy to see *why* these people were assessed on land at all, when so many other small people were assessed on their goods; secondly because, as we shall see in due course, they were much more numerous in some parts of the Riding than in others. Let us for the moment concentrate on the first point. It is to be noted that in their definition of 'lands' in this context the subsidy statutes did not limit the term to freehold property, but explicitly included all lands

[1] P.R.O.: C 142/57/88 (Wm. Raynor), and E 150/243/25 (Wm. Killingbeck).

whether held in fee, in tail, for life, for years, at will, or by copy of court roll. Where land was held for a substantial annual rent, the subsidy commissioners presumably calculated the difference between the rent (together with other charges such as tithes) and the theoretical annual value of the land, judged according to its quality and the price of grain. If they found that the theoretical annual value was no greater than the rent and other charges, they would have to conclude that as far as they were concerned the land had no value. They would then turn to the holder's goods. As we have seen, they might decide that the land was worth over £1 a year, and yet still return an assessemnt based on goods, because that would lead to a higher tax-payment. Assuming that they had all the relevant information, they would only tax a man on his lands if their annual value was great enough to yield a payment of tax at least equal to that which the same man would have paid on his goods. Two possibilities emerge from this discussion: *either* the men who were taxed on lands worth between £1 and £5 had fewer goods than their fellow-villagers who were taxed on goods; *or* their lands were for some reason worth more than the lands of other peasants. We have not so far found any reason for supposing that the peasant taxed on lands in this group was richer or poorer than his fellows. It is at this point that the failure of the subsidy rolls to record assessments on both lands and goods for the same person can be seen for the misfortune that it is. When a man was assessed on lands of an annual value between £1 and £5, we simply do not know the value of his goods at that time; and when he was assessed on goods we do not know the value of his lands. One possible way out of the deadlock might be to compare the rolls of 1546 with those of the previous year. Although a complete comparison is not possible, we can say that of the 1,358 people taxed on lands worth under £5 in 1546, at least 800 had been taxed on lands the year before as well. This shows that at least 800 families were not affected by the change in assessment rules between the two years. On the other hand some households *were* affected, being assessed on goods in 1545 and on lands in 1546; this would imply that some people at least, in the category which we are discussing, had goods worth under £5 and therefore were not liable to taxation on goods in 1546.

A more promising approach, despite the complexities involved, is to look at the rates of taxation on different values of land and goods, as laid down in the subsidy acts. If a man had lands worth £1 a year, in 1545 he would pay 8*d*. in tax; he need only have goods worth £3 to be liable to contribute 12*d*. With lands worth £3, he would pay 2*s*. in that year, an amount which he would not have paid on goods unless they were worth over £5; with lands worth £4 he would also have had to have goods worth £5 to be taxed on goods rather than lands. The 800 or more people taxed on lands under £5 in 1545 therefore *must* have had goods worth under £5, or they would have been taxed on their goods in that year. In 1546 the rates were changed as well as the minimum qualifications. But even in that year, a man with lands worth under £5 would only have had to have goods valued at £10 to be taxed on his goods. Therefore we can say with some firmness that, assuming the commissioners were not hopelessly ill-informed, all the 1,358 people assessed for taxation on lands worth between £1 and £5 in 1546 had goods of a lower value than £10; and that a great many of them had goods worth under £5. If nothing else, we can now place these people on an economic level lower than that of peasants and farmers with goods worth over £10. At the same time they were better off than most of the 10,000 people taxed on goods worth under £5 in 1545; for if those people had had lands worth more than £1 they would not have dropped out of the picture in the following year. That is as far as we can take the analysis for the moment. More will be said about this interesting group of people when we come to consider regional differences in the pattern of assessments.

Meanwhile a sixth group of people should not be ignored: those who were too poor to be recorded in the subsidy rolls at all, even in 1545. We saw that at Selby this group may have numbered as many as a hundred households, compared with the 113 who were taxed. Its size can be estimated at other places. Ripon, with a population about the same as Selby's or slightly larger, had 118 taxpayers in 1545. In

Tanshelf (part of Pontefract), there were sixty-five dwellings
in a survey of 1548, but only thirty-two people were taxed
three years before. The proportion of people too poor to pay
was probably higher in the towns than in some rural areas:
at Barwick-in-Elmet for instance, there were sixty-three
taxpayers for about eighty dwellings. But at Giggleswick
(in Craven) only thirty-seven people contributed in 1545,
out of the fifty-five householders (i.e. dwellings) counted in
a survey of about 1540.[1] Looking at the West Riding as a
whole, if there were 100,000 persons at this period, (or
20,000 households) then as many as 5,000 households up
and down the Riding would fall into this category of poorer
people. Very little can be said about them beyond the
observation that they were there. It would not be surprising
if some of them were dependent on charity, which before the
Dissolution was largely provided by religious houses and
hospitals. Most of them were probably cottage labourers
with little or no land of their own, who depended on
employment by other people if they were fit enough to
work.

V

In an area so economically diverse as the West Riding,
one would expect pronounced regional differences in the
pattern of social structure. In Table XII, I have broken down
the analysis of the 1546 subsidy into seven regional analyses,
using the same divisions as those in Tables III and VI
above. This will enable us to compare the subsidy evidence
with other regional patterns discussed in earlier chapters.
Regarding the subsidy evidence itself, four observations can
be made. First, there were some small differences in the
proportion of people taxed on lands worth over £20 in
different regions; but they were not sufficiently great to
indicate more than that in certain parts of the Riding there
were a few more gentry families than in others. Secondly,
there were some marked differences in the proportion of
people assessed on fees: in Skyrack, Barkston and the

[1] For the relevant surveys see: Gascoigne Coll., Leeds City Library: GC/DL/9
(Tanshelf and Barwick); and Skipton Castle MSS, Y.A.S. Library, Leeds: DD 121/
Bundle 29. (Giggleswick).

TABLE XII

Regional Pattern of Subsidy Assessments, 1546.

	Total assessed	Lands			Fees	Goods		
		£20 up	£5–£19	£1–£4	£1–£9	£20 up	£10–£19	£5–£9
Strafforth and Tickhill	662	18 (2·7%)	47 (7·1%)	166 (25·2%)	—	6 (0·9%)	66 (10·0%)	359 (54·4%)
Osgoldcross and Staincross	667	16 (2·4%)	54 (8·1%)	160 (24·0%)	2 (0·3%)	18 (2·7%)	84 (12·5%)	333 (50·0%)
Agbrigg and Morley	1360	34 (2·5%)	90 (6·6%)	561 (41·2%)	3 (0·2%)	118 (8·7%)	136 (10·0%)	418 (30·8%)
Skyrack	294	10 (3·4%)	13 (4·4%)	86 (29·2%)	13 (4·4%)	7 (2·4%)	28 (9·6%)	137 (46·6%)
Barkston and the Ainsty	520	21 (4·0%)	20 (3·0%)	101 (19·5%)	20 (3·9%)	23 (4·4%)	93 (17·8%)	242 (46·5%)
Claro, Ripon and Knaresborough	604	20 (3·3%)	31 (5·2%)	219 (36·2%)	13 (2·1%)	11 (1·8%)	31 (5·2%)	279 (46·2%)
Staincliffe and Ewcross	524	15 (2·8%)	16 (3·0%)	65 (12·5%)	2 (0·2%)	17 (3·3%)	32 (6·1%)	377 (72·0%)
Whole Riding	4,631	134 (3·0%)	271 (5·8%)	1358 (29·4%)	53 (1·1%)	200 (4·4%)	470 (10·1%)	2145 (46·3%)

Percentages read across.

Ainsty they represent a significant proportion of people assessed, whereas elsewhere they are absent or insignificant. The numbers of people were not great however, and it may simply be that in those areas the subsidy commissioners paid more attention to distinguishing people with an income from fees than did their fellows in other wapentakes. Thirdly, the proportion of people paying tax on goods worth £20 or more was noticeably greater in Agbrigg and Morley than anywhere else; it is highly likely that the explanation for this was the cloth industry. It was moreover a proportion of numerical significance, since Agbrigg and Morley had a far larger number of contributors than any other division. It will be recalled that this area contributed a third of all the tax-money drawn from the West Riding between 1543 and 1547.[1]

The fourth observation is the most remarkable, however, and also the one which will prove most difficult to explain, for it takes us back to the problem of the householders who were taxed on land worth under £5. The table shows that this group was present in all parts of the Riding; but the proportion of people in it was very much greater than average in Agbrigg and Morley wapentakes, and noticeably higher in Claro, Ripon and Knaresborough. On the other hand the proportion was very much lower in Staincliffe and Ewcross, and was also below average in Barkston wapentake and the Ainsty. The converse of these proportions is seen in the last column of the table: in Agbrigg and Morley only 31 per cent of taxpayers paid on goods worth under £10, whereas in Staincliffe and Ewcross that category was as high as 72 per cent. We know that people assessed on lands of under £5 were smallholders of some kind, and we know that they were less well provided with goods than those assessed on goods of £10 or more; let us see now if we can find out more about them by locating them more precisely geographically. For this purpose Table XII provides certain clues, but it is not detailed enough on its own. Table XIII gives the relevant figures for a selected number of localities where the porportion of taxpayers in this group was especially high or especially low. It shows that

---

[1] See Table III, *supra,* p. 29.

TABLE XIII

Areas Where High and Low Proportions of Taxpayers in 1546 Were Assessed on Lands Worth under £5.

	Number of townships	Number of taxpayers	Lands £5–19	Lands £1–5	Goods £10–19	Goods £5–9	Church income in area
First Group:							
Sowerbyshire–Halifax area	15	448	26 (5.8%)	234 (52.4%)	40 (8.9%)	103 (22.9%)	£20
Holmfirth	1	35	—	29 (83%)	1 (3%)	5 (14%)	—
Wakefield and District (Crown wills)	5	166	12 (7.2%)	44 (26.5%)	32 (19.3%)	46 (27.7%)	£9
Hallamshire	6	81	—	39 (48.1%)	5 (6.2%)	34 (41.9%)	£29
Hatfield	7	76	3	26	6	40	£13
Knaresborough, Scriven, and Knaresborough Forest	14	191	10 (5.2%)	141 (74.1%)	6 (3.1%)	32 (16.7%)	£56
Bolland Forest	9	20	2 (10%)	11 (55%)	1 (5%)	6 (30%)	?£10
Total in first group	50	941	50	498	85	226	£124
Second Group:							
Ewcross	9	217	4 (1.8%)	18 (8.3%)	21 (9.7%)	165 (76.0%)	£157
Skipton–Bolton area	15	81	3 (3.7%)	4 (4.9%)	3 (3.7%)	62 (76.6%)	£148
Ripon Lordship	35	183	7 (3.8%)	22 (12.0%)	19 (10.4%)	121 (66.1%)	£89
Marshland (exc. Snaith and Cowick)	10	103	8 (7.8%)	9 (8.7%)	23 (22.3%)	56 (54.4%)	£227
Ainsty	31	144	4 (2.8%)	14 (9.7%)	30 (20.9%)	70 (48.7%)	£428
							£1,740

within Agbrigg and Morley, the townships with the highest proportion were those within the lordship of Wakefield; whilst within the area of Claro, Ripon and Knaresborough, there was a sharp contrast between the high proportion found in the Knaresborough district and the low proportion in Ripon lordship. Likewise in Strafforth and Tickhill, the proportion was high in Hallamshire and Hatfield, and lower elsewhere. Most striking of all, though not numerically important, was the contrast between Bolland Forest and the rest of Staincliffe wapentake.

Almost all of the first group of localities in Table XIII were situated near the margin of settlement, and many included tracts of forest or chase. Could it be that the high proportion was in some way linked with the circumstance of late settlement, in areas where the open spaces on the edge of medieval cultivation offered special opportunities of a kind less often found in the more densely populated parts of the Riding? Possibly. But that can hardly be the whole explanation, because four out of the five localities in the second half of Table XIII were also situated towards the margin of medieval settlement. We must look for other factors. One possibility suggests itself when the regional analysis of subsidy assessments is related to the pattern of property and lordship discussed in Chapter II. If the social group with whom we are concerned were mainly small-holders, whose lands brought them a clear profit of at least £1 a year, then it may be of some significance to ask who were the lords from whom they held their land; we might even go further, and enquire into the terms upon which they held it. Where the tenure was freehold, with rents fixed from time immemorial, the tenant's ability to make an annual profit of £1 is easily understood. But equally, if the tenure was by custom, it might be governed by rules which favoured the tenant rather than the lord. At a time of rising prices, the tenant would be able to make a greater profit from his holding in places where local custom did not permit the landlord to increase his rent at will or to charge a heavy fine on change of tenancy. Can we say then, that the presence in a locality of a substantial number of house-holders drawing profits of £1 a year or more from their land implies either manorial customs which favoured the tenants, or else great restraint on the part of landlords there?

The manorial customs of the sixteenth century were the product of the estate policies of earlier centuries; once again we must look back into the 'medieval' past in order to throw light on the social patterns of the Tudor period. The development of tenurial customs in northern England during the two centuries after the Norman Conquest has not so far received the thorough study it deserves, but this is not the place to try to remedy the omission. We must be content with a few observations relevant to the question in hand. Two points which have been made in recent writing on medieval England are worth noticing in the present context. The first concerns the nature of William I's 'harrying of the North' in 1070, and of the resettlement which followed in its wake. Mr. Bishop, after studying the geography of devastation recorded in Domesday Book, came to the conclusion that the villages said to be 'waste' in 1086 could not possibly have been the same as those laid waste sixteen years before: they were mostly upland places, and it is hardly likely that they would have been destroyed whilst the lowland areas were left unharmed.[1] What really happened, he decided, was that the Conqueror's army 'harried' the lowlands, but that by the time the Domesday survey was made they had been resettled by their Norman lords. In the process the inhabitants of upland areas were either attracted or compelled to move into the lowlands, leaving their own villages 'waste' and worth nothing. The relevance of this for the question of custom is that these upland areas would be gradually resettled over the next two centuries and more, without great pressure from landlords, whereas the new inhabitants of the lowland areas must have been under considerable pressure from their lords. It was in the same article that Mr. Bishop remarked upon the fact that the only reference to 'week-work' was at Tanshelf, near the new Norman castle of Pontefract.[2] The customs of the uplands therefore could very easily have become (or remained) more

---

[1] T. A. M. Bishop: 'The Norman Settlement of Yorkshire' in R. W. Hunt, *et al.*: *Studies in Medieval History presented to F. M. Powicke* (Oxford, 1948).

[2] Cf. *supra*, p. 47.

liberal, from the tenants' point of view, than those of the more low-lying wapentakes. And the upland areas concerned included the wapentakes of Agbrigg, Morley and Staincross; another upland area, Hallamshire, was not 'waste' in 1086, but it had probably not been 'harried' and resettled under pressure. These are amongst the areas of interest to us in our attempt to explain Table XIII. However, the 'waste' areas of Domesday book also included Craven and the area round Ripon, where the subsidy pattern of 1546 was very different; if Mr. Bishop's study of the Norman resettlement is taken as part of the explanation for which we are looking, it is necessary to suppose that in those areas the repopulation was less free from landlords' pressure.

The other relevant point to emerge from research into medieval society concerns the problem of the 'ancient demesne' of the Crown, a favourite topic of legal historians. We need not enter into all the controversies surrounding this concept, for Professor Hoyt has now demonstrated quite convincingly that it became a part of English land law during the thirteenth century, largely thanks to the efforts of Edward I, and that its principal aim was to protect those rural communities over which the King was deemed to have special rights.[1] On all estates which had belonged to the Crown in 1066 a special customary status and tenure existed, known as 'villein socage', which gave tenants various privileges compared with ordinary villeins. In particular men who enjoyed that status were permitted to bring actions in the royal courts using the writ *monstraverunt*, which made it possible for them to resist any claim by their current lord (who might not be the King) to increase their services. At the same time communities within the 'ancient demesne' were liable to heavier taxation by the King: in 1334, when most rural areas paid a fifteenth of their moveable wealth, these communities had to contribute a tenth. Looking at the West Riding, we find only one area assessed at a tenth under the regulations established in 1334: the Soke and Forest of Knaresborough, together with the

[1] R. S. Hoyt: 'The Nature and Origins of the Ancient Demesne', *Eng. Hist. Rev.*, lxv (1950).

lordship of Aldborough.[1] But this was not the only part of
the West Riding that had belonged to Edward the Confessor in 1066; the Soke of Wakefield and the Soke of
Tanshelf had also belonged to the King before the Conquest.
(The Soke of Tanshelf was not the same as the later Honour
of Pontefract; it consisted mainly of the dependencies of
that Honour lying in Staincross Wapentake.) It would
require a good deal of research to discover whether these
other areas were ever considered 'ancient demesne', and also
why they did not pay a tenth in 1334 even though they
technically qualified for that status. But it can be observed
that Knaresborough, Wakefield lordship, and also part of
Staincross wapentake,[2] were areas with high proportions of
people taxed on lands worth under £5 in 1545–6; they might
therefore have been areas with favourable manorial customs,
and if they had had 'ancient demesne' status that fact would
be the more easily understood. In the case of Wakefield there
is one additional piece of evidence which points in the same
direction: when James I challenged the claim of his tenants
there to have 'fixity of fines', they pleaded that their entry
fines had been fixed since the fourteenth century.[3] There is
no evidence however to suggest that any of these considerations apply to the other localities in the first section of
Table XIII: Hatfield was in 1066 a part of Earl Harold's
Soke of Conisbrough, whilst Hallamshire belonged to Earl
Waltheof.

So far, we have found two possible reasons for thinking
that the areas in which we are interested may have had
manorial customs favourable to their tenantry: first, they
may have been areas either untouched by William I's
'harrying', or resettled afterwards without serious disruption
of ancient customs; second, that some of them may have had
the protection afforded by later Plantagenet kings to the
ancient demesne of the Crown. The converse of these factors
must also be considered: that where customs did not favour
the tenants it was because medieval landlords in other areas

---

[1] P.R.O.: E 164/7/ff. 282–95; cf. *supra*, p. 58.

[2] Particularly the townships of Brierley, Hemsworth, Cudworth, Barnsley and
Thurgoland.

[3] Cf. *supra*, p. 81 n. 2.

had defined them more harshly, which outside the ancient demesne they were free to do.

It is quite possible that where the customs of 1066 lasted unchanged through the period in which the pressure of population and prices reached its medieval peak in the twelfth and thirteenth centuries, those customs would by the fifteenth and sixteenth centuries be far more favourable to tenants than customs originating when the pressure was at its height. Amongst the landlords who appear to have been most eager to reorganize their estates in the twelfth and thirteenth centuries, to make them more economic, were the monasteries. In another study, Mr. Bishop has indicated the ruthlessness of Cistercian landlords in their creation of granges in the Vale of York.[1] Kosminsky's study of the Midlands also suggests that the great estates of monastic houses like Ramsey Abbey were given their regular patterns through post-Conquest reorganization which bore hard upon the peasantry; and Professor Postan's study of labour services on some major estates carries with it similar implications.[2] It is not at all impossible that manorial custom on the Church estates of the West Riding was far less favourable to tenants than was the case on royal estates like Wakefield and Knaresborough. Such an impression is to a small extent confirmed by certain demands of the Pilgrims of Grace in 1536, which singled out the abbey lands in Nidderdale and Kirkbyshire as places where the King ought to impose fixed gressums.[3] Moreover, turning back to Table XIII and the subsidy evidence in general, it would seem that areas which had a considerable amount of monastic property also had a low proportion of people taxed on lands worth under £5. The point has been incorporated into Table XIII, which gives the amount of Church income from temporal possessions in each of the selected areas. It can be confirmed by other examples. In Agbrigg and Morley wapentakes, for example, seven townships where the Church was an important landlord could between them muster only eight people

[1] T. A. M. Bishop: 'Monastic Granges in the Vale of Yorkshire', *Eng. Hist. Rev.*, li (1936).

[2] E. A. Kosminsky: op. cit., Ch. iii; M. Postan: 'The Chronology of Labour Services', *Trans. Royal Hist. Soc.*, (1937).

[3] Cf. *infra*, p. 204.

taxed on lands worth under £5, a mere 15 per cent of the total.[1] They were indeed the only seven townships where the Church had the largest share of the land, except for Halifax which was owned almost entirely by the priory of Lewes (Sussex). Halifax had seventeen taxpayers in this category; but it is not impossible that being so far away from the house which owned it, it did not suffer serious interference with its customs on the part of its lords. In Barkston wapentake there is an interesting contrast between the estates of the Archbishop of York and those of Selby Abbey. In the four townships of Sherburn Barony kept 'in hand' by the Archbishop, thirty out of sixty-nine taxpayers were assessed on lands worth under £5 in 1546; in the four neighbouring townships where most of the land belonged to Selby, there were only eight out of sixty-five.[2] Again, in the liberty of Ripon, where only twenty-two people out of 183 were taxed in this way, over half of those twenty-two were in the five townships kept 'in hand' by the Archbishop, and hardly any in the townships whose principal landlords were the monasteries of Fountains, Byland, etc. In Craven, however, it is impossible to attribute the low proportion of small men taxed on lands entirely to the presence of the Bolton Priory estates. If manorial custom in that area was unfavourable, it must have been due in part to the estate administration of the medieval lords of Skipton. What is clear from the sixteenth-century evidence is that the Cliffords had no difficulty in raising the fines of their tenants in the 1540s: custom did not stand in their way.[3]

None of this evidence is utterly conclusive, but there is enough of it for a pattern to begin to emerge. It suggests that one of the major factors in the social structure of later medieval and sixteenth-century Yorkshire was the diversity of manorial custom, which can only be explained in relation to developments of the twelfth and thirteenth centuries. It suggests too, that the diversity was reflected, very indirectly, in the pattern of subsidy assessments.

[1] The townships were Ackton-cum-Snydale, Armley, Bramley, Crofton, Huddersfield (including Bradley), Slaithwaite, and Whitwood.

[2] The four townships of the Archbishop were Sherburn, Wistow, Cawood and South Milford; those of Selby Abbey were Monk Fryston, Hambleton, Hillam, and Selby itself.   [3] Cf. *supra*, p. 80.

VI

The relationship between the pattern of subsidy assessments and the pattern of landownership is extremely
interesting. What of its relationship to the regional economic
pattern? One aspect has already been touched upon, namely
the contrast in social structure between town and countryside. The towns of the West Riding, small as they were
compared with the northern capital of York, had an economic pattern of their own and the opportunities for making
money there are indicated by their higher proportion of
people taxed on goods worth over £10. They probably also
had a higher proportion of families too poor to be taxed,
and probably a very much larger number of indigent poor.
The social contrast between rich and poor was probably
greatest in the towns, but it would be offset by the greater
social mobility there. Most of the Riding, however, was
countryside in the sixteenth century. The economic geography of the rural areas suggests that we should look for
two kinds of contrast between different regions: between
the better agricultural opportunities of the lowlands and the
agriculturally poorer uplands; and between the areas which
developed rural industry and those which remained purely
agricultural. The former contrast is reflected in the much
greater taxable wealth of lowland areas by comparison with
upland areas which had no industry, such as Craven.
Especially noticeable is the high proportion of households
taxed on goods worth over £10 in Barkston and the Ainsty:
they seem to have been mostly farmers of larger holdings, and
were probably producing food for the markets of York.
Osgoldcross and Staincross, despite the indications of
economic decline around Snaith, also had a larger proportion of such people than Claro and Ripon, or than Craven
and Ewcross; the arable land round Pontefract was reckoned
to be as rich as any in the Riding.
    The industrial areas which are most interesting from the
point of view of social structure are the textile and metal-
lurgical manufacturing areas; for these were cottage
industries, whereas mining was an estate industry. It so
happens that the most important cottage-industry districts

were amongst those whose subsidy pattern we have just been discussing at length, for both Agbrigg and Morley (and also Hallamshire) were areas with high proportions of house-holders taxed on small amounts of land. If the explanation which has just been offered is acceptable, then we can also say that they were areas of light manorial custom. The idea that manufacturing was a cause of the peculiar subsidy pattern must be dismissed, for the pattern is not limited to industrial areas. But is it possible that the presence of this special group of smallholders represents a factor in the development of rural industry? Dr. Thirsk has recently attempted a bold reassessment of the location of industry in sixteenth-century England in which she laid special stress on inheritance customs as a factor in the growth of rural manufactures.[1] She showed that in a number of localities where rural industry flourished by 1600 the ancient customs of partible inheritance, gavelkind or 'Borough English', prevailed longer than in other parts of England. An impor-tant consequence of this, she argued, was that such areas experienced an increase in population far beyond the level which their own agricultural resources could support, especially since they were often areas near to the agricultural margin. Thus they became areas of cheap labour, and they found an outlet for this labour in the cottage-production of textiles or some other manufacture. One of Dr. Thirsk's localities was in the West Riding: Dentdale (Ewcross), where hand-knitting became an important occupation in the second half of the sixteenth century. There were other parts of north Yorkshire which still had partible inheritance at this period, though it was slowly dying out. At Arkengarth-dale (N.R.) in 1612 there was a dispute in which one party held that the custom of the manor demanded partition of land at death, whilst the other believed that the custom was one of primogeniture.[2]

It is difficult to apply Dr. Thirsk's thesis to the more southerly parts of the Yorkshire Pennines. Both Agbrigg

---

[1] Joan Thirsk: 'Industries in the Countryside' in F. J. Fisher (ed): *Essays in the Economic and Social History of Tudor and Stuart England in honour of R. H. Tawney* (London, 1961).

[2] P.R.O.: E 134/10 Jas I/Mich 26.

and Morley and Hallamshire lay on the margin of settlement, and in the former area at least there are signs that in
the fifteenth and sixteenth centuries population was increasing faster than in the lowlands; it may even have been
attracting immigrants from the declining area of lower
Osgoldcross.[1] But I have been able to find no evidence that
the custom of partible inheritance survived in this region
in the sixteenth century, or even that it had ever existed.
There is however another way in which custom might have
influenced industrial growth there. It used to be said that the
principal reason why the textile industry gradually moved
away from the towns into the countryside in later medieval
England was that restrictive practices by urban guilds
inhibited its growth, whilst the freer situation in the
countryside favoured expansion. The first half of this
explanation cannot be adequately discussed in the present
context; but the suggestion that industry moved to areas of
greater freedom deserves to be taken seriously. It is particularly relevant to the question why the West Riding textile
industry developed in Agbrigg and Morley rather than in
Nidderdale, which was also a millstone grit area and which
had an easy commercial outlet in the market town of Ripon.
The men of York believed that the reason was mainly to do
with fuel supplies, Agbrigg and Morley being close to or
on the coal measures.[2] But the industry did not flourish in
every area which had plentiful supplies of fuel. Might it not
have been that in Agbrigg and Morley the presence of a
class of smallholders with unusually light manorial customs,
and an opportunity of making relatively substantial profits
on their land each year, meant that there was capital available
for small-scale investment in looms and other textile equip-
ment? And both for new families resulting from population
growth and for newcomers to the area, these same favourable
customs meant that they could settle down on uncleared
land without the fear that some unkind landlord would one
day come and demand exorbitant rents, or make large
increases in inheritance fines. Labour was only one require-
ment for the development of manufacture, and in a region

[1] Cf. *supra*, p. 31.
[2] A. G. Dickens: 'Tudor York', *V.C.H.Y. City of York*, p. 125.

whose industry was carried on by independent small clothiers without powerful middlemen, as the 'Halifax Act' would have us believe, labour was not necessarily a more important factor than capital and the freedom to use it as one chose. If this argument holds good—and a parallel argument might be used to explain the metallurgy of Hallamshire— we have an interesting example of the way in which land-ownership and medieval estate policies influenced not only social structure but even the very nature of economic development.

IV

'MEN OF POWER AND WORSHIP': THE FRAMEWORK OF LOCAL POLITICS

I

L ET us return now to the small group of people whose control over substantial areas of land gave them, one would suppose, a dominant position in West Riding society: the people who were responsible for its government and had power over its inhabitants. This is not the place to attempt a new summary of the development of early Tudor government, still less to try to fill in the many gaps that still remain in our knowledge of it. But it would be absurd to pretend that the West Riding was a self-contained unit whose politics and institutions can be discussed without reference to the kingdom of England as a whole, and in the chapters which follow the national framework must be continually borne in mind. The King was far from omnipotent, and the real measure of his power was his ability to have his decisions executed at the level of the county and village. Generally speaking this was possible only with the acquiescence of those who, in the words of one sixteenth-century Yorkshireman, were 'of most power and worship' in their own locality. The King ignored such men at his peril in selecting his servants, and the latter were never mere slaves of the royal will. So much is well enough known. But what was the nature of the local power and worship which these people enjoyed? And how was it related to the patterns of land-lordship and social structure discussed in previous chapters?

There is unfortunately no simple equation that will enable us to turn a statistical analysis of income and property into a measure of influence and power. Politics is a matter of control over people, not over acres or pounds, and the subject requires an approach quite different from that of the foregoing chapters. We must turn to the institutional framework of the West Riding, and then consider the role of particular individuals within it. There existed two almost distinct hierarchies of institutions embracing the whole kingdom from the highest peaks of authority down to the humblest village: the monarchical State, headed by the King and his Court; and the Church, whose ultimate head until 1534 was the Pope in Rome. The relationship between their respective jurisdictions was one of the principal political issues in the period of the Reformation and the Pilgrimage of Grace. But also there existed a framework of lordship and patronage which was the cement of medieval English society, and which frequently cut across the boundary between Church and State rendering it somewhat less distinct at the local level than at Westminster. Lordship was by this time far more important than kinship. The feudal custom of primogeniture had supplanted that of partible inheritance in most (though not quite all) parts of England, and by leaving younger sons to fend for themselves it tended to put individuals in a position where they were likely to gain more by following a lord than by reliance on their families. Family it is true still counted for something, but within the framework of lordship and often as a buttress to it; in this respect England may be contrasted with sixteenth-century Scotland, where kinship was still the basis of a clan system. When private lordship began to decline, it was to the State that it lost ground, not to kinship groups. But the decline was in any case far from sudden, and in the sixteenth century it would be truer to say that lordship was gradually being transformed into a different form of patronage than to say that it was ceasing to exist altogether. Nor does this observation apply merely to so-called 'backward' areas like Yorkshire: patronage was as important for Wolsey as for the northern Earls.

The complicated inter-relationship between the institutions of Monarchy, Church and lordship in the administrative system of early sixteenth-century England are briefly outlined in the diagram opposite. Relationships between the two hierarchies of jurisdiction and administration, from the King down through the county to the township, and from the Pope (or Archbishop) down through the diocese and deanery to the parish, were complicated by a number of factors.

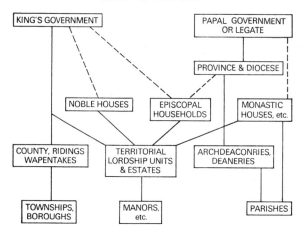

First, the bishops were part of the English nobility, so that both nobles and bishops sat in Parliament and the King might choose either noblemen or Churchmen to serve as his officials. Moreover, both the lords temporal and the lords spiritual were men of no small wealth and power in themselves, and had households which imitated the King's on a smaller scale. A second complication was that the religious orders had a considerable degree of independence from episcopal jurisdiction, and their monastic houses sometimes had under them parishes that were equally independent of the diocese. Monastic heads too played a part in the temporal affairs of the realm, with great institutional wealth which down to Henry VIII's reign was beyond Crown interference. Thirdly, we find that at the level of the wapentake, the deanery, and the great lordship, the pattern was one not of twofold but of threefold jurisdiction: to the authority of the royal official and the priest or bishop must be added that of the lord or owner of the soil, who might be a cleric or a layman. It is with this threefold pattern that we are concerned when we come down to the level of the township, the parish and the manor.

The township, sometimes confusingly called the 'civil parish' since the Local Government Act of 1888, was the smallest unit of local administration under the Crown. Its community was held responsible by medieval statutes for keeping the peace, and for maintaining a local militia properly armed, and the sixteenth century saw the addition of other responsibilities such as dealing with the local poor. The principal township official was the annually appointed constable; some Yorkshire townships also had a tithing system. It has generally been believed that the system of frankpledge, which assigned every household to a tithing group for purposes of village security according to a custom going back before 1066, never existed in Yorkshire. This is not quite true. In the wapentake of Strafforth and Tickhill there is evidence that the view of frankpledge was held in Doncaster lordship as late as 1506.[1] Elsewhere in the West Riding frankpledge is not found; but unfortunately the scholars who long ago convinced themselves of its absence there have made little progress towards discovering what took its place. The constable was also charged, by the statute of Winchester of 1285, to ensure that the King's subjects in his township kept certain weapons and brought them regularly to the musters; muster rolls of Henry VIII's reign show that the practice was still kept up in the West Riding as elsewhere. Another township responsibility was to answer the summons of the subsidy commissioners whenever a tax-assessment was due; the Tudor subsidies were assessed on individuals, but the statute of 1334 granting a fifteenth and tenth to Edward III had fixed a quota for each village and left the inhabitants to decide amongst themselves how the burden should be distributed.

Occasionally the muster rolls tell us who the constables were in particular townships, and from the 1539 roll for Skyrack wapentake we can identify a few of those who held the office in the villages around Barwick-in-Elmet.[2] The constable was sometimes a man of middling substance in the village, like William Sampson, at Parlington, who in 1546 had goods worth £16. 13s. 4d. At Osmondthorpe the

[1] *Calendar of the Records of the Borough of Doncaster*, ii (Doncaster, 1900) pp. 17–19. On the subject of frankpledge generally, see H. M. Cam: *The Hundred and the Hundred Rolls* (London, 1930, reprinted 1963), p. 124.

[2] The roll of the muster taken by Sir William Gascoigne, Sir William Middleton and Sir William Malleverer at Wyke Moor in March of that year is printed in W. P. Baildon: 'Musters in Skyrack Wapentake, 1539', Thoresby Society, ix (1899); esp. pp. 255–60.

constable was even a gentleman, Henry Skelton, whose lands were valued at £12 a year when he died in 1544; but that was probably a virtually depopulated township by this date. In other places the constable was at the other end of the village social scale, as at Seacroft and Newsam whose constables were described in the roll of 1539 as 'poor', which probably meant that they were indigent. Differences in the status of the constable were not without some significance, for a substantial farmer was more likely to enjoy local respect than a poor cottager reminiscent of Shakespeare's Dogberry. He might also be more capable of standing up for the villagers against more powerful outsiders. It is a pity that we cannot discover the names of enough constables to make a thorough survey; nor can we say whether the same people would hold office as constables and as manorial officials at the same time.

The manor was the smallest institution of territorial lordship and we have already seen how its customs were of the greatest importance for all those who held land within it. In matters concerning the land, the manorial court had jurisdiction over all the customary tenants; and the lord's bailiff or collector of rents was a familiar figure in those manors which lacked a resident landlord. The farmer of the manorial demesne or park if any, would also be seen as a representative of the lord, and might even combine the positions of farmer and bailiff. There was no uniform pattern of arrangements in manors; they varied depending on the lord and his estate policies. Manorial boundaries seldom coincided with those of the township or those of the parish, and this formal division between lordship over the land and the administration of royal government left no scope for the development in England of any sort of peasant commune, owning its own land and managing its own affairs. The one exception to this was the incorporated borough, which had special privileges. There were two of them in the West Riding: Doncaster had been incorporated in 1467 by Edward IV and Pontefract in 1484 by Richard III.[1] The mayor and council in each place was virtually lord of the manor, and in the case of

[1] M. Weinbaum: *British Borough Charters, 1307–1660* (Cambridge, 1943), pp. 126, 129.

Doncaster lord of a surrounding lordship as well. But most places which called themselves 'borough' in the sixteenth-century records were no more than manors in which the lord had created a number of burgage tenures.

The ecclesiastical parish was in theory part of a system quite separate from either the township or the manor. Its church and priest were under the jurisdiction of the bishop of the diocese, and his conduct as a pastor was governed by the canon law. However, most if not all of the parish churches in the Riding had been founded and endowed by laymen at an early date, and whilst the common law prevented any subsequent lay interference with ecclesiastical property, the appointment or advowson of rectors was still sometimes in lay hands. In other cases it had been impropriated together with the rectorial tithes to a monastery or cathedral, which gave the abbot or prior, or some other cleric, the position formerly enjoyed by the lay lord. The nature of parochial origins explains why the distribution of parish churches is somewhat uneven, and why there were only about 170 parishes in the West Riding in 1535 compared with about 600 townships. The map of medieval parishes often shows a marked relationship to that of territorial lordships. The largest parish in the Riding, Halifax, was large because it covered a very wide area of the ancient division of Sowerbyshire; Spofforth too, which had the richest rectory in the Riding, was a parish designed to serve a barony not just a village.[1]

Now let us turn to the level of the county and riding, and in particular to royal administration at that level. (The Church had its own separate territorial divisions, the West Riding being mainly within the Diocese of York but partly in the Archdeaconry of Richmond.) Size alone made Yorkshire a more complicated county than most in this respect, and its division into three Ridings took place at a much earlier period than that with which we are concerned here. In consequence it was treated as a single unit for some purposes, but for others as three. In addition

[1] Cf. *supra*, p. 93.

there was the City of York, which had for long been a separate county with its own sheriffs, and which included as a sort of *banlieu* the area known as the Ainsty.[1] Thus, although the Ainsty is included as part of the West Riding in the present study, it was administratively separate from it; in what follows we shall be dealing for the most part with the West Riding as an administrative entity, referring only when necessary to the special circumstances of the Ainsty.

By the sixteenth century, English counties had two kinds of offices: what might be called the ancient offices, established in the twelfth century or before; and others of more recent origin. In Yorkshire the ancient offices were appointed for the county as a whole, whilst the more recent offices existed separately in each riding. The most important office in the former category was that of sheriff; others were those of coroner and escheator, and in addition one should count under this head the bailiffs or constables of the wapentakes. The work of the escheator was concerned mostly with land and the conduct of inquisitions *post mortem* and will be discussed in some detail in Appendix I. The functions of other ancient offices were mostly connected with the administration of royal jurisdiction in the county. The coroner, usually appointed for several years, had a variety of duties arising from criminal proceedings, as well as responsibility for investigating sudden deaths, treasure troves and (where there was a coastline) shipwrecks.[2] There were five coroners in sixteenth-century Yorkshire, but without a systematic analysis of legal records which have not been used in the present study, it is not possible to say very much about their work. The sheriff was a man of more substance and less expertise, being appointed annually on the morrow of All Souls, when the King went to the Exchequer to 'prick' his

---

[1] For a full account of the government of the County of the City of York in this period see A. G. Dickens: 'Tudor York' in *V.C.H.Y. City of York* (London, 1961), pp. 135–42.

[2] cf. R. F. Hunnisett: *The Medieval Coroner* (Cambridge, 1961); he refers to the office in Yorkshire in the thirteenth and fourteenth centuries, pp. 88, 135; and observes that at Doncaster and Pontefract the mayor acted as coroner after the fifteenth-century charters of incorporation, p. 161. These two borough coroners are not included in the five for the county of Yorkshire.

name on a prepared list of three names for each county. His responsibilities included the serving of royal writs, the summoning of juries, arrangement of the sittings of royal courts (when justices came round on circuit), the carrying out of sentences and the collection of fines. He still rendered his account to the exchequer in the form of a 'pipe roll', a document which retained all the antique complexity of a system devised in the twelfth century.[1] Since he himself was not a professional he must have leaned heavily upon a deputy or under-sheriff, who would be a man with legal training.[2] In each wapentake the sheriff had in principle a local deputy, or bailiff; but since the wapentake courts were no longer of any importance, the duties of the latter appear to have been limited to the collection of wapentake 'fines' (for respite of suit) which he sent up to the sheriff for payment to Westminster.[3]

Sometimes wapentakes were in the hands of a private lordship. The Honour of Pontefract included the wapentakes of Osgoldcross, Staincross, Agbrigg and Morley, and parts of those of Skyrack and Barkston. Another part of Skyrack paid wapentake fines to the Abbot of Kirkstall, as lord of Headingley. In Craven the whole wapentake of Staincliffe belonged to the lord of Skipton.[4] Lordships which included private control of these ancient jurisdictions (which must not be confused with the baronial or feudal jurisdiction of a lord over his vassals) were often referred to

---

[1] On the sheriff and his pipe roll see J. S. Wilson: 'Sheriff's Rolls of the Sixteenth Century', *Eng. H.R.* xlvii, (1932), 31–45; and S. C. Newton: 'The Pipe Roll of a Cromwellian Sheriff of Yorkshire', *Y.A.J.*, xli, pt. 1 (1963), 108–16.

[2] We know the name of the deputy in one year: in 1537 Sir Brian Hastings died whilst in office as Sheriff and his place was filled by the under-sheriff Francis Frobisher; the latter was a lawyer of Doncaster and for a long time recorder of that town, and may have had other connections with Hastings.

[3] The 'wapentake fine' was said to be peculiar to Yorkshire, by H. M. Cam: *The Hundred and the Hundred Rolls*, p. 173. It appears to have been the same as 'blanchefarme'. In 1654, 'blanchefarme' was collected by the sheriff only from the lordships of Spofforth, Harewood and Drax, and from the lordship which had once belonged to Kirkstall Abbey; presumably elsewhere these dues belonged to the owners of private franchises; *Y.A.J.*, xli, pt. I, 110–11.

[4] For the accounts of the feodary of Pontefract and of the baliffs of the wapentakes pertaining to that Honour, see the ministers' accounts, e.g. P.R.O.: DL 29/515/8293; for Kirkstall's lordship of Headingley, SC 6/Hen VIII/4590; and for Craven, the accounts of the bailiffs of the Honour of Skipton, Skipton Castle MSS, Y.A.S. Library: DD 121/Bundle 38.

as liberties. But a liberty might also include more than just
wapentake jurisdiction (which by the sixteenth century had
no real value). The most notable liberty in the West Riding
was that of the Archbishop of York at Ripon, which
consisted of two tiers: within the inner liberty, extending for
one mile on all sides of the Church, he had a very wide
franchise indeed, with his own coroner and justices of the
peace; the rest of the liberty, several townships, was probably only a private wapentake.[1] The two incorporated
boroughs of Doncaster and Pontefract also had some of the
features of a liberty, their mayors and councils being
authorized to carry out the duties of coroner within the
borough; at Doncaster the mayor also took the view of
frankpledge.

These private franchises, and the relative insignificance of
wapentake jurisdiction under the sheriff, reflect the decline
of the ancient system of jurisdiction that had existed before
the establishment of Anglo-Norman feudalism. But by the
sixteenth century private jurisdiction had suffered its own
decline, with the rise of a new system of royal courts and
commissions. It was characteristic of the new system, from
its beginnings in the fourteenth century, that the King
delegated his authority not to a single individual like the
sheriff or coroner, but to a group of county men who had to
act in concert. The county commission was used regularly
in the earlier sixteenth century for three purposes: the holding of quarter sessions to keep the peace, the assessment and
collection of subsidies, and the array or muster of the militia.
Henry VIII also used commissions on an *ad hoc* basis, for
example in the valuation of Church wealth in 1535 and in
the actual suppression of the monasteries. He even issued
commissions to small groups of people to act in place of the
escheator in the holding of an inquisition *post mortem*. The
most important of the commissions was usually that of the
peace, which by the sixteenth century was appointed
separately for each of the three ridings. In Yorkshire,
however, there also existed the Council in the North, which

---

[1] M. D. Lobel: 'The Ecclesiastical Banleuca in England' in F. M. Powicke (ed.):
Oxford Essays in Medieval History presented to H. E. Salter (Oxford, 1934), pp.
126–7.

effectively began life in 1525 as the Council of the Duke of
Richmond and which sat either at Pontefract Castle or at
Sheriff Hutton. The detailed study of this body by R. R.
Reid shows how it gradually developed by 1545 into the
Council at York.[1] Its jurisdiction for most of the time was
confined to the three Yorkshire ridings and the City of York,
and in many respects it was rather like a superior commission
of the peace. But its competence was wider than that of the
normal commission of the peace, embracing as it did some
of the features of conciliar jurisdiction in Chancery and Star
Chamber. Since neither the sessions rolls nor the records of
the Council survive for the first half of the century, we have
unfortunately no means of knowing what was the relationship between Council and commission at that time; but we
know there was some overlap in membership.

The commission of array had the responsibility of inspect-
ing the arms and men which each township was obliged to
have ready in case of war, under the terms of the Statute of
Winchester. The muster rolls of 1539 indicate a state of
preparedness in the West Riding which would support
Professor Powicke's thesis that the commons became better
organized and better armed as a result of the civil wars of the
fifteenth century.[2] In Yorkshire there was the additional
factor of endemic warfare against the Scots. As long ago as
1138 parish levies had been made for the campaign in
which the Archbishop of York led an army to victory at the
Battle of the Standard. When Thomas Lord Darcy led an
army northwards in 1523 he was thus continuing a long
tradition.[3] The local noblemen and gentry who carried out
the musters were still at this period quite often soldiers
themselves, and actually led the forces they raised in time of
emergency. In 1513 eight West Riding gentlemen were
knighted on the field of Flodden, and another three at
Tournay in the same month; and in 1544 seven gentlemen
of the Riding were paid conduct money for a hundred men
each for the homeward march from Berwick-on-Tweed to

---

[1] R. R. Reid: *The King's Council in the North* (London, 1921).
[2] M. Powicke: *Military Obligation in Medieval England* (Oxford, 1962), pp.
220–3.
[3] Ibid., 44 (1138); and P.R.O.: E 36/vol. 43 (1523).

their homes.¹ The men they led on these campaigns were
probably not all drawn from township levies; some were
raised by written indenture, and some were the household
servants and possibly tenants of their leaders. (Darcy's force
in 1523 certainly included some members of his household.)
A man who led to war soldiers raised from his own locality,
under whatever form of service, must have considerably
enhanced his prestige in the eyes of the local population,
regardless of the fact that he did so entirely on the authority
of the King. Both this fact and the state of readiness revealed by the muster records should be kept in mind when
we come to look at the events of the Pilgrimage of Grace.

II

The pattern of territorial lordship, the honours, baronies
and liberties of the West Riding, was analysed in some detail
in Chapter II. We must now place that pattern in the
perspective of personal relationships, and the system of
patronage which was the essence of lordship in the sixteenth
century. Whereas in the twelfth century the relationship
between a lord and his followers was explicitly based on
tenure and service, by the sixteenth century what counted
was a lord's ability to secure or guarantee offices and
emoluments for his clients either in his own employment or
in that of some greater man, possibly the King himself.
Nevertheless, there was still an element of regionalism in the
situation, and other things being equal a young man (or his
family) would look to the large landlords of his own county
when in search of a patron. There were also personal factors
involved, and in any part of the country the distribution of
this kind of power might change considerably from one
decade to the next. Thus the situation in the West Riding
was completely transformed by the upheaval of 1536–7,

¹ The Flodden knights from the West Riding were George Darcy, William
Middleton, William Malleverer, Brian Stapleton, William Gascoigne, jr., Guy
Dawney, Richard Malleverer, and Christopher Danby; those knighted at Tournay
were Thomas Fairfax, John Nevill of Liversedge, and Richard Tempest; W. A.
Shaw: *The Knights of England* (London, 1906), ii, pp. 37–9. The seven mentioned in
1544 were Sir William Fairfax, Sir Robert Stapleton, John Tempest, Sir Thomas
Waterton, Thomas Slingsby, Sir John Nevill, and Thomas Malleverer; *L.P.*,
XIX (i), no. 532 (9).

TABLE XIV

The Leading Noblemen and Gentry of the West Riding, c. 1535.

Area of most influence	Name	Residences	Stewardships	Landed income	Sheriff of Yorkshire	West Riding Commission of Peace:			Behaviour in Pilgrimage of Grace
						1528	1530	1538	
Hallamshire	George Talbot, 4th Earl of Shrewsbury (earl, 1489–1538)	Sheffield Castle	None here	£1,533 (1537)	—	x	x	x	Loyal throughout
Strafforth and Tickhill	Sir William Copley	Sprotborough	—	£133 (1546)	—	x	—	—	On jury of indictment, 1537
Hatfield	Sir Brian Hastings (d. 1537)	?Hatfield	?	?	1536–7	—	x	x	Loyal throughout
Pontefract Honour (all) and Snaith	Thomas, Lord Darcy (att. 1537)	Temple Hirst Temple Newsam	Pontefract, Knaresborough (1509–37); Snaith (1497–1537)	£333 (1537)	—	x	x	x	Surrendered Pontefract, Oct. 1536; executed, 1537
Staincross	Sir Thomas Wentworth (d. 1543)	West Bretton	Wakefield (1542–3)	?	—	—	x	x	Not known
Staincross	Prior Comyn of St. Oswald's (d. 1538)	Nostell	—	—	—	—	—	—	Not known
Agbrigg and Morley	Sir Richard Tempest (d. 1537)	Bolling by Bradford	Wakefield, Sowerby (1521–37); Bradford (1524–37, jointly)	£100 (1523)	1516–17	—	x	x	Appears to have followed Darcy; died in prison 1537
Agbrigg and Morley	Sir Henry Savile (d. 1558)	Thornhill Tankersley Soothill	(Pontefract, 1537–49)	£400 (1546)	1537–8, 1541–2	x	—	x	Loyal throughout
Agbrigg and Morley	Sir Robert Nevill (d. 1543)	Liversedge	—	£50 (1524)	1540–1	—	x	x	Followed Darcy; but on jury of indictment, 1537
Agbrigg and Morley	Sir John Nevill (brother of last; att. 1541)	Chevet	(Lord Darcy's lands, 1537–41)		1518–19, 1523–4, 1527–8	—	—	—	Apparently loyal
Marshland and Howdenshire (E.R.)	Sir Robert Constable (att. 1537)	Flamborough (E.R.)	Marshland (for Abbot of York); Howdenshire (for		—	—	—	—	With Darcy throughout; executed, 1537

Area of most influence	Name	Residences	Stewardships	Landed Income	Sheriff of Yorkshire	West Riding Commission of Peace:			Behaviour in Pilgrimage of Grace
						1528	1530	1538	
Barkston wapentake	Abbot Rogers of Selby (1526–39)	Selby	—		—	—	—	—	Not known
Barkston, Ripon and Otley Ldp.	Archbishop Edward Lee of York (1531–44)	Cawood; Bishopthorpe	—		—	—	—	—	With Darcy in early stages; later tried to minimize his support
The Ainsty	Sir William Fairfax (d. 1558)	Steeton	—	£180 (1546)	1534–5 1539–40	—	—	—	Captured near Wakefield in Oct. 1536; followed Darcy reluctantly
The Ainsty	Sir Oswald Wilstrop	Wilstrop	—	?	—	—	—	—	Joined revolt, Oct. 1536; on indictment jury, 1537
Skyrack	Sir William Gascoigne (d. 1551)	Gawthorpe	—	£533 (1546)	—	x	?	—	Not known
Skyrack	Sir William Malleverer (d. 1551)	Wothersome	—	£230 (1546)	1521–2	—	x	x	Not known
Skyrack	Abbot John Ripley of Kirkstall (1528–39)	Kirkstall	—		—	—	—	—	At Pontefract 'convocation', Dec. 1536
Southern Claro (Spofforth)	Henry Percy, sixth Earl of Northumberland	Wressle (ER), Topcliffe (NR); and Spofforth	—	£1,000 (1537)	—	x	x	—	Unclear; he did not openly support revolt
Southern Claro (Spofforth)	Sir William Middleton (d. 1555)	Middleton	—	£267 (1546)	1526–7	—	x	x	Not known
Kirkbyshire and Nidderdale	Countess of Derby	—	—		—	—	—	—	Not known
Kirkbyshire and Nidderdale	Sir William Mallory (d. 1547)	Studley	—	£180 (1546)	—	—	—	x	Drawn into revolt, Oct. 1536; on indictment jury, 1537
Kirkbyshire and Nidderdale	Abbot William Thirsk (retired 1536; executed, 1537)	Fountains	—		—	—	—	—	Involved in second rising, Jan. 1537; so executed
Craven, or Staincliffe	Henry Clifford, 1st Earl of Cumberland (earl, 1525–42)	Skipton	(Knaresborough, 1537–42)	£1,333 (1537)	1522–3 (before succeeding)	—	x	—	Loyal throughout
Craven, or Staincliffe	Sir Stephen Hamerton	Wigglesworth	—	£60 (1524)	—	x	x	—	Joined rebels, Oct. 1536; executed, 1537

having previously undergone less dramatic changes only a few years earlier, following the fall of Wolsey. The first question we must ask therefore is who the leading figures were within the Riding in the period with which we are concerned.

There were some English counties whose political life at this period was dominated by a single noble house: that was the position enjoyed by the Howard family in Norfolk and by the Percy in Northumberland. In the West Riding, which was larger and included a remarkably large number of ancient lordships and castles, the situation was more complicated. A single family could have dominated the whole Riding only by uniting all these lordships under its own control. The Crown had by 1500 acquired quite a number of them, having united the Duchies of Lancaster and York. But the King could not use this control in quite the same way as a nobleman: not only did he have to delegate administrative authority to others, but he was anxious to do so in such a way that not all stewardships went to the same person or family. Outside the area of royal control—notably Craven and Upper Nidderdale—there was hardly any Crown land at all, and the influence that attached to possession of a great lordship belonged to men who did not depend on the King (except to the extent that a nobleman who broke the law might be attainted). It is this absence of a single dominant family which makes the Riding such an interesting area for the study of the nature of local power and worship.

Table XIV lists twenty-four people who could be described as powerful figures in one part of the Riding or another about the year 1535. Five of them were clerics, whose position will be considered a little later in the chapter; of the other nineteen, four were peers of the realm and a fifth was a dowager countess; fifteen were thus gentlemen without any noble titles, but their degree of influence was by no means uniform. Three of the gentry stand out above the rest: Sir William Gascoigne the elder, Sir Henry Savile, and Sir Richard Tempest. If we add these three men to the four noblemen (the Earls of Shrewsbury, Northumberland and Cumberland, and Lord Darcy) we may fairly claim to

have identified the seven most important laymen in the
Riding at this time. The fact that two of them, Darcy and
Tempest, owed their positions at least in part to their tenure
of Crown stewardships, need not trouble us for the
moment.

The three elements in the patronage of a leading nobleman or gentleman were his household, his estate administration, and the rather wider circle of men who looked to him
for advancement. For three of these seven men there is
documentary material concerning their households. Lord
Darcy's private papers, confiscated by the King on his
attainder after the Pilgrimage of Grace, are still kept in the
Public Record Office; the papers of the fourth, fifth and
sixth Earls of Northumberland have been studied by Dr.
Bean; and there is material concerning the Clifford servants
in the Skipton Castle Manuscripts at Leeds. Detailed knowledge of a man's household in this period is rare. How
valuable therefore that the Darcy papers should include a
'cheker roll' of his household servants in 1521, as well as a
number of documents which help us to identify some of the
people named in it: eighty members of the household are
listed, of whom twenty-one were gentlemen, thirty-six
yeomen, and the rest menial servants. Another list, made two
years later, gives the names of over a hundred men who
served in Darcy's household contingent in the force he took
to Scotland in 1523.[1] Twenty-four people appear in both
lists, but the surnames show that a good many others who
fought in the army against Scotland were relatives of the
household yeomen. Many of these household followers
were either tenants on Darcy's estates or else sons and
brothers of tenants who found occupation in his service.
Unfortunately the only full Darcy estate record that survives
is the one made just after his attainder in 1536. But despite
the time-lag it shows that thirteen of the men named in the
1523 list still had holdings on Darcy's lands in 1537; and
again there is a much wider coincidence of surnames. The
most prosperous of the tenants was Lawrence Baynes,
farmer of a large part of Roundhay Park and of a tenement
called Caldcotes near Temple Newsam. One member of the

[1] P.R.O.: SP 1/22/ff. 185–6 (summarized in *L.P.*, III, no. 1330) and E 36/43.

household can be identified as also holding an estate office
under Darcy: Matthew Oglesthorpe of Thorner who drew
a fee of £3. 6s. 8d. as bailiff of Becca in 1528.[1]

The gentlemen in the 'cheker roll' were not of the richer
sort such as appear in Table XIV above. Typical of the more
prosperous of them was Gilbert Scott, esquire, who in
1524 was living at Potter Newton and contributed to the
subsidy for lands worth £20 a year. He was captain of the
household forces raised in 1523, and later appears as
Constable of Pontefract Castle, presumably as Darcy's
deputy.[2] Of a similar status, William Hungate the younger
of Saxton had not inherited his family's estate at this period;
but in 1546 he was assessed on lands valued at £33 a year.[3]
In general both the gentlemen and the yeomen of the household were inhabitants of the region where Darcy's own
West Riding estates lay, that is between Leeds and Selby.
One man, however, stands out above the rest in a number of
ways, and as steward of Darcy's household in 1521 at the
age of about twenty-six he was probably its most important
member; this was Thomas Gargrave, who had ahead of him
one of the most distinguished careers in sixteenth-century
Northern history. He seems to have left Darcy's household
for one of the Inns of Court, and in 1539 became one of the
legal members of the Council at York; for the last nineteen
years of his life he was Vice-President of that Council and
an unexceptionally loyal subject of Queen Elizabeth I. His
service to Darcy therefore was just the first step on a tall
ladder.[4]

The form of patronage which was most frowned upon by
the early Tudor kings was not the mere maintenance of a
household, but the maintenance of a body of retainers, who
having no household or estate functions were nonetheless
bound to a lord by means of annuities or fees payable for
life and wore his livery. A retinue of this kind, led by a great
noble and including substantial knights who brought
followers of their own into his service, might easily be

[1] P.R.O.: SC 6/Hen VIII/4308.
[2] *Y.A.J.*, ii (1873), 289–96.
[3] P.R.O.: E 179/207/190.
[4] For his career, see *Dictionary of National Biography*.

transformed into a private army. This form of patronage was no doubt in the mind of Sir John Fortescue when he wrote about 1476 that: 'the people will go with him that may best sustain and reward them.'[1] Whether Lord Darcy retained knights in this way can only be guessed; his lands were not so extensive as those of a Percy or a Nevill, and his scope for such grants was limited by his income. There was however an occasion in his youth when he came up against Henry VII's statutes against the wearing of livery. In 1496 Sir Thomas Darcy was indicted in the court of King's Bench for giving badges in the form of a silver buck's head to nineteen men of the country round Leeds, Whitkirk, Selby and Rothwell. Another man indicted at the same time was James Stanley of Manchester whose token of an eagle's head was said to have been worn at Bradford, Halifax, Almondbury and Wakefield.[2] The practice may have been both more widespread and of longer duration than indicated by the few legal proceedings so far unearthed. Unfortunately there is no firm evidence to tell us whether Darcy's followers still wore bucks' heads at the time of his rebellion in 1536.

Lord Darcy was not only patron of a household, and perhaps a wider clientele, by virtue of his position as a wealthy landowner; he was also the King's steward and constable of Pontefract and Knaresborough from 1509 till shortly before his death, and steward of Snaith from 1497. As such he was almost a viceroy in the wide stretch of country dominated by Pontefract, and enjoyed too a considerable influence in the wapentake of Claro. In 1523 the force which he took to Scotland consisted only partly of his own household contingent: the greater part of its 1,750 men were drawn from the six wapentakes between the Wharfe and the Dearne. Without Pontefract Darcy was no more than a baron and a fine soldier; with it he was placed on the level of an Earl, at least as far as his West Riding power was concerned.

[1] Sir John Fortescue: *The Governance of England* (ed. C. Plummer, London, 1885), p. 129.
[2] P.R.O.: *Baga de Secretis* document, printed in Deputy Keeper's Third Report, Appendix ii, p. 219.

There is further material on the practice of livery and maintenance in the Percy family archives. The document which goes under the promising title of the 'Northumberland household book', begun in 1512, is somewhat disappointing since it deals almost entirely with regulations and official functions and says hardly anything about particular individuals in the Percy service.[1] The estate accounts are more helpful, insofar as they tell us not merely about receipts but also about expenditure. Dr. Bean found in the accounts of 1442–3 the record of extraordinary fees or annuities paid under grants made by the second Earl of Northumberland; they were sometimes of as much as ten marks or even ten pounds a year and were valid for life. Some of the recipients were West Riding men whose families may still have been associated with the house of Percy in the sixteenth century: Sir William Plumpton, for example, whose manor of Plumpton was held of Spofforth Barony; Walter Calverley; and Sir John Tempest. Twenty years later, in 1461, Dr. Bean calculated that the third Earl spent about a third of his annual estate income on fees of this kind; and the proportion was still a substantial one as late as 1489. But sometime between then and 1518 there was a marked decline, and by the period with which we are mainly concerned it seems to have been most unusual for a Percy to grant fees or annuities outside the family to anyone but officers performing a specific function in his household or on his estates.[2] A not improbable explanation is that Henry VII had at last prevented this practice by the statute of 1504, which not only forbade maintenance of feed men but also gave royal judges the right to take their own initiative in starting proceedings against it.[3] The employment of local gentlemen as officials, however, was still an important form of patronage, as we have seen, and there is a little information about the sixth Earl of Northumberland's estate officers in the accounts made for the Crown shortly after his death in 1537. They

---

[1] T. Percy (ed.): *The Earl of Northumberland's Household Book* (London, 1905).

[2] J. M. W. Bean: *The Estates of the Percy Family 1416–1537* (Oxford, 1958), pp. 92, 136.

[3] *Statutes*, ii, 19 Hen VII, cap. 14. Cf. also 1 Ric. II, cap. 7, and 8 Ed IV, cap. 2.

included men like William Stapleton, the feodary of Spofforth Barony, as brother of Christopher Stapleton of Wighill;
and William Skrimshire, a lawyer who was 'retained of
counsel' and acted as steward of the Earl's courts at Tadcaster and Spofforth.[1] The Park-keeper of Topcliffe (North
Riding) was Sir Thomas Johnson, one of the sixth Earl's
great favourites, who was made a virtual gift of the
West Riding manors of Leathley and Walton Head;
similarly extravagant gifts were made to Sir Thomas
Wharton and to the sixth Earl's physician Dr. Wendy, at
Healaugh and in Langstrothdale respectively.[2] For a patron
to make actual grants of property to his followers was very
exceptional for it meant dissipating the noble family's own
fortunes; but the sixth Earl of Northumberland was an
unusual man, and he ended by destroying the family's
position almost completely for a generation.

The evidence relating to Clifford patronage, though more
limited than that concerning the Percy Earls, is also found in
accounts of expenditure. Two men who received fees from
the Earl of Cumberland in 1528 were John Lambert, a
lawyer and steward of the courts in Craven, and Christopher
Aske, Receiver of Skipton, who also figures in other sources
as the Earl's servant.[3] Lambert was a Craven man and
belonged to a family settled at Calton; either he or a relative
of the same name was assessed there on lands worth £50
in the subsidy roll of 1546.[4] Christopher Aske on the other
hand came from the East Riding; he was a brother of the
Robert Aske who emerged as a leader of the Pilgrims of
Grace. His presence in Craven raises the interesting
question why individual gentlemen entered the service of
one master rather than another. It seems that Robert Aske
was in the household of the fifth Earl of Northumberland
before he went to London to study law; the reason why his
brother went to Skipton was almost certainly the marriage
between the first Earl of Cumberland and Margery Percy;
connections by marriage probably explained a number of

[1] P.R.O.: SC 6/Hen VIII/4283, 4287.
[2] J. M. W. Bean, op. cit., pp. 146–7.
[3] Skipton Castle MSS, Y.A.S. Library, Leeds: DD 121/Bundle 29.
[4] P.R.O.: E 179/207/188, 201.

gentlemen's choice of patron.[1] But another factor was of
longer standing, that of territorial lordship. The great noble
patron was often not only lord of the local castle, but also the
man from whom his leading gentlemen followers held their
original estates. Thus Sir William Plumpton's link with the
fifteenth-century Earl of Northumberland was not only the
financial one of an annual fee, but also the fact that he held
his manor (and residence) of Plumpton from the Percy
barony of Spofforth; William Skrimshire also held some
land from that barony, though he had other more important
estates when he died in 1557. John Lambert, again, held
Calton and Airton from the Honour of Skipton. Insofar as
the pattern of territorial lordship still influenced the choices
of knights and esquires in this way, one can say that the old
feudal pattern was still not completely dead in sixteenth-
century Yorkshire, despite the decline of tenure by knight
service. The history of English patronage is one of gradual
evolution, not of sudden change.

The position of the great ecclesiastical figures of the
Riding was not unlike that of the leading laymen. They had
their households and estate administrations, and even
granted annuities and fees. The most powerful of them in
Yorkshire was The Archbishop of York. From early in the
reign until 1530 the Archbishop was Thomas Wolsey, and
although he did not enter his northern diocese until shortly
before his death, his power and influence there was always a
factor in his national strength. The subsidy roll of Wolsey's
household in 1524 shows a number of West Riding names,
notably Henry Savile, Richard Redmayne, Robert Scargill,
and a John Lambert who may or may not have been related
to the man of that name in Clifford's employment.[2] Wolsey's
successor Edward Lee was a less forceful personality, but
one of the letters he claimed to have written during the
Pilgrimage of Grace in 1536 implies that he was a man of
some weight at Ripon, as well as at York itself and at Beverley

---

[1] On Aske's connection with Northumberland, see *Notes and Queries*, 11th ser.,
iv (1911), 441–3, which cites B.M.: Add. MS 38133; the author suggests that the
Sixth Earl is indicated, but the document is dated 17 May 1527, and the Fifth Earl
died on the 19 May of that year.
[2] P.R.O.: E 179/69/10.

in the East Riding.[1] We must return in a moment to the way in which Wolsey tried to use his influence with the King to carry through a policy which affected the whole balance of power in the North.

Of the Yorkshire abbots, two were spiritual lords of Parliament before 1539: William Dent of St. Mary's at York, and Robert Rogers of Selby.[2] They were both heads of houses with extensive lands, and dominated small areas of the West Riding; whether their power was enhanced by their being summoned to Parliament cannot be judged. The three other spiritual men included in Table XIV were the Abbots of Fountains and Kirkstall and the Prior of St. Oswald's. Marmaduke Huby, Abbot of Fountains until 1525, was the only regular cleric to sit on the West Riding commission of the peace in the sixteenth century; we do not have details of his other temporal activities, apart from a Star Chamber case involving a conflict with Sir William Gascoigne, but his extensive estates in Nidderdale and Craven would entitle him to respect in much of the northern half of the Riding. He was probably a supporter of Wolsey.[3] His successor, William Thirsk, seems to have used his influence on the side of the rebels in 1536 after being forced out of his abbacy by the king's commissioners in January of that year.[4] Less is known of the heads of Kirkstall and Nostell, but both had the estates and income to justify local influence in their respective areas. The employment of lay gentry and even noblemen by the larger monasteries has been noticed in Chapter II. Darcy's position as steward of Selby, Pontefract and Fountains in 1535 is worth recalling in view of what we know of his influence elsewhere. It raises the question whether the granting of monastic fees to laymen was an aspect of lay or of monastic patronage. Where the layman employed was a minor gentleman from within the monastery's own area of influence, there are good reasons

---

[1] The claim was made in his subsequent confession, *L.P.*, XII (i), no. 1022; the importance of this letter, which does not itself survive, will be considered in Chapter V, *infra*, p. 176.

[2] *Journals of the House of Lords*, i. 1–125, *passim*.

[3] *L.P.*, IV (i), no. 1610 (11), etc.; the Star Chamber case is printed in Y.A.S.R.S., xli, no. 7.

[4] *L.P.*, X, no. 137.

for seeing the situation as one where the abbot or prior was bestowing a favour on a lesser man. But when the feed man was a Darcy it is easy to imagine that the situation was the reverse. Darcy would afford the monks the protection of his established influence in the realm (and also locally) in return for their payment of his fee; he cannot have owed much of his own authority to such appointments.

III

The seven laymen referred to earlier as having the greatest power in the Riding each had a sphere of influence, where in most cases his superiority went unchallenged; the same might be said of such religious figures as the Abbot of Fountains or the Archbishop of York. But occasionally spheres of influence overlapped, or cases arose of two powerful men seeking to dominate the same area. When this happened, there was liable to be feuding, and it is at this point that we must begin to enquire about the state of law and order in Yorkshire. The King was not merely concerned that his own commands should be obeyed in the counties and that there should be no danger of private armies challenging his will: he saw it as a necessary prerequisite to these things that there should be no part of the realm that was beyond his jurisdiction, and no area where his subjects were prevented from getting justice in royal courts. The leading figures in the West Riding were not above trying to prevent this and pervert the course of justice for their own ends, and the most flagrant cases arose when two local magnates were at feud with one another.

A very lamentable picture of the state of law and order was painted by the writer of a letter to Cromwell about the year 1534:[1]

Touching the king's right in Yorkshire, he says, every man claims liberties . . . [with the result that] the king's felons, murderers and outlaws are cloaked, coloured and maintained by stewards and bailiffs of liberties, so that the king's process has no place and he is not answered of any profits on the said offenders, which causes his laws much less to be dreaded; there are many of them in the shire out of all sanctuary. . . . Touching the keeping of the king's peace the truth is that there is no

[1] P.R.O.: SP 1/88/ff. 119–20, summarized in *L.P.*, VII, no. 1669.

manner of matter which hath bearing but it is only (tried?) by the justices of the peace, and there is of them a great number in every Riding. And such as be of the most power and worship bring their juries to the sessions and reformeth the sheriff's returns; wherefore if these persons were discharged thereof in every Riding I think it should much quiet the shire . . .

The authorship of the letter is not known; possibly it was Sir William Fairfax who served as sheriff in 1534–5, or possibly his immediate predecessor in the office, Sir John Constable of Burton Constable. But we know the identity of some of those men 'of most power and worship' whom he criticises, for he gives the names of three men in each Riding. In the West Riding they were, not the noblemen whose patronage we have just been discussing, but the three most powerful knights in the county: Sir Richard Tempest, Sir Henry Savile, and Sir William Gascoigne the elder. Possibly the writer did not dare to criticise men of the highest rank; but there is some indication in the evidence we are about to examine which suggests that these men were in fact much worse than the noblemen in this matter of law and order. All three were accused in Star Chamber at some time during Henry VIII's reign. The difficulty of obtaining justice before the commission of the peace was no doubt the reason why Yorkshiremen with the most serious grievances, and with money enough to go to London, sometimes took their cases before Star Chamber in order to get a fair hearing and at least a pronouncement in their favour. Enforcement was another matter.

Sir William Gascoigne was in 1534 a man of about sixty-five years, who had come into his inheritance in 1490. With estates as far apart as Gawthorpe (near Harewood), Thorpe Arch and Burghwallis, as well as some East Riding manors, he had as much substance as many peers; and indeed at the subsidy of 1524 he refused to be assessed in his own county on the grounds that he was rightful heir to the Earldom of Westmorland.[1] The bid came to nought but it illustrates well the man's idea of himself. The eight suits brought against him in Star Chamber between 1499 and about 1535

---

[1] *Y.A.J.*, ii (1873), 292. One must be careful not to confuse this man with Sir William Gascoigne of Cardington, Bedfordshire, a servant of Cardinal Wolsey.

show him—though of course one-sidedly—as a man capable of imposing his will on lesser men by threats or if necessary by action.[1] A typical example of his methods is seen in the series of incidents between Gascoigne and John Saintpole (or Sampole) of Carcroft; the point at issue being whether or not the manor of Carcroft was held of Sir William's manor of Burghwallis. In April 1530 forty of Gascoigne's men came to Carcroft and distrained some cattle belonging to Saintpole's tenants; then a month or so later Saintpole was chased by some of the Gascoigne retinue and attacked at Norton church. He tried to bring the whole case before the justices of the peace at Wakefield, but on the appointed day Gascoigne himself turned up with a hundred of his men to prevent Saintpole being given a fair hearing. There were further incidents at Carcroft between then and 1533, when the case was taken to Star Chamber, and on the 27th October of that year the Bishop of Durham and others were commanded to hear the answers of witnesses.[2] The final outcome of the proceedings is not recorded; quite possibly Gascoigne got away with it. Certainly it would be a brave man who would have given evidence against him, for he was widely feared in the central parts of the Riding. Even if some of the descriptions of violence were exaggerated in order to ensure that the case fell fairly within Star Chamber jurisdiction, the lack of justice for a man like Saintpole is clearly demonstrated. An interesting sidelight is the fact that Gascoigne should think it worth taking so much trouble to assert his claims to this kind of lordship over a mesne lord; the relationship cannot have been an entirely dead one. Another illustration of Sir William's attitude to law and order comes from the bill of complaint made against him (again in Star Chamber) by John Fletcher, constable of Harewood, concerning events that took place in December 1534. The trouble began with an affray between a servant of Richard Redmayne, one of the joint-lords of Harewood Castle, and a stranger to the village called George Wade. Wade claimed that he had been attacked and went off to get

[1] Printed in Y.A.S.R.S., xli, nos. 4, 7, 9; xlv, nos. 16, 17; 32, 52; and li, no. 73.
[2] Ibid., xlv, no. 16 and li, no. 73.

a warrant against Redmayne and his servants from one Richard Chaloner (probably a mistake for Robert Chaloner, a justice of the peace who lived at Wakefield) when Redmayne's men intercepted him and took him back to Harewood Castle. According to Fletcher what happened was that as constable he himself arrested Wade because he had started the initial affray. At this point Wade's brother sought the help of Gascoigne whose house at Gawthorpe was within the township. Gascoigne, at this time a justice of the peace himself, summoned Fletcher to Gawthorpe and demanded an explanation of the proceedings. Fletcher pleaded that he durst not take Wade from the custody of Redmayne, and that he could do nothing to prevent the prisoner being taken off to York Gaol. Gascoigne insisted in binding over the constable to produce Wade, and when this was not done he demanded payment of the £20 stipulated in the bond. Fletcher, who probably did not even have such a sum, was thereupon seized by Sir William's men and imprisoned at Gawthorpe for three days before being taken to York to await trial before the justices of assize. Since the case was brought to Star Chamber, we may suppose that Gascoigne's case was upheld at common law when the justices arrived. Once again the result of the complaint is not known, and the documents which survive are too fragmentary for us to judge the rights and wrongs of the case at this distance of time.[1] But it shows very clearly the general atmosphere of the West Riding on the eve of the commotions of 1536, and how far the King was from being able to control what went on there.

The Star Chamber evidence against Sir William Gascoigne mostly shows him in conflict with lesser men, who crossed his path at their peril. The cases which relate to Sir Richard Tempest and Sir Henry Savile are more interesting because they show these two 'magnates' in conflict with one another. Sir Richard, who was born in 1479 and was the elder of the two by just over twenty years, rose gradually to prominence in the Riding during the first quarter of the sixteenth century, being knighted in 1513, pricked for Sheriff of Yorkshire in 1516–17, and appointed

steward of Wakefield and Sowerbyshire in 1521.[1] His rise
was made easier by the fact that the death of Sir John Savile
in 1505 left the other prominent family of the area without
an active head until the coming of age of Henry Savile in
1521. Unlike Tempest, young Henry Savile was on good
terms with Wolsey and served in his household; a mark of
the relationship being Savile's appointment to the commission of the peace in 1528, though he was removed after
the Cardinal's fall.[2] Savile was a wealthier man than Tempest
and it was hardly surprising that he should wish to recover
the position once enjoyed by his grandfather. The first
mention of a feud between the two men occurs in a report
written by the Earl of Surrey for Wolsey in 1523, and it
continued unabated till Tempest's death in 1537.[3]

An important element in their conflict was Sir Henry's
claim to the mesne lordship of Stansfield, Wadsworth,
Barkisland and a number of other townships within the
lordships of Wakefield and Sowerbyshire; he was in fact
reviving a claim which his grandfather had made long before
but had been unable to prove beyond dispute. About 1530 a
group of tenants in these townships alleged in a Star
Chamber complaint that Savile had reasserted his false claim
to be mesne lord by impanelling there a jury of his own
tenants and servants, and that on the strength of their ruling
he had begun to enclose the commons of three townships.
The tenants' challenge became more serious in 1534 when
a new bill of complaint was laid against Savile by the men of
seven townships, and when in June Sir Richard Tempest
wrote to Cromwell describing how Savile had entered into
an eighth township, Holmfirth, and had driven off the
cattle of the King's copyholders there. Tempest was bound
to defend the interests of the King whose steward he was,
quite apart from any desire to reduce his rival's influence.
In 1535 or 1536 (none of the documents concerned bears
any date), the steward took up the litigation himself and laid

[1] He was knighted at Flodden, cf. *supra*, p. 133n.; for his appointment as
sheriff, see P.R.O.: *Lists and Indexes*, x (1898), 163; for his Wakefield stewardship,
L.P., III (ii), no. 1451 (20).

[2] *L.P.*, IV (ii), no. 5083.

[3] *L.P.*, III (ii), no. 3240. For Henry Savile's coming of age, see ibid., no. 2297
(12).

his own bill against Savile in Star Chamber. In addition to
the matter of the mesne lordship, Tempest made five other
accusations. Two concerned the protection from justice of
a couple of suspected felons, Nicholas Ellestones who had
been charged with murder, and a false coiner called Thew-
lace. The third, in similar vein, alleged that Savile had
'maintained' a group of his own men after they had murdered
the deputy bailiff of Halifax. Fourthly Savile was said to have
been responsible for the theft of some money and plate from
Sir Thomas Tempest, Sir Richard's son; and lastly he was
accused of hunting the King's deer in Wakefield New Park.[1]
Sir Henry replied with more than just a denial: he lodged a
series of counter-charges. Some accused Tempest of abusing
his authority as steward: he was alleged to have taken illegal
fines for new enclosures on the waste of Wakefield and
Sowerby lordships, and to have claimed conduct money for
soldiers whom he had never actually taken to Scotland.
More serious charges were that Tempest had maintained the
murderers of five men in the Wakefield area during the
previous few years, and there was insinuation that in some
cases he might actually have procured the murder. For good
measure Savile added the accusation that the steward had
maintained in his own fee and livery people who were not
his household servants. These counter-charges coincided
with another suit against Tempest in Star Chamber in 1536,
in which Isabel Jepson stated that her husband, after starting
legal action against Sir Thomas Tempest in London, had
been murdered at Wakefield by one of Sir Thomas's
servants. Despite Sir Richard's assurance that the murderer
had been arrested and sent to London by the Council in the
North, Mistress Jepson was convinced that he would
eventually be acquitted, so great was the Tempest power.[2]
It is quite impossible to estimate what degree of truth was
contained in these mutual recriminations, but whilst one
must bear in mind the natural tendency for exaggeration in
such circumstances, there is no inherent reason to doubt the

[1] Y.A.S.R.S., li, pp. 117–20 and 138–40 (suit of tenants of various townships
against Savile); and xli, pp. 189–92, xlv, pp. 46–8, 63–7, and li, pp. 28–30, 104–6,
113–7 (suit and counter-suit between Savile and Tempest).
[2] Y.A.S.R.S., li, pp. 53–6, 145.

main substance of either set of allegations. Before the Star Chamber proceedings reached any conclusion they were overtaken by the events of the Pilgrimage of Grace in which Tempest sided with Darcy whilst Savile was loyal to the King; afterwards Savile came out on top, for Tempest was imprisoned and died in the Fleet.

Another West Riding figure who used violence and defied the law when it suited him was the first Earl of Cumberland. It did so chiefly when he was faced with opposition from John Norton of Norton Conyers (North Riding). In 1528 Norton appeared in Star Chamber with the complaint that Clifford had hunted his (Norton's) deer in the manor of Rylstone and had sent some of his men to enclose Speldersden Moor where the tenants of Rylstone had rights of common pasture. Two years later tension between the two men increased when the Countess of Derby made Norton steward of her lordship of Kirkby Malzeard and Nidderdale. In 1531 Norton went to Kirkby as steward to hold the lord's court, but was prevented from doing so by sixty of Clifford's men led by Christopher Aske. Cumberland's version of the incident is slightly different: he claimed that when he sent his son Lord Clifford to hold the court of Kirkbyshire on that same day, the latter had been attacked by John and Richard Norton with the help of William Mallory of Studley. According to the Earl the sequel to the riot was the indictment of Norton and his friends at Leeds quarter sessions, which no doubt explains why Norton took the case to Star Chamber. As usual the result of the litigation is not known.[1] Once again the conflict played its part in the Pilgrimage of Grace, when the contenders took opposing sides. Further evidence of Cumberland's lack of scruple is revealed by the proceedings concerning the lease of Winterburn, a grange in Craven belonging to the Cistercian Abbey of Furness. It seems that in 1531 shortly after the death of Abbot Bankes, the Earl conspired with a monk of the house to forge an eighty-year lease to himself of the farm of Winterburn and to confirm it with the seal of the deceased abbot. His successor, elected a little later, knew nothing of the lease, or chose to ignore it, and appointed as farmer and

[1] Y.A.S.R.S., xlv, no. 15; li, nos. 86–7.

bailiff of Winterburn one Gabriel Proctor. But three years later the Earl produced the forged lease and had Proctor evicted on the strength of it; whereupon Proctor took the matter to Star Chamber. In 1536 the Doctors Layton and Legh came to Furness during their tour of visitation, and their enquiries yielded a confession from the monk who had been Clifford's accomplice. It seemed as if Proctor's case was won, and in 1537 the Augmentations official Robert Southwell confirmed the story of the forgery. Yet in the end Clifford got his way by securing a formal confirmation of his lease in the Court of Augmentations. On another score, however, he was unsuccessful: the Earl of Derby in 1536 denied Cumberland's claim to be steward or bailiff of Winterburn on the grounds that he himself was steward of all the Furness estates. Derby was powerful enough to stand up to his fellow-Earl and Clifford had to back down.[1]

IV

We have come far enough in this account of the nature of lordly power in the West Riding to be able to put in more personal terms the question raised at the beginning of the chapter about the relationship between the King's authority and the power of the local magnates. To a large extent it is a question about the administration of justice and about the position of those county officers whose task it was to administer royal justice. Writing of Lancastrian England Professor Jacob formed the impression that the sheriff, who had to serve writs and call juries, was more often than not a mere tool of some overmighty subject, just another of the instruments used by a great earl or baron to impose his wishes on the county regardless of royal policy.[2] Since the sheriff could never be of higher status than a knight this situation was difficult to avoid. But there are two reasons for believing that the sheriff was less dependent on a single magnate in early Tudor Yorkshire, one of which applies to England generally whilst the other is peculiar to Yorkshire.

[1] Y.A.S.R.S., lxx, nos. 24, 61; A. G. Dickens (ed.); *Clifford Letters of the Sixteenth Century*, Surtees Soc., clxxii (1962), pp. 59–61 and 124.
[2] E. F. Jacob: *The Fifteenth Century* (Oxford, 1961), pp. 448–9.

The first is that the principal link between noblemen and substantial knights was that of the 'extra-ordinary' fee, and as we have seen this method of retaining was in decline by 1520. But secondly, there was no single family in the three Ridings capable of dominating the whole of Yorkshire. If the sheriff was 'in the pocket' of a local magnate, it is hardly likely to have been the same one all the time; and since the choice of sheriff was in principle a royal one, this at least left the King in a position to play off one group against another.

It may well be significant that between 1516 when Sir Richard Tempest was sheriff and 1537 when Sir Henry Savile was pricked for the office, none of the three knights whose 'lawlessness' has just been discussed held the shrievalty; Sir William Gascoigne never held it at all under Henry VIII. There were, however, two years in which the son of a leading nobleman was made sheriff, and he presumably would have some loyalty towards his father's house: in 1522 Sir Henry Clifford, who succeeded to the barony the following year and became Earl of Cumberland in 1525; and in 1535 Sir George Darcy.[1] Twelve West Riding men were pricked for sheriff between 1520 and 1546, one of them twice. With one possible exception, they all had lands worth at least £50, and some of them are in the group of fifteen gentlemen judged influential enough for inclusion in Table XIV. They were not mere household gentry therefore.

An interesting question is whether the sheriff was able to make money out of his office. The man who held it twice was Sir John Nevill of Chevet (in 1518 and 1527), and in 1528 we find him writing to Wolsey complaining that over the previous year he had incurred serious losses owing to the great dearth. But the fact that in the same letter he went on to beseech the Cardinal to secure his appointment for a second year in order to recoup his losses suggests that it was more normal to make a profit.[2] If there was money to be had from being a sheriff, where did it come from? Partly no doubt from small fees on writs, paid by small men; but was

---

[1] P.R.O.: *Lists and Indexes*, x, 163.
[2] *L.P.*, IV (ii), no. 4838.

there, one wonders, an element of straightforward bribery
in the execution of the office? No Yorkshire sheriff was
charged with such corruption, but both the Savile–Tempest
evidence and the case of Sir Leonard Beckwith which we must
discuss in Chapter VI leave the impression of a society in
which illicit profits were a not uncommon thing.[1] They do not
usually leave records. Another possibility, however, which
would reduce our need to fall back on explanations of that
kind for the apparent lack of justice in Yorkshire, is that
the sheriff was not really the man over whom the ruthless
magnate most needed control. Those who wished to pervert
the course of justice had two other means at their disposal,
which may have been more effective: the coercion of juries
and control of the commission of the peace. It is impossible
to know how strictly the jury principle was interpreted in
Tudor England; but practice did not always correspond to
theory. Jurymen were often small people and in a situation
where natural deference to greater men was reinforced by
fear of their power, such folk would not lightly run the risk
of offending an Earl or an influential knight. We shall see
in Appendix I how in the non-judicial matter of the inquisition *post mortem* juries often did little more than endorse
what had already been agreed between the escheator and the
family of the deceased man. Might juries not have been
equally passive in other kinds of proceeding, at least where
powerful interests were concerned?

The relationship between local magnates and the commission of the peace was a more complicated matter, and it
cannot be discussed without reference to the whole question
of Henry VIII's policy towards the North. The commission
was appointed at Westminster by the Lord Chancellor.
What part if any was played in its selection by patronage and
bargaining by local leaders can only be guessed; but that its
membership reflected royal policy to some extent—and even
the balance of power at Court—can be seen from Table XV,
which analyses the composition of five West Riding
commissions between 1513 and 1545. It can be seen that
between 1513 and 1525 the whole character of the commission changed, and the reason is not far to seek: Thomas

[1] *Infra*, pp. 236–8.

TABLE XV

Analysis of Five West Riding Commissions of the Peace,
1513–45

	1513	1525	1530	1538	1545
Laymen:					
I: *West Riding Men:*					
Nobles:	4	3	5	4	2
Knights:	8	0	8	15	14
Lawyers:	6?	4?	7?	9	9
Others:	11	8	3	14	22
II: *Outsiders:*					
Nobles:	1	4	6	9	9
Knights:	1	5	2	2	2
Lawyers:	0?	6?	4	8	5
Others:	3	0	0	0	1
Clergy:	1	6	3	3	3
Total:	35	36	38	64	67

Note: The category 'West Riding men' is made up mainly of residents; but a few people are included
there because they had substantial estates in the Riding.

The figures do not include the Lord Chancellor, who sat on all the commissions.

Sources: L.P. I (ii), Appendix, p. 1547; IV (i), no. 1610 (11); IV (iii), no. 6803 (12); XIII (i), no. 1519 (39)
and XVI, no. 580 (16).

Wolsey, Cardinal Archbishop of York had risen to power
and become Lord Chancellor in the interval, and had begun
to impose a new policy on the North. Three principal
differences between the list of 1525 and that of twelve years
before may be noticed. First, the number of West Riding
men was reduced from twenty-nine to sixteen, and a group
of influential knights disappeared from the commission
completely. Some of them, like Sir Thomas Fairfax (d. 1521)
were removed by death; but the disappearance of Sir
Richard Tempest and Sir William Gascoigne the elder can
only have been the result of deliberate policy and may have
been a cause for resentment on their part. Second, the
number of outsiders was increased from five to fourteen, and
in some cases we know that the newcomers had specific
connections with Wolsey: the most noticeable example was
Sir William Gascoigne of Cardington (Bedfordshire) who
was treasurer of the Cardinal's household. How active a
part the outsiders played in the work of the commission in

the Riding itself is impossible to judge in the absence of any record of its actual proceedings. Third, by 1525 the number of clerics on the commission had risen from one (the Abbot of Fountains) to six; and since they were mostly ecclesiastical lawyers they were probably among the more active members. It was perhaps no accident that the last ecclesiastical Lord Chancellor should assign an important role to clerics in the administration of justice. Wolsey's policy was one of conflict on two fronts: against the overmighty subjects who opposed his interference with their local influence, and against common lawyers who opposed the introduction of civil (that is, Roman) law. In both conflicts the clerical men trained in civil law were his natural allies; but in the end it was the common lawyers who won the day. The same reliance on clerics is seen in the appointments to the Council in the North (or rather, the Duke of Richmond's Council) created in this same year of 1525. Of the eighteen members of that council, five were church lawyers and three of these held senior offices, including Brian Higden, Dean of York, who was virtually president. There were also seven common lawyers, but only one of them held an office in the Council.[1] Wolsey's fall not surprisingly led to a number of changes in the composition of both the Council and the West Riding commission. Five new members were appointed to the Council in the North in 1530, and the presidency was given to Bishop Tunstall of Durham. Then in 1533, when the Earl of Northumberland became President, another five names were added, this time including that of Darcy. In the meantime seven of the members of 1525 were dropped from the list after 1530, including several known to have had connections with the Cardinal. On the West Riding commission of the peace, the changes are even more marked. In 1530 the knights reappeared, although they were not in all cases the same men who had sat in 1513: Sir Richard Tempest returned at this time, and Sir William Gascoigne of Gawthorpe in 1532. The number of West Riding men altogether rose to twenty-three, whilst that of outsiders fell slightly; and the number of clerics dwindled to three. The next transformation of the commission (which

[1] R. R. Reid: op. cit., 490 ff.

coincided with yet another reform of the Council in the North) followed on the defeat of the Pilgrimage of Grace and was more drastic than ever. None of the earlier changes had involved much alteration in the size of the commission, but in 1538 the number of members was increased from under forty to sixty-four. The King was anxious to revert to a policy of firmer control in the North, but this time he did not do so by choosing clerics. He increased the number of outsiders a little, but apart from Cromwell the newcomers here were mostly men from other parts of Yorkshire, not from the South. The most striking change was the expansion of the list of West Riding men from twenty-three to forty-two, and more especially the inclusion of many more men of the lesser gentry class. This tendency became even more marked by 1545 when about a third of the whole commission was made up of West Riding men who were neither knights nor lawyers. Some of them were men who can have barely attained the minimum property qualification of lands worth £20 a year, fixed for membership of commissions by a statute of 1439. Typical of the new class of justices was Charles Jackson of Snydale, farmer of the former Kirkstall Abbey demesnes in that place and assessed for the subsidies of both 1524 and 1546 on lands worth £20. He was steward of the courts of Monk Bretton Priory on the eve of its suppression, and also steward of Pontefract Priory's manor of Ledston. He was promoted to the commission of the peace in 1538, and served as escheator for a year in 1543–4.[1] Such men were not simpletons and would be quite capable of carrying out the duties of a justice provided they were not interfered with by men of the stamp of a Gascoigne or a Tempest. In the latter part of Henry VIII's reign it was Government policy to draw more and more men of Jackson's sort into local administration, and on the whole it seems to have been a more successful policy than Wolsey's.

One important element in the make-up of every commission of the peace has so far not been mentioned: the common lawyers. They must have borne a large part of the routine burden of work and do not seem to have been

---

[1] P.R.O.: E 179/207/196; *Y.A.J.*, ii (1873), 43–60; *L.P.*, XIII (i), no. 1519 (39); and 'List of Escheators', in typescript at P.R.O.

seriously affected by the political ups and downs, except that their numbers increased and they were probably given a freer hand after 1530 than in Wolsey's day. Some of them were outsiders, either from other Ridings like William Babthorpe and Robert Bowes or from the South like Sir Richard Lister and Sir Anthony Fitzherbert. But an important group of them were residents of the West Riding. One of these, Thomas Grice, sat on every one of the commissions recorded between 1511 and his death in 1546, and despite the fact that he had been closely associated with Darcy was not affected by the changes of 1538. Another was Robert Chaloner, who was retained of counsel by both Darcy and the Earl of Cumberland, and who sat on all the commissions between 1528 and 1545. Grice and Chaloner both lived at Wakefield, as did Thomas Gargrave, and all came of legal families.[1] Already Wakefield was becoming something of an administrative capital in the Riding, a position which it later consolidated and still holds. If Pontefract was the chief focus of lordship in the central parts of the Riding, Wakefield was becoming the focus of royal government: the fact that Pontefract never wholly superseded Wakefield and was later overtaken by it in importance, is almost symbolic of the rise and decline of feudal lordship in the area. It would be wrong, however, to suppose that at this stage Wakefield was formally more than just one of a number of places where the commission met. Another lawyer who sat on a great many West Riding commissions between 1509 and his death in 1544, as well as on the Council in the North from 1525 was Sergeant Thomas Fairfax, a scion of the legal family of Fairfax of Steeton, whose offices included those of recorder at Doncaster and attorney at Lancaster.[2] The fact that common lawyers were often associated with noblemen as their private legal advisers suggests that they were not always so independent of influence as their profession would in theory demand; but

---

[1] Thomas Grice was mentioned in Chapter III, *supra*, p. 89. Robert Chaloner was probably the man of that name who appeared as autumn reader at Gray's Inn in 1521; *Gray's Inn Admissions Register, 1521–1887*, col. 2.

[2] R. Somerville: *The Duchy of Lancaster*, i, pp. 483, 525; he belonged to the Walton branch of the Fairfax family, and his active career stretched from about 1509 to 1540.

neither were they completely dependent on it for their
livelihood, and when conditions favoured it after 1537 they
were probably of great assistance to the King. In themselves
they cannot be said to have wielded great power at this
period.

The transformation of the commission in 1538 was only
one aspect of a local revolution in the distribution of power
in Yorkshire consequent upon the rebellion of the previous
two years. Some local leaders of 1535 lost their 'power and
worship' if not their heads in this revolution. Darcy was
executed, and Tempest died in prison a little later; and the
same year the sixth Earl of Northumberland died in his bed,
leaving the King as his heir. In the central wapentakes of the
Riding the only major figure left for the time being was
Sir Henry Savile, who became steward of Pontefract in
Darcy's room, as well as sheriff of Yorkshire for the year
1537–8. But the King was careful to withhold from him the
stewardship of Wakefield, and in 1543 Sir John Tempest
took the place once occupied by his father in that office.[1]
The other man who gained in power from the events of 1537
was the Earl of Cumberland, who succeeded Darcy as
steward of Knaresborough and whose rival in Nidderdale
(John Norton) was eliminated by the crushing of the revolt.
He took over the Percy fee in Craven, and after acquiring
the main estates of Bolton Priory became the largest private
landlord in the Riding. Both men were added to the Council
in the North, Cumberland in 1537 and Savile in 1542.[2] In
the years after 1537, the position of the Church in the
temporal affairs of the Riding, as of England at large, was
likewise changed. Abbots would never again grace either
the House of Lords or the commission of the peace, and
their households would no longer be foci of patronage. The
Archbishop of York, though not affected by these changes,
also lost some of the basis of his local power before the reign
was out. In 1545 he had to exchange his lordships of Ripon
and Sherburn for a grant of spiritual revenues, and though
the loss was partially reversed in the reign of Mary I, it meant
for the time being that the new Archbishop in that year,
Robert Holgate, had to accustom himself to a situation in

[1] *L.P.*, XVIII (i), no. 981 (11).   [2] R. R. Reid: op. cit., 490 ff.

which his power in the county, and his presidency of the
Council in the North, were dependent on the King and not
on his own local prominence.

The general trend therefore in the period between 1513
and 1545 was towards greater royal control over affairs in
the North. Where Wolsey had failed, Cromwell began to
succeed. But we must be careful of exaggerating the King's
new influence too much. Savile and Cumberland were still
at the helm of West Riding affairs, and though they no
longer had equals with whom to feud (for neither had any
need to quarrel with old Gascoigne) there was not very much
external control over their treatment of less powerful men,
and no compulsion on them to be any more just in their
dealings than before.

V

In concentrating upon the role of leading landowners in
the working of the political and legal institutions of the West
Riding, we have so far ignored one of the aspects of Tudor
local politics about which much has been written in the
past: the relationship between landlords and tenants. Tudor
sovereigns became increasingly aware of this problem as
time went on, and their interest in it was the same as in the
field of conflict between overmighty subjects and lesser
gentlemen; namely to keep the peace and to prevent powerful men from flouting the law to such an extent that the
grievances of the commons became a danger to the realm.
The two fields of conflict were not unrelated, for the real test
in both cases was whether the King's justice was effective in
the counties. But the possible results were quite different.
The overmighty subject was a threat because he might one
day head a coalition to claim the throne; the commons might
become an even more serious threat if, as in 1381, they
challenged the very foundations of lordship and nobility.
The policy of both Wolsey and Cromwell was that, whilst
the commons must be restrained from revolt, landlords
who enclosed land or otherwise interfered with the reasonable rights of their tenants should also be restrained. Under-
lying this approach was the framework of Christian ideals
analysed by Tawney. But already the ideals were being

12

undermined by economic development. When prices were
stable there may have been some possibility that landlords
would accept the role of Christian trustees in an ordered
society; but a combination of inflation and the spread of
expensive new tastes led inevitably to the nobility and gentry
demanding more and more from their tenants in the way
of financial return. The opportunities for lesser men to raise
their status in society led them to follow suit. The consequence for tenants was the disruption of time-honoured
customs, and their resentment was sometimes very strong.

The first occasion on which we can observe conflict
between enclosing landlords and their tenants in the West
Riding is in the enquiry of 1517, whose results were
examined in their economic context in Chapter I.[1] Thirteen
people were 'presented' before the commissioners at York,
for enclosures involving the conversion of West Riding
arable to pasture, or the eviction of tenants, or both. Four of
them were men included in Table XIV, as leading figures
in the Riding in the year 1535: Thomas Lord Darcy, Sir
Stephen Hamerton, Sir John Nevill of Chevet, and the
Abbot of Kirkstall; a fifth, already dead in 1517, was Sir
John Savile, whose son Sir Henry Savile appears in that table;
whilst a sixth was Sir Christopher Danby, a man of some
importance in the North Riding where he spent more of his
time. Notable amongst the others was Henry Pudsey of
Barforth (N.R.), who had an important estate around
Bolton-by-Bolland: he was accused of converting 240 acres
and of evicting 42 people, the most serious charge against a
single person amongst the thirteen. An additional number of
West Riding men were 'presented' for enclosing pasture,
including Henry Lord Clifford (father of the first Earl of
Cumberland), Sir Richard Tempest of Bolling, and the
(fifth) Earl of Northumberland. It is worth noticing that
none of the alleged offenders in 1517 were members of the
enclosure commission for Yorkshire: so far as one can see it
was composed of Wolsey's friends, and out of a membership
of five it had two clerics and one common lawyer. It was a
characteristic instance of Wolsey's use of friends and clerics
to do a job which if left to the local nobility and gentry

[1] *Supra*, p. 18.

would in all likelihood never have been done at all. On the other hand it may well be that as a result the people who suffered most were the Cardinal's enemies. Darcy was certainly amongst these, and at least two of the gentry accused of conversion belonged to families which had at one time been connected with the house of Percy.[1]

Apart from the returns of 1517, most of the evidence concerning agrarian conflict between landlords and tenants comes from court records or from occasional references in letters to village disturbances. Sometimes litigation was started by the lord of one manor or lordship in order to protect his tenants against enclosure by the lord of another manor. One such case was John Norton's plea in Star Chamber against the Earl of Cumberland's enclosure of Speldersden Moor, which we have already seen was part of a wider conflict; another was Sir Richard Tempest's defence of the tenants of Stansfield and Holmfirth against Sir Henry Savile. Cases of dispute over common rights were bound to arise in a county where intercommoning had been widespread for centuries and where the combined pressure of population growth and enclosure were making men ever more anxious to have their rights defined in terms that allowed economic individualism. It was equally natural that wherever the tenants of one township felt that they were being unjustly treated by either the lord or the tenants of another, they should appeal to their own lord to protect them. This kind of situation cannot accurately be described as class conflict.

There were other cases, however, where wronged tenants pitted their strength against their own landlord, or else directly against the neighbouring landlord who was depriving them of their rights. A well-documented example is the case brought by the tenants of the Duchy of Lancaster at Rothwell against the farmer of the park of Rothwell Hay, Lord Darcy.[2] The latter had enclosed a large section of the

---

[1] Sir Stephen Hamerton and Henry Pudsey. Against this must be weighed the presentation of Sir John Savile for converting 60 acres at Thornhill; he was by then deceased, but his grandson Henry Savile appears in 1523 in the service of Wolsey.

[2] *L.P.*, IV (i), no. 1285; VI, no. 355; XII (ii), no. 186; P.R.O.: DL 3/25/D1; DL 5/5/ff. 368, 378, 494–5.

park and thereby excluded the cattle of the Duchy tenants and also those of the tenants of William Legh esquire of Middleton. Legh organized a combined opposition to the enclosure by persuading the tenants to levy a rate on every oxgang amongst themselves, and using the money to appeal to the Duchy Court at Westminster. Their case was upheld by two decrees of that court, in 1529 and again in 1532. But the decrees were either not enough or not enforced, and on a number of occasions, including three in the first half of May 1532, the tenants assembled to pull down the offending enclosure and let in their beasts. In April 1533 Sir William Gascoigne, Sir Richard Tempest and Robert Chaloner, all justices of the peace, were appointed to examine Legh and other disturbers of the peace at Rothwell. The outcome is not recorded, but Darcy was a powerful man and unless he gave way it seems unlikely that the tenants would get satisfaction. A similar case came before the Duchy court in 1532, when the tenants of Barwick-in-Elmet complained that their rights on Winn Moor had been ignored by Sir Thomas Metham, William Ellis and other landowners in Thorner.[1]

The most serious case of conflict between landlord and tenant was in Craven in 1535. In the second week of June of that year a number of anti-enclosure riots took place in different places, which may have been linked by some kind of peasant organization. At Rathmell tenants of the Earl of Northumberland and of the Abbot of Furness pulled down enclosures made by John Catterall; and at other places round Giggleswick tenants of the Earl of Cumberland pulled down the enclosures of the Earl himself as well as those of his legal counsellor John Lambert. Eighty people were arrested for these disturbances and indicted before a court, and were then imprisoned at Wressle, Sandal and Skipton castles. Some of them were still in custody in August or early September when we find the Earl of Cumberland expressing anxiety lest his own tenants fail to gather in the harvest and so be unable to pay their rents.[2] The discontent of the Craven men found an outlet in the Pilgrimage of Grace, as did that

---

[1] P.R.O.: DL 1/7/B13.
[2] *L.P.*, VII, no. 1315; VIII, nos. 946, 969, 991–2; 995; IX, nos. 150, 196.

of the inhabitants of Dent, Sedburgh and Kirkbyshire. One
of the articles drawn up at Pontefract in the autumn of 1536
demanded enforcement of the statute against enclosures,
and another called for limitation of entry fines.¹ The Craven
disturbances, although specifically directed against enclosures, may have been occasioned by both grievances for we
know that the Earl of Cumberland's policy in the matter
of rents and fines was not a lenient one. This case, interestingly enough, did not produce litigation. A likely reason is
that it was a poor man's riot, whereas litigation was usually
initiated by free tenants of some substance. The majority of
the peasantry had no protection beyond the custom of
the manor, and in a region like Craven, so completely
dominated by one high nobleman, they probably had little
opportunity to bring the kind of case that the men of Rothwell began against Lord Darcy. The contrast could be a
significant one: it may well be that in the areas of the Riding
where there was most unrest there is least indication of the
state of feeling in the records of the courts.

Nevertheless, one must always beware of exaggeration;
and in case too much has been said about disorder and lawlessness in the West Riding under Henry VIII it will be
fitting to close this chapter with some observations which
point in a different direction. To begin with, in the matter of
relations between landowners and ordinary farmers it should
not be supposed that on the eve of the Pilgrimage of Grace
practically every village in the county was on the brink of its
own civil war. There were slightly over six hundred townships in the Riding, and over the whole period from 1520
to 1546 there is evidence of agrarian discontent in only
about thirty of them. Nor should the disquieting letter of
Cromwell's correspondent in 1534, quoted above, be allowed
to imply that no justice was to be had for anyone. The
colourful cases which have been quoted relate to only a
handful of instances when rich men quarrelled, either with
one another or with less powerful folk. But when ordinary
yeomen, peasants or trades people were at loggerheads with
one another, there was no reason for 'men of power and

¹ Cf. *infra*, p. 204.

worship' to concern themselves unduly. The cases in Star Chamber which have been discussed in detail will appear in better perspective if they are set beside the records of other courts. More research is needed on all kinds of law court in sixteenth-century England; but there are indications, from the work already done by public archivists, that at least the volume of litigation was increasing in those courts at London where there was most hope of obtaining a quick and equitable settlement. For example in Chancery, between 1500 and 1551 as many as 727 suits were begun involving West Riding people.[1] The average number of suits per year increased from eleven or twelve in the first decade of the century to around twenty-seven during the Chancellorship of Lord Audley (1532–8). There was a small decline after 1538, but that could well reflect the increasing effectiveness of the Council in the North under Holgate's presidency. It is a great misfortune for historians of Tudor Yorkshire that the records of proceedings in that conciliar court have been lost. Other courts where 'poor men' might seek justice were the Court of Requests and—for those who could claim its jurisdiction—the Court of the Duchy of Lancaster. It is in the pleadings and depositions of such tribunals as these that we are likely to find the best evidence of the growing importance of royal justice in Yorkshire, as in other counties, during the period which has been regarded as that of the decline of feudalism.

[1] Counted from the calendar in P.R.O.: *Lists and Indexes*, xxix, xxxviii and xlviii: *Early Chancery Proceedings* iv–vi (London, 1908, 1912, 1922).

V

THE WEST RIDING IN THE PILGRIMAGE
OF GRACE, 1536-7

I

A N unsuccessful revolt is one of the most difficult
subjects for historical study, for it is in the nature of
things that it should leave behind it very little 'inside'
evidence. Not only will the movements of the rebels be
shrouded in secrecy, before and during the revolt, but in the
aftermath of failure, when the Government is collecting
evidence, participants will be anxious to conceal their own
part and lay blame at someone else's door. Thus even the
evidence that exists is likely to be seriously distorted. In the
case of the Pilgrimage of Grace, too much of the source
material consists of letters written to or by the King during
the rising, or of confessions made afterwards under cross-
examination, for the historian to believe everything he sees
on parchment. Too little is known about the secret organization of the Pilgrimage for him ever to feel confident that he
has the full story. Yet in spite of all this a study of the events
of 1536-7 in the West Riding can make a valuable contribution to our understanding of its society. For in time of crisis
a society often reveals aspects of its character which in
more normal times lie hidden from view. Furthermore, the
analysis of the social framework and its political implications, which has been our concern in previous chapters, may
help us to throw light on some of the more puzzling aspects
of the Pilgrimage itself; those who have studied it before
have done so in the absence of detailed knowledge about the
structure of Yorkshire society. In the present chapter, I do
not propose to offer a factual narrative of the revolt, for that
has been well done already with only occasional errors by
the sisters Dodds; and in any case it would lie beyond the
scope of the present book to take in all the regions which

rebelled.[1] But the West Riding included, in whole or part, four of the most important areas of unrest: a study of events in those four areas, seen in the perspective of the economic and institutional pattern already discussed, will provide us with an interesting cross-section of the revolt.

Historians writing on this period of English history have tended to waver between two almost incompatible interpretations of the Pilgrimage of Grace.[2] Both of them can be supported, up to a point, by citing contemporary opinions. The first is that the rising was begun by the commons and that the nobles and gentry were drawn in and swept along against their will; it is hardly surprising that this view was argued by the nobles themselves after the event. A more important piece of evidence in favour of it is the letter which Lord Darcy sent to the King on the 17 October 1536, some days before he himself joined the rebels.[3] All Yorkshire was 'up' by then (except for some areas which as we shall see never joined in at all), and Darcy was trying to explain the rebels' initial success:

all those commons openly favour them that do arise, and many come to them on their own courage so that no man dare trust his tenants; and scarce we may trust our own household servants, and they say plainly they will not fight against them [i.e. the rebels].

Darcy described how the commons would come to a village, swear every man in it including the priests, and charge them to muster at a certain place and time on pain of death. At the muster the rebels would pick out the best men for their army, any who refused to come or to be sworn being threatened with execution if they were caught; Darcy was sure that a

---

[1] M. H. and R. Dodds: *The Pilgrimage of Grace* (2 vols., Cambridge, 1915). A brief summary of the main events of the revolt as it affected the West Riding will be found in Appendix V, *infra*, p. 294. The most recent assessment of the rebellion will be found in A. G. Dickens: 'Secular and Religious Motivation in the Pilgrimage of Grace' in G. J. Cuming (ed.): *Studies in Church History*, iv: *The Province of York* (Leiden, 1967), pp. 39–64.

[2] A. F. Pollard (in *Henry VIII*, London, 1919, p. 354), for example, begs the question of Darcy's involvement with the sentence: 'though there is little doubt that they [Darcy and his friends] were the movers, the ostensible leader was Robert Aske, a lawyer'. J. A. Froude, in *History of England*, vol. ii, *Henry VIII* (London, 1872) set the pattern for this ambivalent interpretation (p. 550).

[3] P.R.O.: SP 1/108/ff. 167–70; *L.P.*, XI, no. 760 (2).

good many joined the revolt only out of fear of death or loss of their goods. The implication throughout the report is that Darcy himself may eventually have no choice but to surrender Pontefract Castle to the rebels. But it is precisely that circumstance which makes the letter suspect: for this is surely just the kind of letter Darcy might have written, in order to cover himself, if he had already made up his mind to surrender. The historians who have accepted this first interpretation have, by implication, been willing to take Darcy at his word; but their case is far from watertight.

The other interpretation would place responsibility for the revolt firmly on the shoulders of Darcy and the other noblemen and gentry involved. It implies that they were able to use their control over local institutions (including the musters procedure in the wapentakes) to create a mobilization of the commons, which they made to appear spontaneous so as to have the excuse of acting under duress if things went wrong. An allegation that this is what happened in the case of the Archbishop of York, Edward Lee, is contained in a letter from Sir William Fairfax to Lord Cromwell in January 1537. He made several charges against the clergy generally, including the observation that the three towns where the rising had started were Louth, Howden and Beverley, of which the first belonged to the Bishop of Lincoln and the two latter to Archbishop Lee; he seems to take it for granted that the commons of these places would follow the inclinations of their lords.[1] As for Darcy himself, the Dodds were of the opinion that when in January 1537 he took pride in his ability to keep his country quiet, he was in fact laying himself open to the charge that he ought to have been able to do so equally well three months before.[2] The choice between these two interpretations is not an easy one to make, and if the present chapter ends by leaning towards the second rather than the first, the conclusion will be no more than a tentative one and the subject will be by no means exhausted.

One factor in the situation has been firmly established by the Dodds: there were several members of the nobility who

[1] P.R.O.: SP 1/115/pp. 2-4: L.P. XII (i), no. 192.
[2] Dodds: op. cit., ii 109.

in 1536 had no love for either the King, his minister, or his
policies. Lord Darcy was amongst them.[1] He had been out
of favour with the King since 1515, when Wolsey compelled
him to surrender his captaincy of Berwick; and his resentment was increased ten years later by the appointment of
the Duke of Richmond's Council, which Wolsey made the
supreme judicial authority in Yorkshire, and to which a
number of outsiders were appointed whilst Darcy was not.
He must have felt the insult especially keenly when the
Duke and his household were in residence at Darcy's own
castle of Pontefract. In 1529, when the Cardinal was at last
losing his grip on power, it was Darcy who led the way in
attacking him by drawing up a list of articles covering such
matters as heavy taxation, the pulling down of monasteries
for Cardinal's College, and the debasing of the currency,
which had reduced the value of England's treasure.[2] When
Wolsey fell, the first results in the North were to Darcy's
advantage, for the Cardinal's men were eliminated from the
Council in the North and from the commissions of the peace
in Yorkshire. But after a year or two it became clear that in
the affairs of the kingdom as a whole it was not the views of
Darcy and his friends that were prevailing but those of
Thomas Cromwell. In 1532 Darcy spoke out openly against
the project for a divorce sanctioned by royal supremacy in
spiritual affairs. By 1534 he was completely alienated from
the King and his plans, and it was at that point that he
entered into communication with Chapuys the Imperial
ambassador in London. Already in September 1533, not
long after the Pope's excommunication of Henry VIII came
into effect, we know that Chapuys was suggesting to Charles
V the idea of intervention to make Reginald Pole King of
England.[3] The chief supporter of such a plan in England
itself was at that stage Bishop Fisher of Rochester; but
before any action had been taken the latter was imprisoned
in the Tower, along with Sir Thomas More, for refusing to

---

[1] His career is described in some detail in the *Dictionary of National Biography*; see
also Dodds, op. cit., i. 18 ff.

[2] *L.P.*, IV (iii), no. 5749.

[3] *L.P.*, VI, no. 1164. The Chapuys letters are calendared in *L.P.*, but the originals
are in the Vienna Archives and could not be used for the present study: their contents were presumably quite unknown to the King or Cromwell.

take the oath of supremacy, in April 1534. Another dissident
bishop, Gardiner of Winchester, went into exile about the
same time. A third, the Bishop of Durham, was suspected of
disloyalty, but the Earls of Westmorland and Cumberland
searched his palace at Auckland in May 1534 without
finding any evidence against him. Then in June and July of
that year came an event which appears to have shaken the
loyalty of several prominent lay noblemen, apart from Darcy.
This was the Earl of Cumberland's action in accusing Lord
Dacre of Gilsland of treason, and the trial which followed.
Dacre was acquitted by his peers, but he was not saved from
being heavily fined and deprived of most of his important
offices.[1] This was the background to Chapuys' report to his
master in September 1534 that a number of English peers,
including Lord Darcy, were seriously disaffected.

According to Chapuys, Darcy intended to return home
that autumn and to animate the people of the North against
the measures proposed for the November session of Parliament. With the Emperor's support he would raise the
crucifix as his banner and lead like-minded people into open
revolt, seizing those who, like the Earl of Northumberland,
were supporters of the King's policy. All the assistance he
asked of the emperor was a small force of arquebusiers,
landed in the North, together with munitions and the
money with which to pay an army: he reckoned on being
able to raise an army of 8,000 men. In the hope of adding to
the confusion, he suggested that the Emperor might induce
the Scots to cross the border, and perhaps also to send a
small force into the Thames estuary in order to keep London
occupied.[2] The King and Cromwell cannot have known the
full extent of Darcy's plan, but they probably suspected
something and prevented him from returning home. About
this time he complained to Cromwell that he had been kept
in the capital ever since the beginning of the Parliament.
The usually accepted view that this meant ever since 1529
is hardly credible; more likely he meant since March 1533,
or since January 1534. Being unable to ride and having no
reliable friends nearer than Pontefract, he was in no position

[1] *L.P.*, VII, no. 962.
[2] *L.P.*, VII, no. 1206.

to make a breakaway without permission. He was not allowed to leave until at least July or August 1535. By the time he was allowed to go, the political situation had changed considerably and there was less chance of his being able to make a successful rebellion. The Statutes of Supremacy, of Treasons, and of First Fruits and Tenths had been passed in December 1534; and a new subsidy had been granted. The royal supremacy had been proclaimed in every corner of the realm by the bishops and parish clergy, and its principal opponents, including Fisher and More, had been executed. Most significantly of all, in January 1535 Charles V had informed Chapuys that no imperial troops could be spared for an adventure in England. As for Darcy himself, his letter from Temple Hirst dated 13 November (probably 1535) suggests some kind of reconciliation with Cromwell, who had obtained the King's permission for the Lord to return home and not to attend any further Parliaments or Feast days in London for the time being.[1] He made no effort now to raise the North, for without allies he was helpless.

Darcy was not the only nobleman mentioned by Chapuys as disaffected. He also noted Lord Dacre, whose ill-feeling towards the King can hardly be doubted, but who was probably reluctant to risk worse misfortune than had already befallen him; and the Earl of Derby, whose presence in this context is intriguing for we have no other indication of his political views save that he subsequently wavered when the Pilgrimage began and then decided to support the King. Another peer who had direct communication with Chapuys in 1534 was Lord Hussey, whose home was at Sleaford in Lincolnshire; but the ambassador tells us nothing of any plans he may have had for open revolt. Three years later Hussey himself confessed to having dined with Darcy and Sir Robert Constable about midsummer 1534, but the limit of their disloyalty on that occasion was, so he said, that they had agreed never to become heretics. Early in 1535 Chapuys apparently received messages from two other peers who said

---

[1] *L.P.*, VII, no. 1426: Gardiner at first thought that this letter belonged to 1534, but later he suggested 1535 as its date, *L.P.*, VIII, p. iii. Darcy was unable to ride, owing to a war injury, but could travel in a carriage.

they were displeased with the King: the Earl of Northumberland (surprisingly) who had personal reasons for
disliking Anne Boleyn, and Lord Sandys of the Vyne, Lord
Chamberlain and Captain of Guisnes, who retired to Hamp-
shire feigning illness early in January 1535.[1] Sandys was an
uncle of the Earl of Westmorland. This last report of
Chapuys must have been made just about the time when the
Emperor was making up his mind to do nothing: in his
view the extent of disaffection against Henry VIII was not
enough.

Mention of the Earl of Northumberland raises the
question of the attitudes of the northern nobility in general
towards the political situation. Darcy was probably the most
outspoken northern opponent of the King, but he was not
the most powerful man in the North country despite his
control of Pontefract. What of the position of the five
northern earls: Northumberland, Westmorland, Cumberland, Derby and Shrewsbury.[2] None of them took the rebel
side openly in 1536, but the first two were much less forth-
right in their opposition to it than were the other three, and
in order to understand their position better we must look at
the activities of their families and clienteles. The sixth Earl of
Northumberland is usually dismissed as a creature of Cromwell, and in 1534 Darcy thought him a firm supporter of
royal policy. Even so, by 1536 it is possible that his relationship with the King was less than happy. Early in 1535 he
was accused of having neglected his duties on the borders
with Scotland, and that was just about the time when
Chapuys reported him disaffected; then in February of that
year he wrote to Cromwell saying that he had decided to
make the King his heir. Who knows what pressure might
have been brought to bear on him in the interval? But if he
was discontented in 1536 it may have been for more personal
reasons: as a young man he fell in love with Anne Boleyn,
and his former feelings might well have been revived by the
trial and execution of the Queen in May 1536, for which no
one but the King himself was to blame. It seems extremely

[1] *L.P.*, VIII, nos. 1, 48.
[2] Except where otherwise stated, information about the careers of these five men
has been taken from the *Dictionary of National Biography*.

unlikely that the Earl was a man upon whom the King could rely at this point to resist a rebellion in the North, even if he was not the man to make one.

When the Pilgrimage began, in late September and early October, the Earl of Northumberland was in fact in London, settling affairs arising from his proposed will, and also trying to get three suppressed northern houses for his favourites. He was still there on the 4 October when news came that one of those houses, Hexham Priory, had resisted suppression; which may well have been his first intimation of revolt. He left London but did not reach Yorkshire until the 17 or 18 October, and by that time any contacts he may have had with the rebels could quite reasonably be attributed to coercion; there is no evidence that he ever took the Pilgrim's oath, or did anything else save grant permission to Robert Aske to use Wressle Castle as the rebel headquarters in Howden-shire. However, it is by no means certain that the sixth Earl enjoyed real leadership of the families which had traditionally been adherents of the house of Percy, or rather of the members of those families who had served the fifth Earl before his death in 1527. Whatever authority he had had over that clientele must have been severely shaken by his decision to negotiate with Cromwell to make the King his heir; for in taking that decision he not only excluded his brothers from the succession, but also virtually abdicated responsibility for those knights and gentlemen who had looked to his father and himself as their patron. A small group of intimates received favours from the sixth Earl, and his gifts to them meant that they were well looked after: notably Sir Reynold Carnaby, Sir Thomas Wharton, Sir Thomas Johnson, and his physician Wendy.[1] The rest were left to share the resentment of the Earl's brothers Sir Thomas and Sir Ingram Percy, and his uncle Sir William. The reactions of Sir William Percy to the situation of 1535–6 are unknown: he was a powerful man in the East Riding, but he does not figure in the documents concerning the Pilgrimage. Sir Thomas and Sir Ingram were much more openly hostile to their brother, or perhaps towards Cromwell and the King who had forced him to capitulate: their entry

[1] Cf. *supra*, p. 141.

into the rebellion needs no further explanation, and the King subsequently had Sir Thomas Percy executed. What is especially interesting is that they were joined in the rebellion by a number of men who had served their father: Robert Aske, the 'captain' of the Pilgrims; William Stapleton, their leader at Beverley; Sir Stephen Hamerton, prominent in Craven who like Aske was later executed for his part in the affair; William Babthorpe; John Norton, whom we met earlier in the service of the Countess of Derby; and Thomas, son or brother of Sir William Middleton.[1] Sir Thomas Johnson was also on the rebel side at one point. Sir Thomas Wharton, although he did not actively join the revolt and eventually proved his loyalty to the King, was clearly not trusted by the Cliffords to defend Carlisle of which he was captain. On the whole, the Percy men who joined in the rebellion played key roles in its development; it is by no means impossible that they were among its first instigators, and certainly they were likely allies in any attempt by Lord Darcy to raise the North.

The Earl of Westmorland held himself aloof from the rebels, but he permitted (or perhaps could not prevent?) his young son Lord Nevill to accompany them on their march south from Durham to Pontefract and Doncaster. In his case there is no reason to suppose any estrangement between the Earl and his family. Perhaps his principal motive was to insure against both the defeat of the rebellion and its success. If so it was a wise move, for when failure came the Earl was able to assure the King of his own loyalty throughout, and was welcomed in London as one of the pillars of the future security of the North. In that way he was able to save from serious harm the various Nevill supporters or clients who had been directly involved in the Pilgrimage: John Lord Latimer, and his brother Marmaduke; Robert and Richard Bowes; and Sir William Mallory of Studley.[2] Latimer was the leading personality in Mashamshire, which was one of

---

[1] P.R.O.: SC 6/Hen VIII/4289. In addition to the fees noted earlier (*supra*, pp. 140-1), William Babthorpe appears in that account as steward and constable of Wressle Castle. On Robert Aske's connection with the fifth Earl, see *Notes and Queries*, 11th ser. iv, p. 441.

[2] For a letter implying some connection between Sir William Mallory and the Earl of Westmorland, see *L.P.*, XII (i) no. 139.

the most prominent areas in the revolt. As for the motives of this Nevill group of rebels, it is less easy to be specific than in the case of Darcy and Percy supporters. There is nothing to suggest that Cromwell had set out to break the Nevill as he tried to break the power of the Percy group. The Earl of Westmorland was, however, related by marriage and blood with the group which the Dodds call the 'White Rose Party' —the surviving remnants of the Yorkist faction. His mother became Lord Darcy's second wife, and Darcy had at one time served the Earl as his steward. His uncle was William Lord Sandys, who had been in contact with Chapuys early in 1535. Alone, the Nevill group would probably not have rebelled; but when Percy and Darcy became involved, the Nevill were their natural allies.

Marriage was not always the basis of political alliance however. The Earl of Cumberland, despite his connection by marriage with the fifth Earl of Northumberland (which explains why Robert Aske's brother Christopher was in his service), seems to have decided that he had nothing to gain by joining in the Pilgrimage, and did in fact gain a great deal by firmly opposing it. It was Cumberland's accusation which had placed Lord Dacre on trial for treason, and the latter's dismissal from his northern offices was followed by Cumberland's appointment as Warden of the Western Marches, making him the most powerful figure in Cumberland. (He was already that in Westmorland, where the Cliffords had long been lords of Appleby and hereditary sheriffs of the county.) Dacre on the contrary had good reason for supporting the revolt, though he did not take an active part in it himself. He probably followed the same cautious policy as the Earl of Westmorland, leaving lesser men dependent on him as patron to play a more open part in it. The rebels included men from Greystoke, where Dacre was Baron, and from Penrith where he was steward; and his brothers-in-law were Lord Conyers and Lord Lumley, both of whom led rebel contingents from the North Riding and from Durham respectively. Lord Lumley's son took part in the second rising of January 1537, and was executed for it. Thus one can see within the alignments of the Pilgrimage enmities and rivalries which had little to do with 'national' issues: Dacre's friends took one side; his enemy Cumberland took the other. And it is significant that when the Clifford castle at Skipton was besieged by rebels in October 1536, probably at the instigation of Percy supporters like Hamerton and John Norton who still had influence in the Percy Fee in Craven, Cumberland never contemplated surrendering to them. There is a noteworthy contrast between his behaviour and that of Lord Darcy in similar circumstances at Pontefract.

The Earl of Derby appears to have hesitated when the rebellion broke out, but he eventually sided with the King.[1] Perhaps it would be more correct to say that he sided with the Duke of Norfolk, who himself is thought to have hesitated before accepting the order to lead an army against the Pilgrims; for Derby had married a daughter of the Duke. Once the Earl of Derby had decided to oppose the rebels, he found it easy enough to raise a force against them. One of the most telling features of the geography of the revolt was the fact that south Lancashire, where Derby was virtual ruler, did not rise; the one area south of the Ribble which did revolt was Blackburnshire, where the steward was Darcy's friend Sir Richard Tempest.[2] If Derby was able to keep his own country quiet, why should not Westmorland or Darcy have been able to do the same? The thesis that the rebellion was a truly spontaneous affair of the commons can only be substantiated if it can be shown that in the regions which rose the commons had strong grievances not shared by the men of Derby's country. The same consideration arises in the case of George Talbot, Earl of Shrewsbury, who also threw in his lot with the King and Cromwell and seems to have had no difficulty keeping south Yorkshire quiet.

From the rebel point of view Shrewsbury's decision was

[1] Although Salley Abbey was reoccupied by the monks on the 12 October, Derby appears to have done nothing about it until he received a letter from the King (dated 20 October), ordering him to go there and suppress the rebellion in those parts. Even then, we find him writing to the King on the 23rd that he intended to proceed to Salley the following Saturday, the 28th; this does not suggest any great urgency, and in fact the Earl allowed Sir Stephen Hamerton and Nicholas Tempest to get to Blackburnshire long before he moved. Moreover, he was still only at Preston on the 30th. For the relevant letters, see *Hist. MSS Comm.*, Fourth Report, p. 445.
[2] R. Somerville: *The Duchy of Lancaster*, i, p. 501. Nicholas Tempest was his deputy in the office.

13

the most fateful of all. With his support they might have
won the day. Without it, they had only a slender chance of
success. Talbot had been an opponent of Wolsey in 1529,
and Darcy may well have hoped that his conservatism would
make him a supporter of the Pilgrimage; his hopes were
probably increased when in June 1536 Talbot heard that he
was to lose his lands in Ireland. But Shrewsbury was not
sufficiently opposed to Henry's policies to contemplate
treason, and on the 5 October he finally set out to suppress
the insurgency in Lincolnshire. If there was still some doubt
in his mind at that point, it was dispelled when he met the
Earls of Rutland and Huntingdon at Nottingham on the
8 October.[1] He carried with him not only southern Yorkshire but also the counties of Staffordshire, Derbyshire and
Nottinghamshire. The significance of his choice for the men
of Yorkshire is strongly suggested by the reaction of the
Archbishop of York, who was at Cawood on the 5 or 6
October when he heard of Talbot's departure against
Lincolnshire. He immediately sent out letters to his servants
at Beverley, York and Ripon, to have the news broadcast
in all three places in order to stay 'light heads' there; he also
sent a messenger to Temple Hirst to inform Lord Darcy.[2]
The implication in Lee's subsequent confession (which is our
source for these actions) is that his loyalty demanded such
behaviour: he must do all he could to prevent trouble. But
it would be equally arguable that his real motive was to
restrain people whom he had previously been encouraging
to rise, because he knew that rebellion without Shrewsbury
would fail.

The Archbishop himself may have had two reasons for
discontent in the late summer of 1536.[3] His liberties at
Ripon, Beverley and York were abolished by a statute that
took effect on the 1 July of that year, and it is noteworthy
that one of the articles drawn up at Pontefract in December
was a demand for their restoration. Secondly, the Archbishop was hoping for the exemption of Hexham Priory

[1] *L.P.*, XI, nos. 536–7, 644.
[2] *L.P.*, XII (i), 1022.
[3] Again biographical information concerning Archbishop Lee and Bishop
Tunstall is to be found in the *Dictionary of National Biography*.

from the suppression statute and at one point believed he had secured it. But the attempt failed and the Prior was in London, continuing his efforts, when at the end of September the canons resisted suppression. The Archbishop later insisted that he had advised the canons to submit, but he cannot have been happy with the situation and they may easily have imagined that he supported them at heart. Lee's actions in the rebellion itself were governed by the caution that is reflected in his response to news about Shrewsbury, already mentioned. But he later had to justify his decision to flee from Cawood in the direction of Pontefract when the rebellion began, instead of to Scarborough where he would have been 'safe'. (Scarborough remained loyal throughout the commotions.) In his sermon before the assembled Pilgrims early in December, the Archbishop spoke out against drawing one's sword against a prince, but that was said at a time when there no longer seemed much chance of easy victory against Henry VIII. He lacked the forcefulness of a Stephen Langton, but given that others were prepared to rebel, his participation was probably not entirely reluctant. Sir William Fairfax, as we saw, was inclined to place some of the blame for the rising at his door. Another ecclesiastical dignitary whose true sympathies may be reflected in the actions of his tenants was Bishop Tunstall of Durham. As soon as the country around Auckland was 'up' the Bishop himself fled to Norham, near the Scottish border. But in January 1537 he refused a summons to court, on the grounds that the journey was too difficult, and it is not impossible that he was playing the same game as his neighbour the Earl of Westmorland: that of 'wait and see'.

II

Thus several leading northerners had reasons for revolt, in particular Lord Darcy and the Percy clientele; certain other northern groups were likely to join in a rebellion, whilst others were almost certain to oppose it. But it is one thing to produce evidence of motives, quite another to show that the rebellion which actually occurred was essentially the noblemen's responsibility. We must look at what actually happened, and at this point our attention must be more narrowly concentrated upon the West Riding. But before we attempt an analysis of the geography of revolt there, we need to take account of two general factors that have bearing on the main question: on the one hand the nature of noble power, on the other the role of the clergy.

An important factor in the deliberations of any potential rebels amongst the nobility must have been the knowledge of their own weakness. Even in alliance they did not have sufficient power to create a sudden and open revolt of the kind which in the previous century had placed a Duke of York or a Henry Tudor on the English throne. To this extent the policies of Henry VII had succeeded: no single overmighty subject had the extensive estates in many different parts of England which had once been enjoyed by the houses of Lancaster and York; and the formal ties of retinue by means of 'extra-ordinary' fees, which once linked important knights to great noble houses had been broken. The disaffected northern noblemen did not between them control even the whole of the North, and in the South they had few close allies. If they were to rebel they must win over other powerful men, such as Derby, Shrewsbury, Rutland, perhaps even the Duke of Norfolk himself. In September 1534, when Chapuys first reported Darcy's plans to the Emperor, there may have been some possibility of overthrowing Cromwell by means of a court conspiracy. Some insight into the nature of court politics under Henry VIII is afforded by Professor Elton's examination of the way in which Cromwell was actually overthrown several years later, when his reforms had become irreversibly established and when the issue of the Church had been settled.[1] In the years 1533–6 the factor of religious principle would have been added to court intrigue and the ambition of Norfolk. But at that time the King and Cromwell were able to defeat opponents of their policies one by one, aided no doubt by the fact that to many leading noblemen opposition at that time must have seemed too much like collaboration with a foreign foe. Since a *coup d'état* in the capital was out of the question the disaffected nobility could only stage a rebellion

[1] G. R. Elton: 'Thomas Cromwell's Decline and Fall', *Cambridge Hist. Journal*, x (1951).

successfully if they could initiate a chain of events in which the country as a whole would eventually be carried along with them. Any attempt to show that the Pilgrimage of Grace was from the outset a rebellion inspired by the nobility must assume that in order to solve this problem the northern lords used their servants or clients to raise the commons, before they revealed their own hand. Such a policy would have carried with it the danger that the commons might seize the opportunity to press their own grievances, which indeed they did, especially in the north-west where noble restraint was at a minimum. But if the bid for power failed, it would be possible to blame the commons for starting the commotion.

If we look at the role of the clergy on the other hand, by which I mean principally the role of the middle and lower clergy, we are likely to find the strongest evidence for the other interpretation; that the rebellion was really spontaneous. Nevertheless, the clergy as a whole were the one group in society most likely to react to a situation by taking sides on ideological grounds, and for the most part the northern clergy were probably conservative. It may be of some importance that in 1534-5, when the danger of lay noblemen opposing the King was at its height, the new policies had barely begun to affect the ordinary clergy. They were probably not greatly worried by the need to accept a theoretical royal supremacy even when it meant swearing an oath to uphold it. To the local priest or member of a monastic community it would become apparent only gradually how the King intended to use his new authority. But by 1536 the ordinary clergy and monks were faced with changes whose immense significance they could understand. The summer session of Parliament that year voided Papal bulls and abolished both benefit of clergy and sanctuary. In July came the Ten Articles; in August the Injunctions issued by Cromwell. In an atmosphere of uncertainty in which wild rumours were circulating about the closure of churches and the confiscation of church plate, the majority of parish clergy may have been weak-willed and willing to compromise, but a minority were bound to react by refusing to change their ways. In the meantime there had taken place the visitation of the monasteries by Layton and Legh, who sometimes interfered in the affairs of individual houses, as at Fountains Abbey where they deposed the abbot and had a new one 'elected' in his place.[1] Then came the statute dissolving the lesser monasteries, and the two counties with the largest numbers of houses valued at under £200 a year were Yorkshire, with thirty-nine (not counting cells), and Lincolnshire with thirty-six; only Norfolk, which had twenty-one, came near to approaching these figures, whilst well-populated counties like Essex and Hertfordshire had only ten or a dozen.[2]

Thus in Yorkshire and in Lincolnshire, where the rebellion first broke out, the parish clergy and the monasteries would have their own reasons for discontent. By September 1536 many monks had been ejected from their houses and had probably begun (in Sir William Fairfax's words) to 'labour and wag the people to put them in and give them aid'.[3] The friars, one of whose orders (the Observants) had been dissolved in 1534, were also likely to be actively opposed to the Government. But it was the parish clergy who were best placed to influence the attitudes of the commons at large, and the spectacle of a parson in his pulpit denouncing the new measures and encouraging resistance is recorded vividly at Louth (Lincolnshire) on Sunday, 1 October 1536.[4] It was doubtless repeated in many places throughout the North during the course of the following weeks. A few parish priests are mentioned by name as supporters of the Pilgrimage, but they may be no more than a small proportion of those actually involved. According to the West Riding lawyer William Maunsell, in a letter to Sir Arthur Darcy by whom he had been engaged to administer the confiscated Salley Abbey estates:[5]

The last insurrection did much come of the report of certain light persons of the Church, and especially of the friars of St. Robert's

[1] *L.P.*, X, nos. 131, 137, 424, 521.
[2] Figures calculated from M. D. Knowles and R. N. Hadcock: *Medieval Religious Houses in England and Wales* (London, 1953).
[3] Letter cited earlier, p. 167 note 1.
[4] Dodd: op. cit., i. 92.
[5] Letter to Sir Arthur Darcy, 11 Nov. 1536; P.R.O.: SP 1/111/p. 74: *L.P.*, XI, no. 1047.

[Knaresborough,] who craftily inscribed and made bills and proclamations in markets that the King should have 6*s.* 8*d.* of every plough, 6*s.* 8*d.* of every child that should receive baptism, and 4*d.* of every beast; which bills was set on Church doors in many parts of the shire. The people was most especially stirred; albeit now by their superiors other oaths are made wherein the people wholly are prefixed and determined, and most especially against the King's most honourable Council.

But Maunsell's brother was himself a priest: Thomas Maunsell, vicar of Brayton (near Selby), who was very active in raising the commons of Barkston wapentake; and he subsequently claimed that he had been acting under the orders of Lord Darcy.[1] That clergy were important in getting the rebellion under way can hardly be doubted; but were they acting on their own account, perhaps within the framework of some secret organization? Or were they the agents of the nobility, who if they wanted to start a rebellion could probably use parish priests just as well as their own household servants? In the end it may prove impossible to choose between these two views of the role of the clergy, and perhaps the safest conclusion will be to acknowledge some truth in both of them.

But now let us look at the actual development of the rebellion in different areas of the West Riding. The first area to rise in strength was Marshland, where events were closely linked to what happened in Howdenshire just across the river in the East Riding. The chief captain of the Pilgrims there was Robert Aske, a former servant of the fifth Earl of Northumberland, who emerged as leader very quickly and issued his first proclamation as captain of Marshland, the Isle of Axeholme and Howdenshire on the 10 October. He summoned the people of all three areas to a muster on Skipwith Moor the following day.[2] Two other names which appeared in the same proclamation were those of William Babthorpe of Osgodby, keeper of the nearby Percy castle at Wressle, which was to become Aske's headquarters; and Thomas Metham, whose father Sir Thomas had received a letter written by Lord Darcy on the 6 October

[1] Cf. *infra*, pp. 183-4.
[2] *L.P.*, XI, no. 622.

warning him against 'hasty follies'.[1] The date of that letter coincides with those written by the Archbishop of York to Ripon and Beverley, already mentioned, and may like them have been inspired by the fear that once Shrewsbury had decided to oppose the rebellion it would be best to abandon any plans. But the warning was not heeded by all the gentlemen of Howdenshire and Marshland, and their failure to do so may be the key fact which explains why there was a rebellion at all in Yorkshire. The importance of this area in any noble plans for revolt may be gauged from the following facts: the Earl of Northumberland owned Wressle and its lordship; Thomas Lord Darcy was steward of the Duchy of Lancaster lordship of Snaith, where his deputy was one Lionel Percy; and a close friend of Darcy, Sir Robert Constable, was steward of Howdenshire and Marshland. Darcy moreover had a house of his own not far away, at Temple Hirst; and Constable had a house at Holme-in-Spalding Moor (East Riding). There is no evidence beyond Fairfax's assertion to suggest that the Bishop of Durham, as lord of Howden, or the Abbot of York who was lord of Marshland, had any direct hand in raising the tenants there; nor were any local clergy mentioned as instigators of rebellion there. Nothing is known of the actions in the crisis of the canons of Drax, recently expelled from their monastery, or of the commandery of St. John at Newland, not far away. All the evidence we have, however, seems to indicate that if the nobility and higher clergy, and their clienteles, were intending to make a rebellion, Marshland and Howdenshire would be an ideal place for it to start, from their point of view. It was too the bridgehead between northern Lincolnshire, which had already risen at the beginning of October, and the central area of Yorkshire.

Robert Aske's movements during the first week of October seem to indicate a close connection between the risings in Lincolnshire, at Beverley, and in Marshland–Howdenshire. At Beverley the chief captain was another Percy servant, and a West Riding man: William Stapleton, feodary of the Earl of Northumberland's lands in Yorkshire and younger brother of Christopher Stapleton of Wighill

[1] *L.P.*, XI, no. 566; cf. Dodds, op. cit., i. 148.

(in the Ainsty). He and his brother and nephew had spent the summer at the Greyfriars in Beverley and were still there on the 9 October when William was called upon (if that is the correct phrase) to lead the commons.[1] A close friend of the Stapletons in Beverley was a former Observant friar called Thomas Johnson, but his role in what followed is not known. On the 13 October the commons of Beverley joined with those of Howdenshire and Marshland in a muster at Weighton Hill; following that, Stapleton led one group to take the city of Hull, whilst Robert Aske led the others to York, which was in their hands by the 16 October.

During the three days between the Weighton muster and Aske's entry into York, the revolt spread to the wapentake of Barkston. Already on the 13th the Archbishop of York wrote that his tenants around Cawood, Wistow and Selby were 'up', and that he had moved to Pontefract to avoid them.[2] The fate (or role) of Abbot Rogers of Selby at this time is shrouded in silence: he was never accused of complicity in the rebellion, nor is there any report of action by the rebels against him or his house. The man who seems to have taken the lead in mobilising Barkston was the priest Thomas Maunsell of Brayton, who held a vicarage there of which Selby Abbey had the rectory. Subsequently he was excluded from the general pardon granted by the King in December, which means that he must have been regarded as a ringleader; but he was included in a later pardon and remained vicar of Brayton till his death in 1555, having in the meantime also survived implication in the Wakefield plot of 1541.[3] (Possibly he was saved by his brother's connection with Sir Arthur Darcy; and it is equally possible that Thomas Maunsell saved William from being sworn as a Pilgrim when the latter was caught by the rebels at York.) On his own subsequent confession the Reverend Maunsell was guilty of treasonous activities throughout the period between the first rising in Howdenshire and the eventual surrender of Pontefract by Lord Darcy on the 21 October.

[1] *L.P.*, XII (i), no. 392.
[2] *L.P.*, XI, no. 689.
[3] His activities are described in some detail in his own subsequent confession, *L.P.*, XI, no. 1402.

On the 11th he attended the muster at Skipwith Moor, where he was apparently suspected by some of the commons of being a spy for the sheriff, who at this time was Sir George Darcy; and indeed the same day he did return to Sir George's house at Gateforth. But later that day he was, he said, at Pontefract where he took orders from Lord Darcy. On the 14–15 October he raised the country around Brayton and further north, then on the latter of those days went to Bilborough where some of the Ainsty musters were traditionally held. On the 17–18 October he was in the vicinity of Wakefield and Pontefract, also raising the commons (allegedly on Lord Darcy's instructions). If we can believe his testimony, he must have been an important link in the chain of rebellion in these crucial days before Lord Darcy risked open defiance of the King. But he too had a skin to save, and just as Darcy had reasons for blaming the commons, so Maunsell had his own reasons for blaming Darcy: the web of conspiracy, if such it was, is inextricably entangled with the web of mutual recrimination.

Meanwhile events were moving in the North Riding and Durham, and what happened in the north-east corner of the West Riding must be seen in relation to movements further north. On the 5 or 6 October we have seen that the Archbishop wrote to his servant Ellis Markham at Ripon, to publish at Ripon Fair the news of Shrewsbury's setting out against the Lincolnshire rebels. He also warned Lord Latimer, his steward at Ripon, to stay the tenants of the Archbishopric. Unfortunately we know nothing about who the 'light heads' at Ripon were, and no confessions of men from that area have survived to give us any insight into what was going on there. But we do know that Lord Latimer, a scion of the house of Nevill, very soon joined the rebels when trouble broke out. So did the two other most prominent figures of the district: John Norton of Norton Conyers, who had at one time been in Percy's service and was steward of Kirkby Malzeard; and Sir William Mallory of Studley who, to judge from a letter he wrote in January 1537, had some kind of connection with the Earl of Westmorland.[1]

---

[1] *L.P.*, XII (i), no. 139 (letter from Mallory to the Duke of Norfolk); *L.P.* XI, no. 729.

Once again we have no means of knowing whether these gentlemen took any secret initiative in the revolt; but certainly Lord Latimer did not succeed if he made any attempt to 'stay' the commons. The commons in Kirkbyshire Nidderdale and Mashamshire (North Riding) first rose on the 11–12 October, of which the latter was St. Wilfrid's Day and doubtless an auspicious one for action in the North.[1] Groups of them gathered at Middleham Castle (N.R.) and near the abbeys of Coverham and Jervaulx (N.R.). The Abbot of Jervaulx was later hanged, despite his plea that he fled the commons at this stage, and the feeling of his monks on the issues of the day may be gathered from the fact that in 1535 one of them had been hanged for speaking out against the royal supremacy. Their resentment was no doubt fanned by the former Abbot of Fountains, William Thirsk, who was living at Jervaulx when the trouble began; he had been expelled by Layton and Legh, and was subsequently executed for his active part in the revolt.[2] Sir William Mallory was amongst those who had tried to defend Thirsk against his enemies when his abbacy was called in question. Of the commons around Ripon we know little save the name of one of their captains, Ninian Staveley, who was probably the son of the Miles Staveley of Ripon Park taxed on goods worth £80 in 1524; Miles was receiver of the Ripon lordship (or liberty) in 1532. Ninian himself, who survived the collapse of the Pilgrimage by turning King's evidence against the Abbot of Jervaulx, was assessed for the subsidy of 1546 on lands worth £12 a year.[3] He may be counted therefore as a prosperous yeoman, not entitled to bear arms but economically on the fringes of the minor gentry.

On the 13 October the rising spread to the country of Richmondshire, and on the 15th Barnard Castle was 'taken'. On the day that Aske rode into York (16 October) another rebel host was assembling north of the Tees, at Oxney field, where the leaders were Robert Bowes, Lord Latimer, and Sir Christopher Danby of Masham (N.R.) and of Farnley

[1] L.P., XI, no. 677; XII (i), no. 1035.
[2] L.P., X, nos. 131, 137.
[3] Interrogation of Staveley, 23 April 1537, L.P., XII (i), nos. 1012, 1035; P.R.O.: E 179/207/191; SC 6/Hen VIII/4409.

(W.R.).[1] They marched on Bishop Auckland, from which Bishop Tunstall promptly fled, and were joined by Lord Nevill (Westmorland's son) and Lord Lumley. This was the focal point of the Nevill contingent to the Pilgrimage. By the 19 October a large force from Durham, the North Riding and the northern part of the West Riding, was ready to march southwards to York, to join Darcy and Aske. A section of it, however, broke away at this point and led by John Norton went across Nidderdale and Wharfedale to help those who were besieging Skipton Castle; Norton's long-standing hostility to the Earl of Cumberland is enough to explain his role in this decision.

During the third week in October the rebels of the two areas we have considered so far consolidated their position and converged upon York and Pontefract. Another group, led by Sir Thomas Percy and Sir Nicholas Fairfax, approached York from the direction of Malton; again, it was claimed by those gentlemen that they had been compelled into this action by the commons.[2] In the city of York itself, there was one party which opposed the rebels completely: they included the mayor, Sir George Lawson, William Maunsell and Leonard Beckwith (a lawyer of whom we shall hear more in due course). This group wrote to the King on the 14 October asking for help, and after the rebel entry into the city they refused to play any part in the Pilgrimage. Leonard Beckwith, the Yorkshire receiver of the new Court of Augmentations, suffered damage to his house and property at rebel hands before the commotion was over.[3] But there were enough supporters of Aske in the city to make his entry there an easy matter. In the Ainsty too he found ready support. Sir Nicholas Fairfax had lands there, but he had made Gilling (in the North Riding) his principal residence, and it is not easy to measure his influence further south. His cousin Sir William Fairfax was a very reluctant participant in the revolt, and for once perhaps we may believe the claims of a gentleman to have been

[1] L.P., XI, no. 760.
[2] Dodds: op cit., i. 230–2.
[3] L.P., XI, no. 704; XII (i), nos. 176, 536; cf. Star Chamber case, printed in Y.A.S.R.S., xlv. 124–33.

'taken' by the commons: on the 21 October he tried to get
away to the South, perhaps to join the Shrewsbury forces,
but was arrested two miles south of Wakefield and prevented
from going further.[1] The gentleman who did most to help
the rebels in the Ainsty was Sir Oswald Wilstrop of Wilstrop: he was a man in debt, and may have had the same kind
of personal reasons as Sir Francis Bigod for joining the
revolt, though the fact that he had sought preferment to one
of the suppressed monasteries suggests that he lacked
Bigod's idealism.[2] He was quick to change sides after the
truce of Doncaster, in December, when the rebel cause
seemed less promising. But his initial commitment was one
of some vigour, for it was he who held the Ainsty musters
at Bilborough and Acomb soon after the 17 October.[3] He
was probably in contact with Thomas Maunsell just before
this, and he may have had the help of other clergymen. Of
the two religious houses in the Ainsty that had been suppressed—Synningthwaite and Healaugh—the latter was
restored during the rebellion; and its last Prior, obviously
not very sympathetic to the reoccupation, later began a
Chancery suit concerning goods alleged to have been
damaged in the process. He had himself returned to the
house for only three weeks, but other canons had remained
there for twenty, which must have been from October 1536
until February 1537.[4]

Another man who was with Wilstrop at York when Aske
arrived is referred to as 'one Plumpton'.[5] This may have
been William Plumpton, or possibly his son Robert who like
Aske was a student at the London Inns of Court. The
Plumptons held their principal possessions of the Percy
barony of Spofforth, and in the fifteenth century (when the
family was much more powerful) had been feed adherents
of the Earls of Northumberland. Conceivably the Plumpton
who was at York at this time led a contingent of rebels from

[1] L.P., XII (i), no. 192.
[2] L.P., XI, nos. 449, 519; for his debts, cf. infra, p. 219. Sir Francis Bigod's
part in the Pilgrimage is discussed by A. G. Dickens, Lollards and Protestants in
the Diocese of York (Oxford, 1959).
[3] Dodds: op. cit., i. 231; cf. L.P., XI, no. 1138.
[4] P.R.O.: C 1/881/31.
[5] L.P., XII (i), no. 901 (p. 404).

Plumpton and Spofforth. Another gentleman from that area was present at the rebel council at Pontefract in December: a Mr. Middleton, who may have been Thomas Middleton, bailiff of Spofforth and brother or son of Sir William Middleton who had ridden with the fifth Earl of Northumberland at Flodden in 1513.[1] If anyone was in a position to bring out the tenants of Spofforth barony it was Plumpton and Middleton. The fact that there is no mention at all of this area, either of commons rising or gentlemen being taken, need not mean that it was completely quiet in the revolt. Nor is there any mention, in the documents concerning the Pilgrimage, of events in the area between Spofforth and Ripon: the Forest and Soke of Knaresborough. And that despite the fact that Lord Darcy was its steward. His deputy was probably Thomas Slingsby, who was not mentioned by Aske as having attended either the York or the Pontefract councils of rebels, although that may have been simply because Aske did not know his face. William Maunsell alleged that the friars of St. Robert's were active participants in the revolt, and that they prepared bills to stick on church doors. But the only evidence to corroborate this is the statement that one of the friars, Robert Eshe (Ashton) was sent by William Stapleton from Beverley to raise the commons in Ryedale (north of Malton) in mid-October.[2] Perhaps the part which the friars played was mostly in other areas of the county than their own, If nothing else, this silence about what was happening at Knaresborough is some measure of its political unimportance at this period.

Lord Darcy went to Pontefract on the 7 or 8 October, before there was any open sign of trouble north of Lincolnshire. On the 11th he must have been aware of the plans of rebels in Marshland and Howdenshire to take York, but the 'central wapentakes' area dominated by Pontefract was still quiet. The King as yet knew only of the Lincolnshire rising, and the royal instructions which Lord Darcy received on the 13 October, by the hand of his younger son Sir Arthur, were simply to arrest anyone guilty of spreading false rumours and to ensure that the Lincolnshire unrest did

---

[1] Cf. *supra*, p. 133.
[2] *L.P.*, XII (i), no. 392.

not spread into Yorkshire. On the same day (the 13th) Lord Darcy wrote to the King telling him that part of Yorkshire was already 'up' and complaining that Pontefract Castle was ill-supplied for a long siege. He made the same point about shortage of supplies in a letter to the Earls of Shrewsbury, Rutland and Huntingdon, dated the 16 October. And the next day he wrote the letter to the King quoted earlier in this chapter, describing how the commons had forced their masters into open revolt. On the 19 October Lord Darcy received Aske in audience at Pontefract, and on the 21st he surrendered the Castle.[1] Some time between the 11th and the 21st, the 'central wapentakes' had joined the revolt, but it is once again not easy to tell whether they rose spontaneously or at the behest of Darcy and the leading gentry.

It would appear that the townships dependent on Wakefield rose before those of the Honour of Pontefract. As early as the 8 October, the rebel council in the chapter house of Lincoln Cathedral heard from a messenger that the men of Halifax were 'up' and were ready to aid their fellows of Lincolnshire.[2] It was said later that the Halifax district had risen long before other parts of Wakefield lordship, under the leadership of John Lacy, son-in-law of Sir Richard Tempest and bailiff of Halifax. Lacy had been foremost amongst the parishioners there in campaigning against the vicar, Dr. Robert Haldsworth, a friend of Sir Henry Savile whom we have seen was Sir Richard Tempest's enemy. The vicar fled the revolt and went to London, leaving his vicarage to be occupied by the rebels, and a pot of gold to be discovered hidden under his stair.[3] At Wakefield itself, Darcy's friend and lawyer Thomas Grice reported on the 12 October that the people were in rebellious mood, and that the King's commissioners, probably those appointed to assess the subsidy, did not dare sit in the town.[4] It was rumoured too, at that time, that bowstaves were being sent across into Lancashire where the Earl of Derby's men were

[1] *L.P.*, XII (i), no. 6.
[2] *L.P.*, XI, no. 971 (p. 396).
[3] Haldsworth's career is dealt with by J. Lister: 'A Life of Dr. Robert Holdsworth', *Transactions of the Halifax Antiquarian Soc.*, i–iv (1902–7). Cf. *supra*, p. 94.
[4] *L.P.*, XI, no. 678.

believed to sympathize with the revolt. But Grice had no
formal authority at Wakefield, even though he later became
captain of the commons there; the steward was Sir Richard
Tempest. On the 14 October, Thomas Tempest (Sir
Richard's son) called the men of Wakefield together in the
moot hall to learn their attitude towards the rebels; it is not
stated whether this meant the town or the lordship of
Wakefield. He subsequently reported to his father that the
Wakefield men would go either with the Commons (i.e.
the rebels) or with the steward, depending who arrived first.[1]
Whereupon the following day Sir Richard Tempest rode
over to Wakefield from his house at Bolling-by-Bradford,
and took control. The same day Thomas Grice heard the
news of the collapse of the Lincolnshire rising, which he
duly reported to Lord Darcy; at the end of the same letter
he observed that one Lawrence Baynes, a known member of
Darcy's household, had been intending to come to Pontefract, 'but now I trust it shall not need'.[2] Was there some
plan, involving Baynes, which would now be abandoned
because of the disaster in Lincolnshire? One cannot tell;
but if Grice expected the affair to be over now, he was
mistaken. On the 18 October Thomas Maunsell was at
Wakefield and raised the town, and Sir Richard Tempest
decided, if he had not always intended, to follow the
Pilgrimage.[3]

In the Honour of Pontefract, we must consider Darcy's
own position very carefully, both in relation to the commons
and in relation to the gentry who held their important
manors from that Honour. If Darcy had direct contacts
with the commons during the ten days before his own
surrender of Pontefract Castle, it was probably through men
like Thomas Maunsell, and perhaps his household servants.
One of the latter was Thomas Strangeways, who went to
York on the night of the 16 or 17 October to meet Robert
Aske; he came back with copies of the rebel oath and the
Pilgrims' demands.[4] It was between then and the 21 October

[1] L.P., XI, no. 702.
[2] P.R.O.: SP 1/108/f. 124: L.P., XI, no. 734.
[3] L.P., XI, no. 1402.
[4] L.P., XI, no. 762.

that the commons of the Honour joined the revolt, but we cannot tell whether Strangeways played any part in the event. What we do know is that on the 17th Thomas Maunsell 'raised' the town of Pontefract, and according to Archbishop Lee prevented any more provisions being sent in to the Castle. The next day Maunsell went on to Wakefield, calling en route at the Priory of St. Oswald at Nostell. From there he went to Doncaster, where he swore in a number of townsmen, and also gave permission to the Earl of Northumberland to pass through on his way to Topcliffe.[1] All this information is derived from his later confession. Unfortunately whoever 'raised' the more northerly parts of the Honour of Pontefract has left no such useful evidence behind, and once more we find an area (that round Leeds and Barwick) where any rebel activity there was has gone unrecorded. In view of the fact that Darcy had a house at Temple Newson and that one of his servants there was the Lawrence Baynes mentioned by Grice, it seems very likely that the commons of that region participated in much the same way as the commons a little further south. One thing about the role of the commons in the central wapentakes, however, stands out and is worthy of comment: none of the evidence we have gives any hint that the clothiers were discontented for economic reasons, and there is nothing to suggest any link between their actions in 1536 and the 'flocking' dispute of three years before. This area was not the most important in the revolt by any means, but insofar as it participated at all it was under the leadership of the gentry and of Darcy himself.

When it comes to Lord Darcy's relations with the gentry of the area, we must examine an interesting document which bears the date 1 October and which appears to have been circulated by Darcy amongst the leading gentlemen of the Honour.[2] Its heading states that it is a list of those who have promised to serve the King, under Lord Darcy or his deputy, at an hour's warning. Save for two later additions, the names

[1] *L.P.*, XI, no. 1402.
[2] P.R.O.: SP 1/106/pp. 234 ff.: L.P., XI, no. 522. Possibly this is the document from Darcy referred to by Sir Henry Savile in a letter to Cromwell, 29 Jan. 1537: P.R.O.: SP 1/115/pp. 130-1: *L.P.* XII (i), no. 281.

are all in the same hand, but next to some of them appear comments in a variety of hands, to the effect that this or that person has promised to come himself, or to send his son, or to send so many men to Darcy if the need arise. Some of those listed made no reply, notably Sir Henry Savile; but forty-four promised aid of some kind, the largest contingent promised being that of Sir William Gascoigne of Gawthorpe who offered a hundred men. Altogether the document shows that a force of about thirty gentry and 240 followers would be forthcoming if Darcy called; in addition of course the steward would have his own household servants and perhaps some of his tenants to draw upon. Darcy's control over the gentry of the Honour is suggested too by a letter of Sir Brian Hastings written on the 3 November, reporting that the steward had charged all the Honour of Pontefract and Soke of Snaith to be ready on an hour's warning and that he had collected money to pay 20s. to every soldier.[1] But that was after the surrender of Pontefract, when the situation had become more clear-cut. The remarkable feature of the document of 1 October is its date. Its form suggests that it may have been sent round the various gentry houses of the Honour, in which case it may have taken several days to complete the information contained in it. But even so, it would all have been written down some days before the beginning of the rising in Marshland and Howdenshire, or even that at Beverley. Darcy was still at Temple Hirst, and on the 1 October itself he can hardly have known about even the Lincolnshire rising or the resistance of the canons of Hexham. It is at least as likely that he made these enquiries about the readiness of the Honour for his own purposes, as that he felt the need to meet some external threat.

The response of the gentry to this appeal for aid is perhaps a measure of their various attitudes towards Lord Darcy; another indication of who were his most willing supporters is the list of those present at Darcy's meeting with Robert Aske in Pontefract Castle on the 19 October.[2] They

---

[1] *L.P.*, XI, no. 966.

[2] *L.P.*, XII (i), nos. 6, 1022; a full list of those present will be found in Dodds, op. cit., i. 345.

were: Sir Robert Nevill of Liversedge, Sir Henry Everingham of Birkin, Sir John Wentworth of Elmsall, and Henry
Ryther of Ryther. Perhaps one should add the name of Sir
William Gascoigne of Gawthorpe, since he offered a hundred
men, but he was not present at Pontefract either on the
19 October or for the great council early in December; his
former quarrel with the Nevill family over the Earldom of
Westmorland may explain his reluctance to become too
openly involved with a cause in which some of the Nevill
clients were very active.[1] He was too no longer a young man
and may have peferred not to travel. Others who were at
Darcy's meeting with Aske, though not of the Honour of
Pontefract, included Sir John Dawney of Cowick, Sir
Robert Ughtred of Bilton Ainsty, William Babthorpe of
Osgodby, and Darcy's closest friend and adviser Sir Robert
Constable. One man who was significantly absent was Sir
Henry Savile, who later asserted that Darcy had not sent out
requests for attendance at Pontefract until it was too late for
many of those invited to reach the Castle before the decision
had been taken to surrender; consequently when they
arrived they had no choice but to take the Pilgrim's oath.[2]
Darcy might indeed have tricked the less reliable dependents
of the Honour in this way, though it was also a good alibi
for those gentry who later wanted to change sides. Savile
himself needed no alibi. At some point in the proceedings,
while he could still do so, Sir Henry fled to Rotherham: a
natural enough place for him to go, since his cousin the
Earl of Shrewsbury was steward there; that is, if one can
accept the assumption that the commons were not likely to
join the revolt if their masters did not actively encourage
them. Towards the end of October, after the first truce at
Doncaster between the rebels and Norfolk, Savile returned
to the Wakefield area. On the 12 November Sir Robert
Nevill reported an incident in which Sir Henry had forced
the constable of Dewsbury to restore money contributed by
Savile tenants towards rebel funds. Nevill offered to prevent
Savile from leaving home again, but Darcy took no action
and, a week later, we find Thomas Grice taking action to

[1] Cf. *supra*, p. 173.
[2] P.R.O.: SP 1/115/pp. 130-1: *L.P.*: XII (i) no. 281.

prevent some of Sir Henry's servants and tenants from going to Rotherham, where their master had fled once more.[1] In view of what we know of the Savile–Tempest feud, all this is hardly surprising; Savile's relationship to Shrewsbury makes it even more understandable.

Amongst the West Riding gentry who viewed the Pilgrimage with some coolness must also be counted Lord Darcy's own sons. Sir George Darcy was sheriff of Yorkshire until November (when his place was taken, at the usual time, by Sir Brian Hastings), which meant that if Aske and the other rebels were to be arrested for high treason it would be his duty to make the arrest. His father sent him to make the arrest, on 10 October, but he did not find the rebel captain. He seems to have spent most of the period of the rebellion at his house at Gateforth, with occasional visits to Pontefract, until he decided shortly after Christmas to ride up to London.[2] Sir Arthur Darcy, who had for many years been a royal servant, was more open about his opposition to the revolt. He went backwards and forwards between his father and the King several times between the 6 and the 21 October, and on one occasion he met Shrewsbury en route and assured him of his loyalty to the King. Sir Arthur became effectively steward of the Honour of Tickhill after the death of Sir Henry Wyatt in November 1536. He visited Tickhill at least once during the course of the rebellion, to put his men in readiness, but he did not see it as his duty to sit tight there as his father chose to do at Pontefract. Apart from these few facts we know little of either his movements or his opinions during the first two months of the revolt.[3] But we know that by the following February he had emerged as a staunch supporter of Norfolk's mission to pacify the North, and he gained considerably in the King's and Cromwell's favour as a result. Perhaps his attitude was that of a great many Yorkshire gentlemen whose only real interest in the revolt was backing the winning side.

Two other men who might have been expected to play

---

[1] *L.P.*, XI, nos. 846, 997, 1051, 1113.

[2] *L.P.*, XI, nos. 1086, 1368; Dodds, op. cit., 168.

[3] *L.P.*, XI, no. 1026. Sir Arthur Darcy's career will be discussed in Chapter VI, *infra*, pp. 245.

a part in the events of the Pilgrimage were Sir Thomas Wentworth of West Bretton and Sir John Nevill of Chevet. Wentworth was probably in London throughout the rebellion, whilst Sir John Nevill stated in a letter of 9 November that he had been with the Lord Steward (that is, the Earl of Shrewsbury) since the first beginnings of the trouble in Lincolnshire.[1] Both were men who, had they been present in Yorkshire at that time, might well have been drawn into the Pontefract group; in the event they were probably glad not to have to make the decision whether to do so or to flee southwards.

The clergy of the 'central wapentakes' were less prominent in the Pilgrimage than their fellows of other areas. They were not, however, wholly inactive. The Prior of Pontefract, James Thwaites, took part in the December council at Pontefract; and on the 18 October his tenants of the lordship of Barnsley were probably among the commons mustered at that place, though that in itself does not prove any complicity on his part.[2] Abbot John Ripley of Kirkstall was also present at the Pontefract council in December, and as one of the more learned of the northern clergy helped to produce a set of ecclesiastical articles. Apart from that he is mentioned in the records of the rebellion only once: in January 1537, when some of his servants were involved in an affray with those of Sir Christopher Danby. In his letter reporting that incident to Cromwell, Sir Henry Savile commented on the 'lightness that is in the man' (that is, the Abbot), and recommended that he be deposed and Kirkstall Abbey confiscated.[3] But the advice was not followed, and Kirkstall survived until 1539. Further north than Kirkstall, in the Archbishop of York's lordship of Otley, there is one piece of evidence that the commons actively participated in the revolt: as late as January 1537 the Archbishop's servant there Lawrence Keighley still had the tenants under arms and was advising them not to surrender.[4]

We have now looked at all the rebel areas of the West

[1] *L.P.*, XII (i), no. 899; XI, no. 1025.
[2] *L.P.*, XI, no. 759.
[3] *L.P.*, XII (i), no. 281.
[4] *L.P.*, XII (i), no. 192.

Riding whose activities were focused on York and Pontefract, where the largest rebel host assembled before advancing
to meet the Duke of Norfolk at Doncaster on the 26 October.
Events at the centre of the Pilgrimage during the following
three or four months are too well known to need more than a
brief summary here. A truce was agreed at this first en-
counter between Norfolk and the rebels, but it amounted to
no more than the purchase of a breathing-space by both
sides. The climax of the Pilgrimage came early in December
when its leaders met in council at York to draw up articles,
and then formally presented their demands to Norfolk at
Doncaster. The latter made a number of promises on behalf
of the King, and announced that the rebels would be
pardoned for all acts committed between the 10 October
and the 10 December. But then in mid-January 1537 the
attempt to make a new rising by the followers of Sir Francis
Bigod in the East and North Ridings gave the King an
excuse to break both his promises and his pardon. He sent
Norfolk to the North once again, not this time as negotiator
but as pacifier: the Duke was at Pontefract on the 4 February,
at York the day following, and by the 19 February he had
reached Carlisle. That was the end of the rebellion. Lord
Darcy, who had refused a summons to London in January,
finally went up to the capital in early April 1537, only to face
trial and execution. He and the other principal leaders of the
Pilgrimage (or such they were at least in the eyes of the
King) were arrested, tried and executed in the period
between April and June.[1]

In the last stages of the revolt, that is in January and
February 1537, there was a noticeable contrast between the
behaviour of the more southerly rebel areas of the West
Riding and the country to the north and west of Ripon. The
commons of Mashamshire, Kirkbyshire, etc. were less
content than their fellows further south to go back home and
settle down after the December agreement at Doncaster.
Unrest in January was followed by new musters early in
February, when news of the advance of Norfolk to Pontefract reached the northern area. One of the leaders in this
new insurrection (which needless to say did not last long) was

[1] Dodds, op. cit., ii, Chapter xx.

Ninian Staveley, who later explained that it was occasioned by fear that the pardon would not be observed. The commons there were especially suspicious of the action of Lord Latimer and Sir Christopher Danby in going up to the capital shortly after Christmas (when a number of other West Riding men did the same), because they saw in this move all the signs of a betrayal.[1] By responding to the King's call Latimer and Danby were able to save their own heads, but their absence from home meant that the restraint which they might have imposed on the commons was lacking. Further south, where Darcy refused the first royal summons to London, he was able to keep his country quiet in January and February. Even this probably counted against him, for it raised the question why he had not been equally effective the previous October. Indeed this contrast between the 'central wapentakes' and the Masham–Ripon area seems to give a little more support to the thesis that the revolt was really the work of the nobility and gentry.

The idea that there was a correlation between the geography of revolt and the pattern of territorial lordship is given further credence by the relative absence of unrest throughout the period of rebellion, in the southern-most parts of the Riding. Thomas Maunsell said he had sworn a number of Doncaster men shortly before the surrender of Pontefract to the Pilgrims; and during the following week the Pilgrims' army advanced as far south as Hampole Priory, just south of the boundary between Osgoldcross and Strafforth wapentakes. But apart from this, and the two meetings between Norfolk and the rebels at Doncaster, there was no stirring in the Wapentake of Strafforth and Tickhill. Hallamshire was firmly under the rule of the Earl of Shrewsbury, and nothing seems to have happened there. Tickhill Castle was officially in the charge of Sir Henry Wyatt (until his death on 10 November 1536); his deputy was Sir Brian Hastings, who in November became sheriff of Yorkshire. Hastings did not attempt to hold the castle against the Pilgrims, nor does there seem to have been any danger that they would attack it. Instead he spent most of the time at Hatfield, where he was deputy steward and where

[1] L.P., XII (i), nos. 173, 1012; cf. Dodds, op. cit., ii. 108.

he could keep a better watch on the activities of the Marshland rebels; he was not, however, able to prevent them from
crossing into Hatfield Chase on one occasion and spoiling
the King's deer, or from stealing some of Sir Brian's own
cattle on another occasion, probably from Norton-in-Osgold-
cross.[1] Hastings' own loyalties were no doubt determined by
his relationship to the Earl of Huntingdon, and he would
presumably follow the lead of the three Earls who gathered
at Nottingham on the 8 October. When Sir Henry Wyatt
died, Hastings appears to have handed over responsibility
for Tickhill to Sir Arthur Darcy, who now became joint
steward with Thomas Wyatt. The younger Darcy is said
to have made the castle ready for action, but like Hastings
he saw no reason to stay there for long. As for the middling
gentry of Strafforth and Tickhill, there is no indication
that they participated in the Pilgrimage: they would follow
the lead of Shrewsbury and Hastings, just as their fellow-
gentlemen in the 'central wapentakes', for whatever reason,
followed the lead of Lord Darcy.

III

The north-western parts of the Riding, Craven and the
country beyond, were referred to by Lord Darcy in his
letters as 'wild parts', and events there were much less
closely bound up with what happened in rebel areas nearer
the Ouse. They should be seen rather in relation to what
happened in Westmorland and north Lancashire. We have
already seen that in Craven there was trouble a little while
before the Pilgrimage year, between the Earl of Cumberland
and lesser inhabitants of the area: there were riots at Rylstone
in 1528, arising partly from the antagonism between the
Earl and John Norton; and the commons tore up hedges at
Giggleswick and other places in 1535, in some cases in
manors of the Percy fee which Cumberland had acquired by
marriage. If we go further back, we find earlier evidence
that Craven and Ewcross were unruly areas, liable to rebel
against established authority. In 1513, the year of the
Scottish campaign which ended at Flodden, there was a
revolt against taxation which began in Richmondshire and

[1] *L.P.*, XI, nos. 1026, 1059, 1088.

spread to Craven. Polydore Vergil described it as:[1] 'a sudden new upheaval of the north country folk caused by the heaviness of the tax imposed a little earlier. . . . These north country folk volunteered their personal services in waging war, but they refused the money because they have so little of it.' Towards the end of May 1513, Lord Clifford (the Earldom was not conferred till later) wrote to Lord Darcy that when the Craven commons heard of the resistance of Richmondshire, they refused to appear before the commissioners or to hand in their bills of assessment. They were still refusing to do so in the autumn when Lord Darcy informed Sir Richard Tempest that all the commissioners would run in the King's displeasure if they failed to return the assessments into Chancery.[2] It was not until January 1515 that Clifford was able to report to the Exchequer that most of the townships in Craven and Ewcross had been assessed; but even then Dent and Sedbergh still refused to appear. In 1516 the commissioners for a new subsidy did not go to Ewcross because, so they said, there was pestilence there. Part of the tax due was never collected; there is no record of the payment of the subsidy of 1513 from Ewcross; and the 'fifteenth and tenth' that had been due in February 1513 was formally written off in 1528, for eighteen townships in Ewcross and Bolland.[3] All this is evidence of a tradition of resistance in these areas, and it is unfortunate that we do not know more about the way the opposition to the taxes was organized, or if there were gentry as well as commoners involved.

In 1536, the trouble in Craven began in the former Percy Fee when the monks of Salley Abbey were restored to their monastery on the 12 October. The fact that this was an area where there was probably a long-standing loyalty to the Percy family is of some significance in view of what has been said earlier. How soon revolt spread to the Honour of

---

[1] *The Anglica Historia of Polydore Vergil*, ed. Denys Hay, Camden Series, lxxiv (London, 1950), pp. 202-3.

[2] Clifford to Darcy, 28 May (year unspecified), P.R.O.: SP 1/31/f. 50: *L.P.*: IV, no. 377 (assigned erroneously to 1524). Darcy to Tempest, undated but probably of autumn 1513, SP 1/31/f. 51: *L.P.*: IV, no. 378 (again mis-dated by editor).

[3] P.R.O.: E 179/279/1/13, 16-17, 25; E 179/279/3/96; and E 404/Box 96/an. 20/114.

Skipton we do not know. On the same day (the 12th) the Earl of Cumberland wrote to the King from Skipton pleading that he could not obey a royal command to go and restore order at Hexham because of the disturbances nearer home: but possibly he was referring only to the rising of Mashamshire and Kirkbyshire, of which he had been informed in a letter sent to him by Lord Scrope the previous day.[1] On the 16 October the Earl was once more contemplating a journey northward, this time to Carlisle to defend the border against the Scots; telling Sir Richard Tempest of this decision, the Earl said that he would leave his son at Skipton to organize a force against the Lincolnshire rebels.[2] It is likely that the news of the collapse in Lincolnshire, only known at Wakefield on the 15 October, had not yet reached Skipton when that letter was written. Perhaps it was after the Lincolnshire situation was known that the Earl changed his mind and sent his son to Carlisle, remaining himself at Skipton. But in all this there is no firm indication that Cumberland's own tenants had yet joined the rebellion. The Craven revolt took on wider proportions in the period 18–21 October, and it was then that a number of gentry began to be drawn into it. On the 18th Sir Stephen Hamerton (of Wigglesworth and Hamerton), according to his own subsequent confession, heard that there was a bill on Giggleswick church door, calling upon the people to join the Pilgrimage. It was probably one sent out by Aske from York, and no doubt others like it made their appearance at other places in the dales about the same time. The next day there was a muster at Neales Ing (probably in the vicinity of Wigglesworth) and it was then that Sir Stephen Hamerton was 'taken' and sworn to the cause. On the 20 October Sir Stephen led a small group of men to Skipton Castle to try and persuade the Earl of Cumberland to join the Pilgrimage, but in vain. Also on the 20th the commons 'took' Nicholas Tempest at Bashall and he too was sworn. On the 21st, Hamerton and Tempest attended a muster of the commons of Ribblesdale and Bolland at a place called Monubent.[3]

[1] *L.P.*, XI, nos. 712, 760 and 784.
[2] *L.P.*, XI, no. 742.
[3] *L.P.*, XII (i), no. 1034.

Still we cannot be sure that Skipton itself was yet involved. But, as we have already seen, on the 19 or 20 October a party of the North Riding forces that had been collected for the march on York broke away from the main column and crossed the hills to join in the siege of Skipton Castle. By the 21st therefore it is very likely that the Earl was besieged in his own residence by a force which in all likelihood included some of his own tenants.

Even so, it was not the Clifford tenants who started it all, and it would be a mistake to see these events as arising from a conflict between landlord and tenants. The real conflict was between Cumberland and some of the leading gentry of his area. Sir Stephen Hamerton and Nicholas Tempest both insisted that they had been coerced into rebellion by the commons, but the King refused to believe them and both were eventually executed. Hamerton was a Percy man, having served under the fifth Earl of Northumberland at Flodden, and he held his lands from the Percy Fee in Craven. Nicholas Tempest, who lived at Bashall only by right of having purchased the wardship of young Thomas Talbot, was the brother of Sir Richard Tempest and appears to have acted as the latter's deputy in his offices of steward of Blackburnshire (Lancashire) and forester of Bolland.[1] By the time of the Monubent muster, Sir Richard had already decided to follow Lord Darcy and had taken the Lordship of Wakefield into the rebel camp. One cannot know whether Nicholas Tempest knew that Lord Darcy would give up Pontefract Castle to the rebels (which he did on the same day, the 21st), but he was probably in whatever secrets there were between his brother and that Lord. As for the people who arrested Tempest, we know some of their names from his confession, and in fact they were substantial yeomen, perhaps minor gentry, rather than very poor tenants. Their leader was John Catterall of Rathmell, whose lands had been valued in 1523 at £10 a year. Moreover, he was one of those whose enclosures had been pulled down the previous year, a small but useful indication that the leadership in the Pilgrimage was not the same as that in the

---

[1] See A. C. Tempest: 'Nicholas Tempest, a sufferer in the Pilgrimage of Grace', *Y.A.J.*, xi (1891), 246-78.

1535 enclosure disturbances. Another man in the group was Anthony Talbot, probably a poor relation of the Bashall Talbots, who lived at Halton (in Ribblesdale) and had lands worth £6. 13s. 4d. in 1523.[1] A third was Richard Hamerton, probably the brother of Sir Stephen, and possibly the same as the 'Mr. Hamerton' who attended the council at Ponte-fract in December. A man of similar class to these, though he is not named by Tempest, also participated in the revolt: Lancelot Marton, son of Henry Marton of Eshton, who by Christmas was lodged in the dungeon of Skipton Castle. His father, whose lands had been put at £10 a year in 1523, was a few years after that receiving a fee of £5 as steward of the Earl of Cumberland's lands in Craven. But Lancelot himself appears in the accounts of the former Percy estates in 1537, as bailiff of Gisburn and Forester of Langstroth-dale.[2] Between them, father and son were probably well-placed to raise the tenants of both the Percy fee and the Honour of Skipton.

In the week following the 21 October the rebels of Craven and Bolland seem to have had two aims. One was to harass the Earl of Cumberland, not so much because he was an unpopular landlord as because he refused to join in the revolt. The Earl reported to the King on the 31 October that the commons had robbed his parks, spoiled his houses of Carle-ton and Barden, stolen some of his money, and destroyed his records.[3] The second aim was to protect the southern flank of the revolt, especially Salley Abbey, from the threatened advance of the Earl of Derby. To that end, on the 22 October Nicholas Tempest and Sir Stephen Hamerton rode over to Blackburnshire to raise the people of Colne and Burnley and to take control of Whalley Abbey.[4] Since the steward of Blackburnshire was Sir Richard Tempest, the area may be presumed to have been less firmly under Derby's influence than the rest of Lancashire south of the Ribble; the Earl was, however, steward of Whalley Abbey, which must have placed Abbot John Paslew in a very difficult position

---

[1] P.R.O.: E 179/206/116.
[2] Ibid. and P.R.O.: SC 6/Hen VIII/4289.
[3] L.P., XI, no. 927.
[4] L.P., XII (i), no. 1034.

when Derby decided to oppose the Pilgrimage. Whalley was as far as the rebels moved in the direction of south Lancashire, and they were saved by the first truce at Doncaster from having to confront Derby's forces in battle.

In Ewcross, and in the adjoining region of Kendal, it is less easy to find close connections between local events and the general pattern of north country and national politics. Since Derby was lord of Burton-in-Lonsdale, one would not expect that area to rise, and there is no evidence that it did, though silence is not strong evidence in a case like this. In Dent and Sedbergh there was no such dominant figure to restrain the commons (even an absentee); there was, however, even there, one tenuous link with the rebels through a landlord. Both at Dent and in Kendal much land was owned by Sir William Parr, brother of Katherine Parr (later queen), who had a castle at Kendal but lived mostly in Northamptonshire. Parr himself answered promptly the royal command to proceed from Northamptonshire to help suppress the revolt in Lincolnshire. Nevertheless, his sister was at this time the wife of John Nevill, Lord Latimer, which meant that he was related by marriage to some leading figures of the Pilgrimage. Whether this was of any significance matters less than the fact that, whatever made the commons of Dent and Sedburgh rise in the first place, they were very soon beyond the control or influence of any gentleman. They in fact rose much earlier than the commons of Craven, Mashamshire or central Yorkshire, for it was reported by one witness that they were taking a rebel oath as early as the end of September and speaking out against the King's pulling down churches.[1] In mid-October they joined forces with rebels from Kendal, and towards the end of the month some of them probably joined the force that marched on Lancaster under the leadership of one John Atkinson. In Kendal and Lonsdale, as in Dentdale, there was a marked absence of support from the larger gentry families. Nevertheless, some of the leaders at Dent and Sedburgh were by no means poor men. At Sedbergh they included James Cowper and John Middleton, who in 1546 paid tax on goods

[1] Confession of Wm. Breyar, who visited Dent at that time, *L.P.*, XI, no. 841; cf. Dodds, op. cit. i, 217.

worth £100 and £60 respectively; and John Hebblethwaite, possibly a relative of the Robert Hebblethwaite, chaplain, whose lands were taxed at £9 a year in that year. At Dent one of the leaders was George Willan, who may have been related to the Ralph Willan taxed on goods worth £40 in 1546.[1] The only clergyman mentioned as an active supporter of the rebels was Thomas Yeadon, vicar of Clapham.

In the north-west generally, the absence of any restraining influence of nobility or gentry may explain why social and economic discontents played a more prominent part in the rebellion there than elsewhere. At the Pontefract council of Pilgrims on the 2 or 3 December, Kendal and Penrith were represented by commoners whereas all other areas had gentry or noblemen present. It was probably they who stood out for the inclusion of a number of peasant grievances in the list of articles that was drawn up there. One of these grievances, concerning the enforcement of the statute against enclosures, was attacked generally by the articles (though it can hardly have been a subject dear to the heart of Lord Darcy). The other was the basis of a demand specifically related to certain areas: for the recognition of tenant-right, and for the statutory limitation of entry-fines ('gressums') to two years' rent, in the lands of Westmorland, Cumberland, Kendal, Dent, Sedbergh and Furness, and on the abbey lands of Kirkbyshire, Nidderdale and Mashamshire.[2] No estate records have so far come to light that explain why gressums on abbey lands in these last three areas differed from those on other estates; it is not impossible that the distinguishing fact was really the ability of Latimer and Danby to keep their own lordships out of the reckoning. These two items in the Pontefract articles are not the only clue to the more radical spirit of the north-western rebels. On 15 November the commons of Westmorland drew up a set of articles of their own. In addition to the demands concerning enclosure and gressums which went into the Pontefract list, the Westmorland articles included a demand for the complete abolition of neat-geld and sergeant-corn, two ancient Northumbrian dues which had either never existed in the

[1] P.R.O.: E 179/207/184.
[2] The Pontefract articles are analysed in detail by Dodds, op. cit., i, 346 ff.

West Riding or had died out by this period; and they called for the prevention of clerical absenteeism, in the knowledge that some of the non-resident clergy of their own area were Cromwell's minions.[1] The suppression of monasteries was not an important issue in Westmorland, which had few religious houses, but there was concern for the behaviour of the secular clergy, a reminder that even left to themselves the commons were not uninterested in the religious aspect of the revolt. It would be anachronistic to see such concern as exclusively a Protestant leaning in the England of Henry VIII.

The Dodds suggested a comparison between these Westmorland articles and those of the peasant rebellion in Germany in 1525, though they did not intend to imply that there was any German influence in northern England. They might equally well have compared them with the demands put forward in the peasants' revolt of south-eastern England in 1381. But the whole character of the Pilgrimage of Grace was different from that of rebellions which we know to have been inspired primarily by the desire of the commons for economic and social reforms and where the principal conflict was between landlords and tenants or between officials and tax-payers. In 1381 the commons took up arms against the nobility and gentry, and some of the higher clergy, and proceeded to sack their houses, to burn their manorial records, and in some cases even to take their persons hostage. The leaders of that revolt were not men of the poorest sort; but neither were they in a mood to accept the commands of noblemen. In 1536 the northerners were acting in defence of old customs, not against them, and their attitude to the highest members of society was one of deference, so long as they supported the Pilgrims' cause. In the West Riding the only people who suffered loss or damage to their property were those who, like the Earl of Cumberland or Leonard Beckwith, refused to join the rebellion.

IV

The contrast between the character of the revolt in the North-West (including Dentdale) and in the North-East (including central Yorkshire) is itself a small additional

[1] Dodds, op. cit., 370 ff.

indication that in the latter area the commons did not act alone at the outset. It must be admitted that the evidence in favour of the view that the revolt was really the work of the disaffected nobility is not conclusive; but it is in the nature of the situation that the secret plotting and organization which preceded the revolt, whatever its character, would not leave behind it hard documentary evidence of the kind which the historian demands as proof. Nevertheless the evidence on this side of the argument is by no means negligible. First, there is the evidence concerning Lord Darcy, who appears to have convinced Chapuys that he could make a rebellion in the North if the occasion arose; and it is his ability rather than his inclination to do so which really matters. If Chapuys's report is correct, the 'good old Lord' must surely have had specific plans for action, which would involve exploiting his position as steward of Pontefract, and which probably depended too on his alliance with the Nevill group. Secondly, there is the evidence concerning the Percy clientele: there can be little doubt that the relationship between Cromwell and the sixth Earl of Northumberland would arouse the resentment of Sir Thomas Percy and of the former servants of the fifth Earl. Their position differed from Darcy's: they could not act in the same way as a single nobleman throwing his weight on one side or the other of a political conflict; rather they were men with small amounts of local influence, but if they acted together they could probably be as effective in raising the Percy country as the Earl himself. There is no evidence to link clearly the Darcy–Nevill position with the activities of the Percy men, and it is impossible to show that the two groups acted entirely in concert. Indeed it is not impossible that the Percy rebels forced Darcy's hand at a time when he would have preferred to hold back. But if Darcy was seriously planning a revolt in 1534 it is very likely that he would at some stage make contact with the group of men in the North who had the greatest grievance of their own. Thirdly, there is the fact of the King's belief that he would only be safe with certain Northern figures out of the way: there may be some significance in the list of those he chose to execute. In Lincolnshire a large number of commons were executed; which may

have been because the King thought it was primarily a
commons' affair, but could equally have been because he
thought that the executions would overawe the commons of
Yorkshire and make them reluctant to follow men like
Darcy. In the case of Yorkshire, most of those executed
were noblemen or gentry: Lord Darcy and his friend Sir
Robert Constable; Sir Thomas Percy; Sir Stephen Hamerton and Nicholas Tempest; Robert Aske; and, for their
revolt after the Doncaster pardon, Sir Francis Bigod and
George Lumley.[1] It is very likely that others would have
been executed had they not had powerful friends to protect
them, or had they not had something to offer in return for
their lives, for example by giving evidence at the trials. But
the King seems to have had no doubt of the guilt of Darcy,
Constable, Percy and Aske; this in itself proves nothing, but
it must be weighed along with the other evidence.

Finally, the documented events of the rebellion itself give
a few hints that in the North-East the moving force behind
it was the nobility and gentry rather than the commons. In
the West Riding we know the names of eighteen men, of a
status less than knighthood, who played some part in the
early stages of the Pilgrimage, before the surrender of
Pontefract Castle. (I am including here the rising in Craven,
but not that in Dent and Sedbergh.) Of those eighteen, eight
were connected in some way with the Percy family and its
estates: Robert Aske, William Babthorpe, William Stapleton, Plumpton, Middleton, John Norton, Richard Hamerton (related to Sir Stephen), and Lancelot Marton. Another
two were connected with Lord Darcy: Thomas Strangeways,
his servant, and the vicar of Brayton Thomas Maunsell;
perhaps one should add here Darcy's lawyer Thomas Grice,
but I have not counted him amongst the eighteen since he
cannot be shown to have been directly involved in the revolt.
Two other men prominent in the rebellion were John Lacy
and Nicholas Tempest. The former was the son-in-law, and
the latter the younger brother, of Sir Richard Tempest, who
was a close ally of Darcy; Sir Richard was not executed, but

[1] Dodds, op. cit., ii, pp. 195-7, 214, 233-4. Several leading monastic clergy were
also executed: the Abbot of Jervaulx, the Prior of Bridlington, and the *quondam*
heads of Fountains and Rievaulx, as well as the Abbot of Whalley, Lancashire.

15

was imprisoned after the revolt and died in the Fleet in August 1537. Anthony Talbot, another of the eighteen, may also have been connected with this group, for he was probably a scion of the Talbot family of Bashall, whose heir was currently the ward of Nicholas Tempest. Ninian Stavely, in the list, was probably the son of Miles Stavely, receiver of the lordship of Ripon; in which case he was connected with the Archbishop of York. This leaves only three of the eighteen who cannot be related to any of the leading noblemen and gentry in the revolt. Two of the three were clerical men: the friar Robert Eshe; and William Thirsk, the *quondam* of Fountains. The last was John Catterall, who played a prominent part in Craven and may have had some unknown connection with the Percy fee there.

The evidence on the other side of the argument is superficially more impressive. But almost all of it derives from statements made after the rebellion had failed, or from letters written in circumstances which leave open the possibility that the writer intended to mislead the King. These sources show Darcy, the Archbishop and others affirming that they were coerced into joining the Pilgrimage, but that is precisely what they would have said if they had deliberately used the commons in order to save their own skins in the event of failure. Even Robert Aske claimed to have been coerced! There are, nevertheless, two general features of the revolt which suggest that its character was not *merely* that of a 'feudal' rebellion in which 'men of power and worship' used their control over the commons to oppose the King. One relates to the education of some of the participants; the other is the oath devised by the rebels to secure the adherence of their followers to the aims of the Pilgrimage. A remarkable feature of the list of eighteen leading figures is that at least four of them, possibly more, had been educated in the Common Law. Robert Aske, and perhaps also William Stapleton, had been at Gray's Inn; Robert Plumpton was currently at the Inner Temple, and William Babthorpe was also of the Inner Temple.[1] Such men may not have acted wholly out of traditional loyalties to the Percy house. They

---

[1] *Gray's Inn Register of Admissions*, col. 6; Dodds, op. cit., i, 48; *Register of Admissions to the Inner Temple*, i, 12; A. G. Dickens: *Lollards and Protestants*, 132–6.

may also have been convinced on grounds of principle that Lord Darcy was right in his opposition to Henry VIII's new interpretation of the relation between kingship and law. The same may have been true of some of the clergy involved, including Robert Eshe and Thomas Maunsell. In this respect the Pilgrimage differs sharply from the fifteenth-century revolts of the Dukes of York and of Henry Tudor. The issues of principle, moreover, were embodied in the Pilgrims' oath, which appears to have been formulated by Robert Aske at York on the 17 October.[1] The Pilgrims swore to take up Christ's cross, to love the Holy Church militant, and to work for the 'restitution of the Church and the suppression of these heretics and their opinions'. The oath did not involve any disloyalty to the Crown; the rebels committed themselves to 'expulse all villein blood and evil councillors against the commonwealth from his Grace and his privy council'. But it was in direct contradiction to the oath of supremacy which the King had made his subjects swear in 1534, when he had sent Sir Thomas More to the scaffold for refusing to take it. The importance of the oath in Tudor politics should not be under-estimated. The coronation oath was the foundation of monarchy, and Henry VIII took it sufficiently seriously to alter it after his attitude to the Church changed.[2] The oath of supremacy signified an attempt to change radically the whole nature of the King's relationship to his people, as well as to the Church. What more natural than that the Pilgrims of Grace should oppose it by an oath of their own? But the fact that they chose to do so reflects the fact that their movement was one held together by something more than traditional feudal ties.

Even if the evidence concerning Darcy and the Percy group is accepted as circumstantial proof that it was they rather than the commons who made the rebellion, the way in which they used the commons meant that the latter were drawn into political life. They had an opportunity to think for themselves about political issues and to contemplate opposition to the Government on a level somewhat higher

[1] Dodds, op. cit., i, 182.
[2] The coronation oath of Henry VIII, showing alterations, is reproduced in L. E. Tanner: *The History of the Coronation* (London, 1952), p. 23.

than the stubborn refusal of a remote area like Craven to
pay its taxes. The significance of this aspect of the Pilgrimage
is to be seen in its aftermath. Murmurs of discontent continued to be heard in the next few years, and in 1541 there
was more positive action. Professor Dickens has described
in detail the Wakefield plot of 1541 and we need refer to it
only briefly here.[1] The conspiracy was centred upon Wakefield, but the focus of action was once more to be Pontefract,
where it was planned to raise a new rebellion at the fair on
Palm Sunday. The plan appears to have been uncovered
by the county authorities around the 22 March, and the
protagonists were arrested. They included eight or nine
priests (one of them Thomas Maunsell of Brayton) and also
the last abbot of Croxton (Leicestershire). Five laymen were
also involved: William Legh of Middleton, who had led the
opposition to Lord Darcy's enclosures at Rothwell in 1532;
Thomas Tattersall of Milnthorpe, whose sales of livestock
were mentioned in Chapter I; Gilbert Thornton, another
yeoman of the district; James Diamond of Wakefield, who
had taken part in the Pilgrimage; and Robert Boxe, of whom
we know only that his father had left lands in Wakefield and
Stanley worth £2. 9s. in 1531. Many of these people were
executed. So too was Sir John Nevill of Chevet, not apparently for any direct part in the plot itself, but for failing to
reveal his first awareness of it to the authorities. Apart from
him, no mention is made in the records of any gentlemen
(still less nobility) having anything to do with the affair: it
seems this time to have been genuinely the work of the commons. When all was quiet, the King decided to appease the
northerners by going to Yorkshire himself. He arrived in
the county on or about the 23 August 1541 and left it about
the middle of October, having spent twelve days at York and
a slightly longer period at Pontefract. He also visited the
former Percy possessions at Leconfield and Wressle, and
spent a few days at Hull.[2] This was the only occasion on

[1] A. G. Dickens: 'Sedition and Conspiracy in Yorkshire during the later years of
Henry VIII', *Y.A.J.*, xxxiv (1939).

[2] *L.P.*, XVI, nos. 1117, 1124, 1130, 1142, 1150, etc.: items showing Privy Council
meetings at Pontefract (24 Aug.–3 Sept.), at Cawood (4–5 Sept.), at Wressle (6–7
Sept.), at Leconfield (8–9, 13–14 and 24–8 Sept.), at Hull (11–12 Sept.), and at
York (16–24 Sept.).

which Henry was seen by his West Riding subjects, except for the small minority who were visitors to Westminster and the Court.

To return to the events of 1536: after the surrender of Pontefract on the 21 October, we are on firmer ground, for the leadership of the north-eastern areas of the revolt was then firmly in noble hands. The council at Pontefract early in December, and the articles drawn up there were concerned much more with their grievances than with those of the commons.[1] The dominant theme was antipathy towards Cromwell and towards his (or the King's) policies regarding both the Church and the North. In the latter respect, there was perhaps a fear that Cromwell would revive the policies of the hated Wolsey, which may have been the real significance of the Dacre trial. Additional demands, all of far greater interest to the nobles and gentry than to the commons, were for the repeal of the Statute of Uses, an end to the extortionate practices of escheators, an end to the undermining of Common Law by the conciliar courts, and the repeal of the Statute of Treason (for words). The articles prescribed an interesting remedy for their grievances: not just the removal and punishment of Cromwell, Audley and Riche, but the summoning of a new Parliament to meet at Nottingham or at York, and for representation in it of Ripon, Beverley, Richmond, Pontefract, Wakefield, Skipton and Kendal. The promise of such a Parliament, which would be free from domination by Cromwell and his friends, was one of the means by which the King was able to win over Robert Aske and to use him to prevent further unrest in the North pending Norfolk's mission of pacification. The constitutional element in the demands of 1536 prompts a comparison between the Pilgrimage and a much earlier revolt by northern nobility and gentry: that of 1213 against John, which has been studied in detail by Professor Holt.[2] On that occasion too a King had to accept conditions imposed by his people—embodied in Magna Carta—and then sought to go back on his word. The revolt against John was much more openly that of the highest orders of northern society, with

[1] Dodds, op. cit. i, 359, 388.
[2] J. C. Holt: *The Northerners* (Oxford, 1961).

no element of independent action by the commons; in that period it was not necessary for the leaders to have such support, nor possible for the commons to supply it. Nevertheless, the King was able in 1215 to drive a wedge between the gentry and the nobility, proving that the latter's control over the knightly class was even then not complete. Henry VIII adopted the same tactics, and when it became apparent that the promises of Doncaster were as much as the Pilgrims could hope for, the knights fell away from the revolt much more quickly than either the lords or the commons. Fifteen of the gentlemen who attended the Council at Pontefract were in the following year sworn as members of the grand juries which indicted the rebels to be tried.[1] Seen in the broad sweep of English history, the rebellion of 1536 was an important turning-point in the complex relationship between the Crown, the nobility, and the gentry, and one whose results were to the advantage of the Crown. It was not until the rise of an increasingly independent Parliament in the seventeenth century that an English monarch would have to face opposition as determined as that of 1536. By that time, the gentry had realized that the medieval type of rebellion was no longer effective, but they had found their own instrument of opposition to the King, which proved more effective than the feudal power of great lords.

---

[1] P.R.O.: *Baga de Secretis*, KB (Crown side), pouch x, bundle 2, printed in A. C. Tempest, *Y.A.J.*, xi (1891), 267.

VI

THE DISSOLUTION OF THE
MONASTERIES AND THE LAND
MARKET: 1536–46

I

H ENRY's victory over the Church and its defenders
had great consequences, not only for the political
scene but also for the distribution of control over the
land. The suppression of the monasteries and the confiscation of their property was the first step in the transformation
of what Tawney, following James Harrington, called the
'balance of property'. That the nobility and gentry between
them controlled a very much greater proportion of the land
of England in 1640 than in either 1535 or 1540 has never
been doubted; the only question at issue between Tawney
and his critics was the relative proportions held by the
nobility and the gentry as separate categories of landlord.[1]
This controversy, which relates to developments after 1558,
need not concern us here. The object of this chapter is
merely to trace the beginnings of the change.

The transformation of the pattern of landlordship
in the West Riding between 1535 and the end of Henry's
reign was dramatic indeed. Table XVI summarizes the
changes of this decade, in terms of the four principal
categories of owner identified in Chapter II. Unlike the
tables in that Chapter, however, it does not distinguish
between spiritual and temporal income. One reason is that
by 1546 spiritual income was no longer the monopoly of
ecclesiastical institutions, and it is not always possible to
separate it from temporal income in tracing changes of
ownership in the interval. The figures given for 1535 are
otherwise the same as those of the earlier tables, the percentages having been recalculated to include spiritual income as
part of the Church's share of the total. For 1546 it was

[1] Cf. *infra*, p. 254.

TABLE XVI

Distribution of Temporal (Freehold) and Spiritual Income in the West Riding in 1535 and 1546.

Category of Landlord	1535	1546
Church	£11,604 (43·8%)	£4,645 (17·2%)
Crown	£2,350 (8·8%)	£7,250 (26·8%)
Nobility	£2,090 (7·7%)	£2,300 (8·5%)
Gentry	£10,616 (39·7%)	£12,830 (47·5%)
Total	£26,660 (100%)	£27,025 (100%)

decided not to attempt a completely new township-by-township analysis, but simply to discover what happened to the land which moved from one category of owner to another in the interval, using mainly the records of confiscation and sale of land by the Crown, together with the Augmentations Accounts of 1546.[1] The values for 1546 therefore are very largely those of 1535. The enquiry could not be perfect, and it was found impossible to take full account of the fact that when parcels of monastic property were sold to laymen by the Crown, the latter reserved a small rent to itself, which was deductible from the revenues received by the lay grantee. These rents are counted in the income attributed to the Crown in 1546, but could not always be deducted from the revenues of the grantee. Hence the slight discrepancy between the totals of revenue for the two dates.

The Church saw its revenue cut to less than half its former level. The Crown, although it had begun to sell confiscated property by 1546, still had more than three times as much landed income at that date as in 1535. For what it is worth, one can also make the observation that the gentry share of land increased far more than that of the nobility in this period. It is not, however, worth a great deal.

[1] P.R.O.: SC 6/Hen VIII/4364, 4405, 4408, 4438, 4450, 4457, 4578, 4583, 4589, 4594, 4600, 4605, 4611, 7310, 7466, etc.

For the nobility of the North underwent a transformation of personnel in the years just after 1535. Before the rebellion the principal noble landlords were Clifford, Percy, Talbot and Darcy; but by the end of 1537 Darcy had been executed and Percy had died leaving the King as his heir. The chief landowning noblemen in Yorkshire in 1546 were Clifford, Talbot, Wharton, and perhaps one may count Latimer.[1] But the Earl of Cumberland had greatly increased his proportion of noble land, from £612 a year in 1535 to at least £1,100 a decade later, not allowing for changes in values. His gain makes up for the fact that otherwise the nobility as a class would have had a smaller percentage of land revenue at the end of the period than at the beginning. To look only at the distribution of annual income in these years, however, is to ignore one of the most important elements in the situation, the flow of large sums of money from the purchasers of monastic lands into the coffers of the King. Over the period from 1538 to 1546, the Court of Augmentations received approximately £37,470 from the sale of lands and spiritualia in the West Riding.[2] It was not spread evenly over these years, but it was equivalent to an annual income to the Crown of £4,160. This was in addition to revenues from the sale of royal wardships, which may also have been higher in 1546 than in 1535, in view of the changes effected by the Statutes of Uses and of Wills. All in all, the King's financial gains from the Reformation were considerable, despite the fact that, given the enormity of his expenses in the last decade of his reign, they were not enough for his needs.

II

How did the transformation come about? To answer that question we must explore in detail the process of Dissolution and the nature of the monastic land market in the West Riding, following to some extent in the footsteps of Dr. Youings' study of the subject in Devon. We must also

[1] On Latimer and Wharton, cf. *infra*, pp. 246–7. Both were purchasers of monastic property in the West Riding.
[2] This figure has been calculated from the details of grants or sales of confiscated property contained in the patent rolls (calendared in *L.P.*), and in the particulars for grants of Crown lands (P.R.O.: E 318).

abandon the idea of looking only at categories of landlords, and begin to concern ourselves with individuals, or at least with particular families. The first point which must be made is that seen in terms of individual landlords the situation of 1535 was itself by no means a static one. People were already familiar with three channels by which land could pass from one lord or owner to another: family arrangements; sale or mortgage; or royal decree. These channels were used more frequently and more extensively after 1535 and in time they produced significant changes in the general pattern; but they were an established feature of the land situation long before.

Transfer of land by family arrangement depended neither on money payment nor on the King's power to enforce his will. Church land apart, all land belonged to a family as much as to an individual, and even the King had to make arrangements for the distribution of revenues from his estates so as to ensure that all members of his family were provided for.[1] The practice of making family settlements at each generation was a compromise between the rigid system of primogeniture implied by military feudalism, and the more ancient system of partible inheritance which it had probably superseded; it was also a necessity in a society where marriage was bound up with the dowry. When a man died, his heir must make provision for the widow (often by assuring her the dower she brought to her marriage), and must make what arrangements for life interests he deemed appropriate to ensure an income to his brothers; at some stage too he might have to provide dowry for his sisters and daughters. But to prevent a disintegration of the family estate, he would make these arrangements by granting lands or annuities for life, or sometimes by entailing them so that they might at some future date return to the patrimony of the eldest line of the family. Often, therefore, the heir's hands would be tied by the testament of his father. Where there was no male heir, the more ancient method of partible inheritance was adhered to, so that the estate went in equal portions to the families into which the daughters married. Where there was

---

[1] For arrangements of this kind affecting the Duchy of Lancaster estates, see R. Somerville; op. cit., i, pp. 199 ff.

a male heir not yet of age, or where the heiresses were not yet married, a period of wardship would follow as we have seen. To imagine a gentry (or noble) estate as a static entity therefore, to be handed down from father to son like a billiard ball or a family heirloom, is to fail to appreciate the nature of sixteenth-century landlordship. Even when there was no partition amongst heiresses and no wardship, one must not suppose that an heir inherited the whole income which his father had enjoyed. An illustration of this is afforded by the feodary's survey made in 1544 on the death of Sir Thomas Johnson. The whole estate was valued at £143; it so happened that young Henry Johnson was too young to inherit and a wardship was declared, but even if he had been of age he would have inherited only about £40 of his father's income immediately. For the rest he would have to wait until the deaths of various people who still had claims to annuities from the estate, even including some to whom the Earl of Northumberland had made grants before he gave the manor of Leathley to his father.[1]

Where there was a failure of male heirs, land passed from one family to another through the marriage of heiresses. This represented a family disaster for the father who could not produce a son, and it was not only the King who was anxious lest he leave only a daughter to survive him. But from another point of view it represented an opportunity, and marriage to an heiress was a means of advancing the fortunes of a rising family. A notable example is the family of Sir Henry Savile of Thornhill. In the fourteenth century Sir John Savile had added to his own manor of Golcar lands in Rushworth brought to the marriage by his wife. A descendant of his, in the fifteenth century, married the heiress of the Elland family, and the son of that marriage added Thornhill to the estate by marrying the heiress of the Thornhill family. Finally, Sir Henry Savile himself, having inherited this large group of manors in 1521, married Elisabeth Soothill and acquired an interest in a large part of the possessions of Thomas Soothill who died in 1535.[2] In this way the Saviles rose to become one of the two or three

[1] P.R.O.: Wards 9/133/f. 87d.
[2] J. W. Clay: 'The Savile Family', *Y.A.J.*, xxv (1920), 1–47.

richest gentry families in the Riding, without making any important purchases of property for cash.

A land market had nevertheless developed by the first half of the sixteenth century, and some families did gain or lose land through transactions for money. The land law had not been devised to allow for such transactions, and consequently the legal formulae available to record changes of title of this kind were clumsy and very technical adaptations of feudal forms. A thorough study of the market in land, at virtually any period of English history, can be made only by someone with both legal expertise and the patience to work out changes in the ownership of land over a wide area and a long period. Such an undertaking lies beyond the scope of the present study, but there is one kind of conveyance which can be used to obtain a rough idea of the overall volume of the land market at different periods. This is the series of records known as 'feet of fines' because they were entered at the foot of the rolls of a court of record (often the Close Rolls of Chancery) in return for payment of a fine. They record in fact collusive law-suits whose sole purpose was to confirm the title of a new owner, and its recognition by the former owner. A chronological analysis of the West Riding 'feet of fines' calendared by Collins is given in Table XVII. Unfortunately the figures in the first column cannot be taken as a straightforward measure of the volume of sales and purchases, for not all the items recorded in this

TABLE XVII

Transfers of West Riding Land Recorded in Feet of Fines, 1510–50

Period	Total number of items	Enfeoffments to use	Cash transactions
1510–14	19	8	11
1515–19	30	9	21
1520–4	36	8	28
1525–9	79	24	55
1530–4	95	27	68
1535–9	114	15	99
1540–4	197	4	193
1545–9	223	3	220

Source: F. Collins (ed.): *Feet of Fines for the Tudor Period*, i: 1485–1570. (Y.A.S. Record Series, ii, 1887.)

way were transactions involving permanent (or even temporary) transfer of land for money. Quite a number of them
were simply confirmations of an enfeoffment to trustees,
for the use of someone within the 'donor's' family, even
sometimes his own son. These 'feet of fines' come under the
heading of family settlements. They can often be identified,
though not invariably, and the second column of the table
shows numbers of 'fines' which seem to belong to this
category. On the other hand many of the records make
specific mention of a cash transaction, and these are noted
in the third column. It is interesting that the number of
enfeoffments to use declines at the point where the number
of money transactions climbs most steeply. The likeliest
explanation for this is that the statute of uses passed in 1536
reduced the advantage to be gained by such enfeoffments,
whose primary object seems to have been to avoid liability
to wardship.

The volume of cash transactions in land increased
markedly during the decade before the suppression of the
monasteries, and this was an important feature of the background against which the first commissions for the sale of
monastic property were issued. It means that already by that
time there were men with money to buy land, as well as
families whose financial circumstances compelled them to
mortgage or sell. Occasionally the 'feet of fines' can be
related to other evidence to reveal more details about such
cases, although not unfortunately the reasons why some
gentry landlords had to sell or to borrow in this way. One of
the moneylender-merchants who made loans to West Riding
landowners was Ambrose Woolley, who in 1536 was
warden of the grocers' company in the city of London; his
name suggests that he may have been a Yorkshireman by
birth. About 1535 Woolley acquired a temporary title to
the manor of Wilstrop and other lands, in return for a loan
of over £500 to Oswald Wilstrop. The mortgage gave rise to
a complicated dispute which landed Wilstrop in prison for
a while, on a statute staple. Eventually, after a suit in Chancery, he seems to have recovered his property.[1] Again, some

---

[1] P.R.O.: C 1/1084/44; Woolley occurs in *List of Wardens of the Grocer's Company 1345–1907* (London, 1907), p. 18.

years later we find Woolley making a loan to Thomas
Langton and Anthony Dryland, on the security of the
manor of Huddleston. It is not clear whether they ever
recovered the property, but probably they did not for in
1556 that manor was sold by another London merchant,
Richard Tyrrell, to one Robert Baker.[1] Yet another West
Riding gentleman who had recourse to the city money-
lender was Sir Thomas Wentworth of West Bretton. In
1533 he sold his lands in Shitlington to John Cotes, salter
and Alderman of London, for £360 and a covenant to the
effect that Sir Thomas might at some later date repurchase
if he wished. Cotes was still lord of Shitlington in 1542, when
he opened a suit in Star Chamber to protect the rights (or
claims) of his farmer there; and in 1545 he resold the
property to Thomas Pymme and Richard Gaywold (Wentworth having died in 1543, which presumably meant an end
to his right of repurchase).[2]

These examples demonstrate that already Yorkshire was
not too far away from London to be occasionally a field of
operations for city financiers; perhaps, on a smaller scale,
Yorkshire merchants lent money on this basis too. But there
was another kind of purchaser who played an even more
important part in the growth of the land market: the man
who had money and wanted to use it in order to become a
landowner and perhaps in time a gentleman. In the decades
before 1540 the most interesting example of this in the West
Riding is the case of John Wirrall of Doncaster. Possibly a
Cheshire man, to judge from his name, his recorded career
begins in Doncaster where he was a prominent merchant
and became mayor in 1524. He was justice or alderman on
a number of occasions between then and his death in 1544.
Between 1519 and 1538 Wirrall made nine purchases of
land, including the manors of Loversall and Stancil and some
property in Tickhill. When he died his estate was valued at
£37 a year. His son Hugh also made a number of land
purchases, beginning in 1536; later, when ex-monastic land
came onto the market, he acquired Monk Bretton Priory's

[1] *Feet of Fines*, Y.A.S.R.S., ii (1897), pp. 84, 95.
[2] *Yorkshire Deeds*, Y.A.S.R.S., lxxvi, no. 449 (p. 135) and Y.A.S.R.S., xli, no. 35 (p. 78).

grange of Carr House, Greasbrough, of which his father was lessee. In 1546, having inherited his father's possessions two years before, Hugh Wirrall was assessed for the subsidy on lands worth £80 a year.[1]

Sales, mortgages and family settlements were responsible for a good deal of mobility of property within the category of gentry landlords in the years before 1535. Although I have not been able to measure it systematically, a sample study of the lordship over seventy-four gentry manors in 1428 and 1535 showed that only forty of them had a continuous history of ownership in the male line by a single family during that interval; all the others—nearly half—passed into the hands of a new family by one means or another.[2] On the other hand transfer from one category of landlord to another was unusual in the fifteenth and early sixteenth century. The land market indicated by the 'feet of fines' did not mean serious instability of the pattern of distribution of land amongst the four principal categories. It required the King's power of changing the ownership of land by decree to disrupt that pattern.

III

The political instability of the fifteenth century had been responsible for a number of significant changes in the distribution of land, as between the nobility and the Crown. The reason why the King's estates were so extensive under Henry VIII was that on two occasions, in 1399 and 1461, the throne had been seized by powerful noblemen who had added their family estates to those of the Crown. But after 1485 this sort of change in the ownership of land was less important. What mattered under the earlier Tudors was the King's power to confiscate land from his subjects by attainder and to add it to his own possessions or to grant it away again to more loyal nobles. This was the power which Henry VIII brought into play after the Pilgrimage of Grace, to confiscate

[1] Y.A.S.R.S., ii, pp. 34, 38, 42, 49, 53, 56, 60, 62, 74–5, 81, 83, 146; P.R.O.: E 150/241/37; E 179/207/198; *Calendar to Records of the Borough of Doncaster*, ii, *Court Rolls 1454–1687*, 37, 50, 61, 67, 72.
[2] The evidence for 1535 is the same as that used in Chapter II; for 1428, see *Inquisitions and Assessments relating to Feudal Aids 1284–1431*, vi, 180–1 and 188 ff.

the estates of such rebels as Lord Darcy and Sir Stephen Hammerton. In the 1530s he also used his power in less conventional ways, perhaps at the instigation of Cromwell. A notable instance was the pressure brought to bear on the sixth Earl of Northumberland to ensure that on his death without male issue in 1537 most of his lands passed by will to the King. At the same period, and a little later, Henry was impressed by the loyalty of the Cliffords and as we shall see, encouraged them to extend their estates. The King was also anxious to reduce the importance as landowner of the Archbishop of York, and in 1545 forced on Robert Holgate an exchange of temporalities (including Ripon, Sherburn and Otley lordships) for a grant of ex-monastic spiritual possessions.[1]

These confiscations and pressures on individual owners, however, pale before the wholesale measures of suppression and confiscation which brought to an end the religious houses of Yorkshire, as of England generally, in the three years between 1536 and 1540. They began in March 1536 with the enactment of the statute dissolving all houses of monks and nuns whose net taxable income, according to the *Valor* of the previous year, was less than £200 a year. Of the ten houses which came within the scope of this statute in the West Riding, five were reprieved and had their exemption confirmed by letters patent as late as 1538; they were all nunneries and meagrely endowed.[2] The other five were formally dissolved by September 1536, including Salley Abbey which had almost certainly been undervalued by the commissioners in 1535. The restoration of Salley, and of Healaugh Priory, by the Pilgrims of Grace meant that this phase of the suppression could not be finally completed until February 1537. Later that year, as a consequence of the rebellion, three other houses which had lands in the West Riding, although situated elsewhere, were surrendered to the King: the attainder of the Abbot of Jervaulx and the Prior of Bridlington was interpreted to mean the forfeiture of both their houses, whilst the Abbot of Furness was

[1] *L.P.*, XX (i), 465 (39).
[2] Arthington, Esholt, Hampole, Kirklees and Nun Appleton, *L.P.*, XIII (i) nos. 646 (17–18), 115 (19) and 1519 (44).

simply persuaded by the Earl of Sussex to surrender his abbey voluntarily.[1]

During the months between the late summer of 1537 and the spring of the following year, it may have seemed as if the royal appetite for Church lands had been satisfied. But gradually during the course of 1538 the policy of wholesale suppression took shape. In the West Riding the second phase of the Dissolution began in June 1538 with the surrender of the abbey of Roche.[2] Earlier that month Sir John Nevill of Chevet had written to Dr. Thomas Legh to report that the Prior of Monk Bretton was also ready to surrender his house, and to ask for a grant of the monastic demesnes if that were to happen. But for the moment Monk Bretton was safe, and in the same month the priory of Nostell went ahead with the election of a new head.[3] It was this new prior, Robert Ferror, who wrote to Cromwell in September expressing the hope that his house might be spared suppression and made into a college for the nourishment of youth in virtue and learning; but in vain.[4] In November 1538 Sir George Lawson and three officers of the Court of Augmentations set out on a commission to travel through Yorkshire and to accept the surrender of any house whose head wished to make it; they also had special instructions to suppress the friaries in the county. By the end of the year they had dissolved thirteen houses, including six in the West Riding: five friaries and the priory of Monk Bretton. In January 1539 Bolton Priory was added to the list.[5]

The remaining houses were given a short respite before the final axe fell. One possible reason is that the royal officials wished to allow the activities of the agricultural year to proceed unhindered, for with one exception nothing further was done until the following November, by which time both the harvest and the Michaelmas rents had been safely gathered in. The exception was the surrender of the nunnery at Esholt in August.[6] In November and December

[1] *L.P.*, XII (i), nos. 1241, 1237, 1257, 832, 840, 880.
[2] *L.P.*, XIII (i), no. 1248.
[3] Ibid., no. 1130.
[4] *L.P.*, XIII (ii), no. 285.
[5] *L.P.*, XIII (ii), nos. 823, 869, 877, 888, 912; XIV (i), 162.
[6] Y.A.S.R.S., xlviii, p. 109.

came the last series of suppressions, which included the
largest prizes of all: Nostell, Pontefract, Kirkstall, Selby,
Fountains, St. Mary's at York.[1] By Christmas 1539 the
monastic life which had graced the Riding for over four
centuries had, in as many years, been obliterated. The final
episode in the disappearance of the religious orders was the
statute of 1540 dissolving the Order of the Knights of St.
John in England and Ireland, which brought an end to their
preceptories at Ribston and Newland.[2] Parallel measures
were taken to dissolve religious houses in other parts of the
country which had held lands in Yorkshire, so that by the
end of 1540 the whole of the £6,800 of West Riding
revenues, both temporal and spiritual, which had pertained
to the religious orders in 1535 was in the firm hands of the
Crown, or of lay grantees.

In order to administer these religious lands the King in
1536 set up a Court of Augmentations, rather than add them
to the estates of any existing administrative court. He staffed
its Northern offices with men who for the most part were
not attached to local power groups, but whose position
depended almost entirely on their skill as administrators, and
the loyalty to the King's new policies which earned for them
their appointments. Among them were Leonard Beckwith,
receiver of the Augmentations of Yorkshire, and William
Blythman who performed similar duties in Durham and the
Archdeaconry of Richmond. The one was a common lawyer,
the other a graduate in civil law. Leonard Beckwith was the
son of a minor gentleman of Stillingfleet (East Riding) and
entered Lincoln's Inn in 1523 having been escheator of
Yorkshire two years previously. He does not appear in the
records again until 1535 when he was noted in the *Valor
Ecclesiasticus* as bailiff for Selby Abbey at Acaster Selby and
Stillingfleet. But he must have made progress in London in
the interval for in 1536 he was simultaneously appointed to
the Augmentations receivership in Yorkshire and to the
commission to suppress the Yorkshire monasteries affected
by the statute of that year. Within the year he had made his
first gain from his new office, by acquiring the lease of Holy

[1] *L.P.*, XIV (ii), nos. 557, 567, 576, 587, 641.
[2] *Statutes*, iii, 32 Hen VIII, cap. 24.

Trinity Priory at York, which he later purchased outright and made his chief residence. In 1537 he furthered his career by marrying the daughter and eventual heiress of Sir Roger Cholmley, Recorder of London.[1] We shall have occasion later in this chapter to pay more detailed attention to his activities as receiver, which appear to have included both peculation and speculation. By 1544 he was a wealthy landowner and a member of the West Riding commission of the peace, and in that year he was knighted. He survived a lawsuit arising from accusations that he had abused his position in the Augmentations, and in 1546 became treasurer of Boulogne and a member of the Council in the North.[2] When he died in 1557 he left an estate worth £181 a year.[3]

William Blythman came of a Durham family. After studying at Cambridge he obtained the degree of Bachelor of Civil Laws in 1520, seven years before the same degree was awarded to the notorious Dr. Thomas Legh by the same university. The two were probably acquaintances of long standing when they became associated with the movement to suppress the monasteries. By 1528 Blythman was Registrar of the Bishopric of Durham, and a few years later he was given a similar appointment in the Archdeaconry of Richmond. But his connection with the Church did not foster in him any love of the monasteries, and in 1535 (after working on the valuation of clerical wealth of that year) he was recommended as a suitable man to be registrar of the commission to carry out the visitation of the Northern religious houses. In April 1536 he was appointed to the Augmentations receivership of Durham and Richmond, whose territory included part of the West Riding. His rise was less meteoric than Beckwith's—perhaps he was more scrupulous—but he did acquire some property, and died at Thorpe Underwood in 1543 the owner of an estate worth £80.[4]

Besides receivers the regional divisions of the Court of

[1] East Riding R.O., Beverley: DD 47/BRA 301; *Gray's Inn Admissions Register*, col. 4; *Valor Ecclesiasticus*, v, 13; L.P., XIII (i), nos. 721 (5) and 1520.
[2] This lawsuit will be discussed at length, *infra*, pp. 236–8.
[3] P.R.O., Wards 9/137/f. 184.
[4] *Alumni Cantab.*, pt. i, vol. i, p. 172; L.P., IV (ii), no. 4877; VIII, nos. 149 (65, 68, etc.), and 955; XIII (i), no. 1520; P.R.O.: E 150/241/25 and Durham 3/177/69.

Augmentations also had auditors. The auditor for Yorkshire, Hugh Fuller, is an obscure figure about whom hardly anything is known. His colleague of Durham and Richmond was James Rokeby, another purchaser of monastic property in the West Riding. Born apparently in the North Riding, he too had played a part in the compilation of the *Valor Ecclesiasticus* and was rewarded for his pains with an appointment as auditor. In 1546 he was living at Newton-by-Ripley and was assessed for the subsidy on lands and fees to the annual value of £40. Two years earlier he had purchased Slenningford, near Ripon, but did not live there.[1]

IV

As early as September 1534, rumours were abroad that Cromwell was pressing the King to 'distribute between the gentlemen of the kingdom the greater part of the Church revenues, that he may thereby gain the hearts and affections of his subjects'.[2] As the policy of suppression gradually materialized over the next few years, the idea of granting the confiscated lands to the nobility and gentry must have been continually in the back of men's minds. In the event, however, the policy of selling lands which the Government finally adopted proved to be somewhat less favourable to the King's subjects than Chapuys had anticipated.

In the spring of 1536 the West Riding gentry were already writing to Cromwell pressing their claims for 'preferment' to one or other of the houses to be dissolved. A typical plea was Sir William Gascoigne's, in a letter of 17 June: 'If the nunnery of Nun Monkton founded by my ancestors go to the King's augmentation, I beg I may have the preferment of it, paying as much as any other will.'[3] Similar letters came from Sir John Nevill of Chevet, concerning Hampole Priory; and from Sir Henry Everingham, who did not specify any particular house.[4] But none of these suits was successful. More begging letters were written in 1537 and 1538. Sir John Nevill tried again several times, on

[1] *L.P.*, VIII, nos. 149 (72), 945; XIII (i), p. 573; XIX (i), 812 (107); P.R.O.: E 179/207/191.
[2] Report of Chapuys, *Cal. S.P. Spanish*, V (i), p. 256.
[3] *L.P.*, X, no. 1152.
[4] Ibid., nos. 621, 633.

one occasion seeking the site and demesnes of Monk
Bretton, but without success. In December 1539 he was
after a lease of the granges of Stainer and Thorpe which had
been kept in hand by the Abbot of Selby, but again he was
disappointed.[1] The reason for his repeated failures can only
be surmised. Was it that he could not afford to pay? Or was
it because of lack of suitable connections in the royal household or at the Court of Augmentations? Oswald Sysson, who
actually secured a lease of part of Selby Abbey's demesnes in
1540, did so through the good offices of Sir Ralph Sadler
and paid him over £100 for the trouble; the purchasers of
the freehold to the property were first Sir Ralph Sadler and
then Leonard Beckwith. Sadler had connections with Cromwell, Beckwith with the Augmentations.[2] Nevill on the other
hand appears to have had no important connections at
court at this time; he may once have been associated with
Wolsey, and perhaps lost his best chance of getting plums
of this kind when the Cardinal fell from power.

Normally the first move by the Crown towards disposing
of the property of a monastery was the leasing of the site and
demesnes. The Court of Augmentations was neither inclined nor equipped to take over a large number of demesnes
and run them on an entrepreneurial basis as the monasteries
had done. Of the nineteen monastic sites and demesnes in
the West Riding, four were granted or purchased before
any lease was made, the remaining fifteen were leased. Only
eight of the lessees were established Yorkshire gentlemen or
nobles, and of these only three or four were men of whom
it can be said that their principal landed interest was in the
West Riding. Another two of the lessees, Blythman and
Rokeby, were Augmentations officials; the other five were
complete outsiders, all members of the King's household.[3]
Why should such men be interested in West Riding
demesnes? As we shall see shortly, there are reasons for
supposing that the demesnes had not always been properly

[1] *L.P.*, XIII (i), no. 1036; XIII (ii), no. 900; XIV (ii), no. 742.
[2] Cf. *infra*, p. 237.
[3] The five were Robert Pakenham (Kirkstall), Robert Darkenall (Nun Appleton),
William Knevett (Esholt), Hugh Ascue (St. Robert's, Knaresborough) and Peter
Mewtas (St. John's, Pontefract); P.R.O.: E 315/211/f. 62; 212/ff. 78–9, 172; and
213/f. 93.

valued, and it is very likely that there were profits to be made from them: if a lease was tantamount to a royal favour, it is not surprising that those who achieved success were those with most influence at court. Neither is it surprising that only five of the seventeen lessees subsequently purchased the freehold of the lands they had leased; some of them probably sold even the lease as soon as they could do so at a profit.

The most remarkable case in which a West Riding grantee seems to have gained a valuable prize through some kind of political influence is that of Salley Abbey, which was granted with all its lands to Sir Arthur Darcy before the Court of Augmentations had even had time to make a preliminary survey of their value. The full story cannot be told, for Darcy covered his tracks so well that there is hardly any documentary evidence of the deal. The grant was not even made, in the first instance, by letters patent, but by an indenture of 28 March 1536; this has not survived, but is referred to in the statute which passed through Parliament later in the year to confirm it. Further confirmation is found in a patent of 1538, but this adds nothing to our knowledge and probably did not add anything to Darcy's title.[1] The speed with which the grant was made is in itself highly suspicious. Our suspicions are to some extent confirmed by two letters written in the summer of 1537. First, Darcy wrote to Cromwell to protest against a suggestion to resurvey his lands at Salley, and defending himself against an allegation that he had deceived the King. He pleaded that he never knew what the land was worth until it was granted to him, and offered to bring up his rentals if the King asked for them. The second letter was also to Cromwell, from Robert Southwell who had been instructed to make the new survey of the Salley estate. He reported that an informer had alleged the true value of the estate to be £600, whereas Darcy himself said it was worth only about £465. Southwell thought Darcy credible enough and Cromwell appears to have agreed, for no further action was taken.[2] But even if Darcy's assertion was correct, the question must still be

---

[1] *Statutes*, iii, 27 Henry VIII, cap. 54; *L.P.*, XIII (i), no. 1115 (13).
[2] *L.P.*, XII (ii), nos. 59, 204 (p. 89).

asked why Salley Abbey was dissolved at all in 1536 if its
lands were worth £465; the statute of that year ordered the
dissolution only of houses with a net income of £200 a year
or less. It is possible of course that the undervaluation was
due to the mistaken cleverness of the Abbot. Or did Darcy
himself not only get the lands at a large profit, but also
arrange for their undervaluation in the first place? These
questions cannot be answered with any confidence. Nor is it
easy to say why Darcy alone amongst the West Riding
gentry, should have been able to pull off a deal like this when
the pleas of men like Gascoigne, Everingham and Nevill,
went unheard. One factor in the situation was Darcy's
position in the King's household and his long years of loyal
service; but is it not possible that his acquisition of Salley
had something to do with his attitude in the Pilgrimage of
Grace, when he seems to have offered very little if any support to his father? Knowing as he did that the elder Darcy
was potentially disloyal, as early as 1534, Cromwell might
well have decided to buy off his son. This cannot be more
than speculation, but it would certainly explain the extreme
peculiarities of the case.

Apart from Salley only five outright grants, or rather
sales, of religious property were made in the West Riding
before the end of 1539. One was to Cromwell himself: the
lordship of Halifax, which was included in the grant of the
whole estate of Lewes Priory to the Secretary immediately
upon its dissolution. Three others were of sites of houses:
Drax, granted to Sir Marmaduke Constable of Everingham;
Nun Monkton, granted to Lord Latimer; and Synningthwaite, granted to the nephew of Sir Thomas Tempest, the
Durham lawyer.[1] These three grants were made in 1538,
and seem to have been normal sales. The fifth grant, the
only one of 1539, was of Appletreewick lordship to Sir
Christopher Hales, Master of the Rolls.[2] The general policy
of selling off the freehold right in ex-monastic property did
not develop until the very end of 1539 when the first regular
commission for the disposal of religious lands was issued to
Cromwell and Rich. It ordered them to sell lands to the

[1] *L.P.*, XIII (i), nos. 1519 (65), 384 (54 and 74); (ii), no. 1182 (34).
[2] *L.P.*, XIV (i), no. 1354 (57).

annual value of £6,000.[1] Others followed in similar vein before the end of the reign, and the method was imitated by Henry's successors. All grants (that is, sales) made by these commissions were recorded on the patent rolls, and the number of entries involving West Riding land will give some idea of the volume of sales in different years. There were twelve in 1540, and during the following six years the number fluctuated between six and eighteen, the peak being reached in 1545. The total annual value of the religious property alienated by the Crown between 1536 and the end of 1546 was £3,025. Of this, land and spiritualia granted back to the Church was worth £455 a year; and the grants to Sir Arthur Darcy and Lord Cromwell, for which there is no evidence of any payment being made, were worth £360. For the remaining £2,210 worth of land, the Crown received about £37,470 in purchase money.

The procedure to be followed by a would-be purchaser, and the way in which the price was decided upon, have been the subject of investigations by Dr. Youings and Professor Habakkuk.[2] The first step for someone wishing to buy a specific parcel of land was to approach the Court of Augmentations with a request. Thereupon the auditors would make a valuation of the land and fix a price for it. For most kinds of property the minimum purchase price in the remaining years of Henry VIII's reign was twenty years' value; for urban tenements with no land attached, it was only ten or fifteen years' value. There was a tendency for the figure to rise above the twenty years' purchase as time went on, probably in order to allow for increases in value which the auditors could not represent in terms of annual income; by the later part of the century thirty years' purchase had become normal. But there were certain types of property where valuation in terms of an annual figure was never possible, notably woodlands and advowsons. In these cases an estimate of capital value was made and a price was based on that. If the would-be purchaser found that he could afford to

---

[1] L.P., XIV (ii), no. 780 (36); cf. XV, no. 436 (38) and XIX (i), no. 278 (5).
[2] J. A. Youings: 'The Terms of the Disposal of the Devon Monastic Lands, 1536–58', Eng. Hist. Rev., lxix (1954), 18–38; and H. J. Habakkuk: 'The Market for Monastic Property, 1539–1603', Econ. Hist. Rev., 2nd ser. x (1958), 362–80.

pay the price fixed, a patent was issued granting the property
to him in perpetuity; he then entered into possession. The
purchase money was often paid in one lump-sum, but sometimes a series of instalments over several years was permitted.[1] In addition, it was normal for the Crown to reserve
to itself an annual rent of one tenth of the yearly value of
the lands granted; this practice continued at least until the
end of Henry's reign. And the patent usually stated that the
property was to be held from the King in chief by knight
service, from the manor of East Greenwich or from some
other royal lordship, which meant that the new owner was
liable to the full rigours of royal wardship. (In 1544 urban
tenements and all parcels worth under £2 were excluded
from the latter rule.) These arrangements are a salutary
reminder that the term 'ownership' can still not be used in
its most modern sense when speaking of the Henrician
period. The insistence on tenure in chief, moreover, had a
further implication, that new owners were not allowed to
alienate their holdings without royal licence, for which the
Hanaper claimed a small fee in order to have it entered on
the patent rolls.

From our point of view this last rule is very convenient, for
it means that the patent rolls record both initial grants (or
sales) and licences for subsequent alienation. The importance
of this lies in the fact that the initial grantee was very often
not the real purchaser. The interval between the grant and
the licence to alienate was sometimes so short that we can
only suppose that the grantee never had any intention
of keeping the land. Two possibilities have been entertained
at different times by historians seeking to explain this
apparent oddity. The first, that the two transactions reflect
speculative profiteering by the initial grantee, is now
regarded with some scepticism. It assumed that the prices
fixed for monastic property in the first instance were lower
than they ought to have been; and it assumed that certain
people had a privileged access to the Court of Augmentations

[1] Of the £11,137 paid by Sir Richard Gresham for lands including Fountains
Abbey, granted in October 1540, half was paid immediately and the rest in five
instalments of £666 13s. 4d., ending in Dec. 1545; P.R.O.: E 315/1/ff. 142–8.
However, three instalments was more usual.

which enabled them to buy lands at a low price and sell them at a realistic one. Dr. Youings and Professor Habakkuk, having reached the conclusion that neither of these assumptions was correct, decided that a second possibility was more likely: namely that the initial grantee was simply acting as agent for the real purchaser, earning a small commission perhaps but not a large profit. Without, for the moment, dismissing the first possible explanation out of hand, let us explore further this idea of the agent. Not all country gentlemen could afford the time, or had the inclination, to travel to London to make arrangements of a complicated legal nature with the auditors of the Court of Augmentations. Those who did not might well entrust the task to agents with special experience of the procedure. Many of the agents, it is true, seem to have acted only once or twice and were probably working for friends or relatives. But a few appear to have specialized in this line of business and to have made their services available to a wider clientele in a particular part of the country. Since the Crown seems to have been more anxious to dispose of small parcels of property than whole manors, the activities of such men was probably encouraged by the Court of Augmentations, for they would enable small country families to acquire property which they might not have been able to purchase had it meant a trip up to London and complicated legal procedures. It so happens that one of the most prominent of these regular agents was a West Riding man, whose career can be recounted in some detail.

William Ramsden belonged to a small yeoman family in the country round Halifax. In 1531 he married Joan Wood, one of the heiresses of John Wood of Longley (near Almondbury), and when Wood died in 1540 Ramsden inherited a portion of his estate, worth about £11 a year.[1] He subsequently made a number of small purchases and sales of land in that locality, which no doubt introduced him to the procedures of conveyancing; later on, between 1544 and 1548 he acquired the leases of a number of watermills on Crown estates in the area. A survey of his property in 1548

[1] Ramsden Deeds, Huddersfield Library: Series ii, no. 4 (N.R.A. Calendar); P.R.O.: C 142/62/33; *Feet of Fines*, Y.A.S.R.S., ii, pp. 100, 116–7, 120.

showed that he had in his possession lands worth £48 a year
(not counting the leases), of which £22 went to the payment
of various annuities.[1] If this were all we knew of him we
should put him down as a rising landlord who succeeded in
moving his family up from the yeoman class to the lesser
gentry. But we know more. The first occasion when Ramsden's name appeared on the patent rolls was in June 1543,
when he was one of two grantees to receive lands to the
value of £1,175 (purchase price). The other man was
Richard Andrews of Hales, in Gloucestershire, who already
had some experience as an intermediate purchaser of monastic property.[2] Most of the lands in this block grant were
situated in Yorkshire and that presumably is why Andrews
wanted the participation of a Yorkshireman. Why he chose
Ramsden is something we shall never know. Between that
date and 1546 Ramsden was recipient of four more grants:
on one occasion he acted alone; on the others, in collaboration with three other Yorkshiremen, Edward Hoppey of

TABLE XVIII

Property granted to William Ramsden, 14 September 1544	Details of alienation	
	Date	Purchaser
Sites of two friaries and other land in Northampton	15 Sept. 1544	Francis Samwell
Messuage in Saxton	15 Sept. 1544	William Hammond
Carr House Grange, Greasbrough	16 Dec. 1544	Hugh Wirrall
Land in Horton and Bolling	14 March 1545	Richard Lister
Lands in Welbourne (North Riding)	15 Sept. 1544	Richard Stansfield (part)
	15 Feb. 1545	Thomas Savell (part)
Loscoe Grange	15 Sept. 1544	Richard Bunney
A messuage in Pudsey	15 Sept. 1544	Thomas Smith
Land in Briercliffe and Extwistle (Lancashire)	15 Sept. 1544	Robert Parker
Lands in Dodworth and Hoyland Swain	March, 1545	Robert Thwaites of Barnby (part) and
Land in Thurlstone	28 Nov. 1560	Richard and John Nichols
Further land in Welbourne (N.R.)	28 Nov. 1544	Thomas Barcroft
Land in Hartshead and Huddersfield	No information	
Tithes of Quarmby	No information	

Sources: Letters and Papers XIX, ii, 340 (26) for grant; ibid: 340 (60); 690 (67); 800 (36); XX: i, 282 (52); 465 (101); XX, ii, 707 (52); and *Cal. Patent Rolls, Elizabeth,* 1560–3, p. 53.

[1] P.R.O.: E 36/161/f. 63.   [2] *L.P.,* XVIII (i), no. 981 (9).

Halifax, Ralph Wise of Redehouse, and Richard Vavasour of Ripon, all men of a social status similar to his own. Altogether, the five grants in which Ramsden was involved had purchase prices totalling £6,715, so that although many of the individual parcels included were very small, the whole operation was on a quite large scale.[1] Many of the items were alienated almost at once, others after an interval: in some cases we do not have a record of the alienation, because after 1544 no licence was necessary for the resale of items worth under £2 a year. In order to illustrate Ramsden's activities, Table XVIII summarizes the information available concerning the grant which he received (alone) on 14 September 1544. One of these items can be set against a background of more detailed documentation. In August 1543, probably not long after Ramsden had returned to the West Riding to dispose of his first grant, he and one Robert Whittel of Elland made an agreement with Richard Lister, a Halifax mercer. Ramsden and Whittel were bound in £100 to deliver to Lister a lawful estate in the messuage and land at Little Horton, worth 44s. a year, 'in such form as the said William [Ramsden] has delivered to divers other persons', and after the form used in the Court of Augmentations. The bond was not fulfilled until 14 March 1545 when Ramsden obtained a licence to alienate to Lister lands in Horton and Bolling.[2] The significant feature of these arrangements is that the agreement was made quite a while before Ramsden obtained the grant of the lands concerned, and before he paid for them. In cases such as this the purchase money was raised by securing advance payment from a client. But other items were probably not spoken for in advance, and in those cases the agent may well have been taking a risk in the hope of finding a purchaser and making a worthwhile profit.

However, before we jump to the conclusion that this was the way in which William Ramsden found the money to buy estates for himself and advance the fortunes of his own family, another piece of evidence must be taken into account. In March 1545 he was appointed by the Court of Augmen-

---

[1] *L.P.*, XIX (ii), no. 340 (26); XX (i), no. 1081 (28); XX (ii), no. 707 (27); XXI (i), no. 718 (4).

[2] *West Yorkshire Deeds*, Bradford Hist. Soc., ii, 27–8; *L.P.*, XX (i), no. 465 (101).

tations to be bailiff of Tadcaster (the former Percy lordship) and woodward of all the Court's woodlands within the receivership of Yorkshire. Seven years later Robert Henneage, Master of the King's Woods in the North Parts, conducted an enquiry into sales and spoils of wood in Yorkshire since Ramsden took up his duties, and miraculously the record of the depositions has survived.[1] They indicate in all three Ridings a long list of occasions when Ramsden or his deputy felled trees and sold them. In none of the years since 1545 had he accounted to the Court for his sales, and it was reckoned that for the West Riding alone he owed £460. We do not know what punishment was visited on Ramsden for his misdemeanours, if any at all; it may be that in the end he was able to pay all he owed, or perhaps he bribed someone to drop proceedings. But whatever happened afterwards, Henneage's discovery means that the woodward must have had in his hands large sums of money embezzled from royal funds between 1545 and 1552. Even if he was not allowed to keep them, he may well have used them in the interval to make purchases of land, for sale at a profit. Or he may have succeeded in preventing the enquiry of 1552 from discovering the full extent of his gains. His rise may therefore have been as much a consequence of his office as of his operations as an agent buying and selling monastic land. In either case his career shows what could be achieved by a small man with the ability and energy to take advantage of the opportunities created by the Dissolution.

If even the apparently innocent activities of agents leads us back to the theme of peculation and profit, we cannot dismiss without further enquiry the possibility that some men were able to make even larger profits out of the disposal of the religious confiscations. Three examples will serve to revive the suspicion that there were indeed opportunities for such gains, and the third will take us much further towards a proper understanding of the situation. The first amounts only to circumstantial evidence. It concerns the grant received in March 1540 by James Gage, a Sussex man and a member of the royal household, of the site and demesnes of Healaugh Priory for which he paid the usual purchase

[1] L.P., XX (i), pp. 673, 676; Gascoigne Coll., Leeds City Library: GC/Fo/2.

price of twenty times the annual value. A month later he sold the same to Sir Arthur Darcy, who already held the rectory and some lands at Tadcaster nearby and who may at that time have intended to keep Healaugh; later he returned the rectory to the Crown as part of an exchange. In December 1540 Darcy resold Healaugh to Sir Thomas Wharton. But Wharton had been lessee of this same property ever since the house was dissolved in 1536: if he wanted the freehold why did he not purchase it directly from the Crown? Why did it have to pass through the hands of two other men before it came to him? We have no information about the prices paid on the later transactions, but it seems most unlikely that either Gage or Darcy would have been involved at all had there not been some profit to be made.[1] The second example is a much clearer case, and again it concerns Sir Arthur Darcy. When Sir Christopher Hales bought Appletreewick for £314 in July 1539 he probably had no serious intention of keeping it. In October of the same year he conveyed it to Thomas Proctor and his heirs for a thousand marks (£667), more than twice what he had paid. But then a month or so later Proctor sold the lands to Sir Arthur Darcy for whom he had been acting in the earlier transaction. Then something went wrong: perhaps Darcy failed to pay as much as Proctor had expected. For whatever reason, Proctor refused to recognize the validity of the second conveyance and Darcy had to sue him in Chancery to have it enforced. The case was not finally settled until 1546 when a foot of fine regularized the transfer of title from Proctor to Darcy.[2] Darcy, moreover, seems to have wanted Appletreewick for himself for he added it to his permanent estate. Clearly he was not always in the most advantageous position to get what he wanted, and by 1540 he had lost any political importance he may have had in 1536.

The third example takes us into the question of Leonard Beckwith's dubious activities as Receiver of the Augmentations in Yorkshire. But to begin with let us look at the circumstances of his acquisition of the site and demesnes of Selby Abbey. He bought the freehold of this property in

[1] *L.P.*, XV, nos. 436 (50), 611 (33); XVI, no. 379 (1).
[2] *L.P.*, XIV (i), no. 1354 (57); P.R.O.: C 1/1117/3; Y.A.S.R.S., ii, p. 120.

December 1540 from Sir Ralph Sadler of Hackney, who four months earlier had paid £736 for the grant from the Court of Augmentations. Immediately after the original purchase Sadler had leased the demesnes to Oswald Sysson and it was later alleged that he bought the property primarily in order to do just this, Sysson having agreed to pay Sadler £100 for his services in the matter. The reason we know this is that almost as soon as he became owner of the demesnes Leonard Beckwith came into conflict with Sysson. In 1544 the conflict came to a head when Sysson joined with the farmer of Selby Mills, John Beverley, to lodge a series of informations against Beckwith in the Court of Augmentations, which had jurisdiction in disputes affecting former religious estates.[1] As a result much dirty linen was washed in public, to the embarrassment of Beckwith no doubt, but to the advantage of the historian. Having made the lease to Sysson, it would seem that Sadler had no further use for the land and he told his servant Henry Whitereason to dispose of it as he would; the only condition he laid down was that Whitereason should obtain a price of at least £110 more than the price paid to the Augmentations. Whitereason said afterwards that he could not raise so much money himself, even though he enquired into the state of the woods at Selby and into the opportunities for selling profitable leases. Since he could not afford to buy the land for himself, he sold it to Beckwith, who was said to have paid £1,040 for it. Whitereason's evidence takes us thus far, and shows that whilst the King was paid only £736 for Selby, Sadler and Whitereason between them obtained a profit of £304 on the resale; and Sadler got an additional £100 for the sale of Sysson's lease. Sysson's accusations, however, were even more damaging to Beckwith, for according to him the real purchase value of the estate was in the region of £2,500. This was because the estate granted in the patent included a large acreage of woodland which had been omitted from the survey used by the auditors to calculate the price. Sysson further alleged that Beckwith knew of

[1] *L.P.*, XV, nos. 1027 (40); XVI, no. 379 (40); P.R.O.: E 315/113 and 125. Cf. G. W. O. Woodward: 'A Speculation in Monastic Lands', *Eng. Hist. Rev.*, lxxi (1964), 778–83.

this, even if he was not responsible for it in the first instance. If this was true it was a remarkably skilful piece of fraud, of a kind probably only open to someone with an official position in the Augmentations administration. Beckwith denied the charge, and countered it with his own allegation that such undervaluation as had occurred in the making of the survey was achieved by Sysson himself, who already at that time intended to be the lessee. The latter's reply to that was that the woodlands were not included in his lease, and that he had no connections with the people who made the survey which might have enabled him to influence them in their work.

Nor did Beverley and Sysson stop there. They made a whole list of other charges affecting lands elsewhere, and also challenged Beckwith's conduct as receiver. At Woollas, near Bolton Percy, Beckwith was said to have repeated the fraud he had committed at Selby, by obtaining the woods of the manor there for only £60 when they were really worth £320. In this case Beckwith sought to shift the blame for undervaluation onto Sir William Fairfax of Steeton who, he said, had been eager to obtain the manor of Woollas for himself. As receiver Beckwith was accused of having made illicit profits from the sale of monastic lead; that is, the lead from religious buildings. They specified a number of instances. One of the receiver's tricks had been to weigh the lead from the friaries at Beverley and Hull by troy weight instead of bringing it to be weighed at the royal cranes, so that whoever bought the lead would be able to make a profit by selling it at the official weight: the purchaser being in this case Beckwith's own brother William. The weight of evidence against Beckwith seems very convincing, much more so than his replies to the charges. But he does not appear to have suffered any serious penalty, and in 1546 he became a member of the Council in the North and also Treasurer of Boulogne. The reason for his escape has puzzled several writers on the case, but Professor Slavin seems to have found the simple explanation: that Beckwith used his influence with Sadler to have the proceedings quashed.[1]

---

[1] A. J. Slavin: *Politics and Profit, A study of Sir Ralph Sadler 1507-47* (Cambridge 1966), p. 198.

The evidence concerning Leonard Beckwith, William Ramsden, and Sir Arthur Darcy suggests an atmosphere in which ruthless men could make considerable profits, and in which connections could be used not merely as the path to opportunity but also as a way of covering up fraud. On the other hand there is every indication that the King was anxious to improve the efficiency of his administration on all fronts, and the opportunities arose from loopholes in a system which was far less lax than that of a century before. What we have, it would seem, is a situation of bureaucratic corruption rather than one of royal largesse. Apart from the embezzlement of royal revenues, most of the opportunities to which the Dissolution gave rise turned on the valuation of land rather than its price. Where land was accurately valued, prices fixed at the rate of twenty years' purchase were likely to be realistic; and this was probably the case with lands from which the monasteries had drawn income in the form of rents. But in the case of sites and demesnes there was no such straightforward rental value. The King's surveyors had to make their own estimate of how much the land was worth. A letter written by Archbishop Cranmer to Lord Cromwell in 1538 or 1539 shows that contemporaries were well aware of the shortcomings of surveyors.[1] The Archbishop wanted one of his servants to have 'preferment' to the demesnes of Pontefract Priory, which probably meant the lease and not an outright grant. To support his claim he observed that the estate was not likely to be much sought after by suitors, by reason of the fact that 'the landes are valewed to the uttermoste'. When the priory was finally dissolved it is noticeable that its demesnes were amongst the last to be leased, though we do not know whether in fact Cranmer's servant was the actual lessee. It is possible to test Cranmer's observation against the Augmentations records. The survey made about the time of the suppression shows that on the demesne of Pontefract Priory the surveyor returned valuations equivalent to an average of 1s. per acre of arable, 3s. per acre of meadow, and 3s. 2½d. per acre of pasture. This last figure is remarkably high, but even the others are much higher than was usual in the West Riding. Compare them for

[1] P.R.O.: SP 1/129/ff. 157–8: *L.P.*, XIII (i), no. 369.

17

example, with the valuations in the survey of Nun Monkton Priory's demesnes: arable at 5*d*. an acre, meadow at 2*s*. 7½*d*. and pasture at only 6*d*.[1] The differences are too great to be due entirely to differences in the quality of the soil. More-over, the average valuation per acre on the demesne of twelve West Riding houses were 8*d*. for an acre of arable, 2*s*. for meadow and 11*d*. for pasture. Cranmer almost certainly knew that undervaluation was a common practice and that Pontefract was unusual amongst Yorkshire houses in having been, relatively speaking, valued realistically. Surely few lessees in the Riding can have made no profit at all.

Occasionally even more direct evidence is to be found. In three cases the values of the Augmentations surveys can be compared with accounts made after the land had been sold, and in all three the rents paid to the new owners were more than the estimated values. Nor was the interval very great, for all three belong to the years 1544–5. The figures speak for themselves:[2]

	Valuation 1539–40	Income 1544–45
Bolton Priory demesne: (Earl of Cumberland)	£53	£116
Fountains Abbey demesne: (Sir Rd. Gresham)	£446	£550
Monk Bretton demesne: (William Blythman)	£28	£55

It may be of some significance that in all three cases the farmer of the demesne was the subsequent purchaser, or else there was no lease at all before the freehold was sold. At Fountains, not all the land included in these figures had been in the hand of the Abbot in 1539, but even where there was a tenant Gresham was sometimes able to raise the rents in 1541; the increase there may be deceptive, however, for sometimes the Abbot insisted that his farmers keep stock belonging to the monks on their farms, and if Gresham

[1] P.R.O.: SC 6/Hen VIII/4584, 7453; E 315/401.
[2] P.R.O.: SC 6/Hen VIII/4542, 4452, 4539; Skipton Castle MSS, Y.A.S. Library: DD 121/Bundle 29; Surtees Soc. xlii, 396 ff (Vyner MS 5501); P.R.O.: E 150/241/25.

TABLE XIX

Purchasers of Confiscated Property in the West Riding, 1536–46.

Purchaser	Annual value of purchase 1546	Family circumstances	Other sources of capital
Earl of Cumberland	£175	Head of noble family; increased estates by marriage	—
Earl of Shrewsbury	£152	Head of noble family	—
Sir Arthur Darcy	£300?	Younger son of a nobleman; married daughter of a City man	Office, royal service
John Nevill, Lord Latimer	£105	Head of noble family in North Riding	—
Sir Thomas Wharton	£40	Head of Westmorland family	—
Sir Marmaduke Constable, senior	£21	Younger son of East Riding family; married heiress of Sir John Sotehill	—
Sir Thomas Tempest (for his nephew Richard)	£12	Younger son of family in Durham	Common lawyer
Sir Thomas Legh	£71	Possibly of a Cheshire family, not its head	Civil lawyer, and royal servant
Sir Leonard Beckwith	£58	Son (younger?) of East Riding minor gentry family; married heiress of London lawyer	Common lawyer; Augmentations official
William Blythman	£50	Possibly younger son of minor family in Durham	Civil lawyer; Augmentations official
James Rokeby	£17	Possibly younger son of minor North Riding family	Augmentations official
Sir Richard Gresham	£450	Of a Norfolk family	London finance
Robert Fermour	£25	Of a Midland family	London merchant
Richard Pymond	£50	Uncertain, but of West Riding origins	Wakefield merchant
Hugh Wirrall	£7	Head of town family, with lands	Son of Doncaster merchant
Henry Goodrick	£71	Younger son of a Lincolnshire family; married daughter of a Merchant of the Staple	?
Sir Gervaise Clifton	£36	Head of Nottinghamshire family	—
Sir William Fairfax	£14	Head of a West Riding family	—
Sir George Darcy	£15	Head of West Riding family, but son of an attainted nobleman; married heiress of Sir John Melton	—

TABLE XIX (*cont.*)

Purchaser	Annual value of purchase 1546	Family circumstances	Other sources of capital
John Tempest	£9	Younger son of a West Riding family	—
Arthur Kay	£23	Head of West Riding family	—
Walter Paslew	£13	Head of West Riding family	—
William Hungate	£13	Head of East Riding family	—
John Storres	£14	Head of West Riding family	—
John Lambert	£7	Of West Riding family, probably head	Lawyer?
Brian Sandforth	£7	Head of West Riding family	—
Richard Paver	£34	West Riding yeoman, who married a minor gentry heiress	—
Thomas Stevenson	£7	West Riding yeoman	—
William Dyneley	£8	West Riding yeoman	—

abolished this practice he was effectively increasing the size of some of the holdings. But the two other examples are not complicated by considerations of that kind: they show clear increases in value of about 100 per cent, which would mean that at 20 years' purchase (based on the Augmentations estimate), the new owners would have recovered their money in ten years. On the other hand the great majority of rents paid by customary tenants on these estates remained unchanged: the only scope for profit there was by raising fines on new entries, a practice which by this time was becoming normal on private estates.

V

The disposal of monastic lands, like the land market generally, depended on there being people with the inclination and the wherewithal to make purchases. In looking at the procedure for the sale of lands by the Court of Augmentations, and the opportunity for profit that sometimes existed, we have already identified some of the purchasers. But they were not necessarily the most typical amongst those who bought such property, and in order to place the information so far given into a better perspective, we must

make a more general survey of the picture. Table XIX is
a list of twenty-nine men who bought religious property in
the West Riding before the end of 1546 and who either still
held it at that date or died earlier. It includes all those who
made substantial acquisitions (of land or spiritualities worth
£20 a year and upwards), but only a sample of the smaller
purchasers. A group who are not represented at all are those
people, mainly yeomen, or perhaps even copyholders, who
made very small purchases. One of them was Richard Lister
of Halifax whom we have seen negotiating with William
Ramsden to obtain a small parcel of property at Horton
and another at Bolling. That such men were buying more
land is a reflection of the social atmosphere in which they
lived, but their purchases did not greatly affect the overall
pattern of landownership. (Nor does the table include a
transaction which occurred between Thomas Malleverer of
Allerton Mauleverer and the Provost and Scholars of King's
College, Cambridge: in 1544 they sold to him their manor
at Allerton, a highly unusual example of a sale by an ecclesiastical institution to a layman, and so far as I know unique
in the West Riding at this period.[1])

The question at issue is why these twenty-nine families
should have acquired land, when so many others did not.
If we look at the list of subsidy assessments in 1546, we can
find as many as 133 inhabitants of the West Riding taxed
on lands worth upwards of £20 a year. Only fifteen were in
any way connected with the disposal of monastic property.
Again, taking the evidence used for the compilation of the
tables in Chapter II, it would seem that about eighty
gentry families with freehold incomes of £40 a year or more
owned land in the West Riding, although they did not all
live there. Of these eighty only four appear in Table XIX,
and there is no evidence that any others amongst them
bought any monastic land before 1546. The question why
twenty-nine people bought land therefore has its obverse
side: why did a hundred and more established gentry
families in the Riding fail to make any purchase? A large
part of the answer may well be simply that they did not want
to do so: one cannot assume that the desire for more land

[1] *L.P.*, XIX (i), nos. 113, 141 (29).

was universal. Land was but one aspect of gentility in Tudor England and those who already had an ample estate probably did not attach very high priority to the acquisition of more. A man who would show his worth to his neighbours must keep a fine house and good hospitality, and such things were not cheap at a time of inflation. The people most likely to spend their money on land were those still rising on the social scale, for whom land was the prerequisite of acceptance into the gentry. The idea seems to find confirmation in the table. Six of the people there were lawyers or professional accountants, and another four were merchants or financiers: all men who had risen in the world in their own lifetimes, by their own efforts combined with a measure of royal favour. A number of the others were lesser gentry or yeomen whose sense of thrift and desire to better themselves had not yet been submerged in the desire to prove their gentility by lavish expenditure on good living. Of the rest, at least four were younger sons of established families, and in a land of primogeniture that often meant making one's own way in the world with only limited support from the head of the family. There was thus a diminishing marginal propensity to spend money on land, the higher one moved up the social scale, though it will hardly explain why three noblemen should have come to be in the list.

Nor will it explain why those who wrote begging letters to Cromwell at the time of the Dissolution did not, on the whole, become purchasers of any of the land which came onto the open market after 1540. Desire for land was not the only factor in the situation. It was also necessary to have the money to pay for it, especially where—as in most cases—the valuation and the price fixed by the Court of Augmentations were perfectly reasonable and did not allow much scope for resale at a profit. Where the opportunity for profit did arise, the further factor of competition for spoils enters into the picture, and there the man who had influence at court or a position in the Augmentations itself was at an advantage over the country gentleman who had influence in his own county but not so much at Westminster. What Gascoigne and Nevill were no doubt seeking when they wrote to the King's secretary in 1536 or 1537 was grace and favours: in that they were disappointed. It was the Beckwiths and the Blythmans who were lucky, for the most part; or else it was the men whom Henry VIII wanted to reward for their loyalty in the crisis of 1536–7, or to strengthen because he was sure of their loyalty in the future. Six of the people named in Table XIX may be described as in some measure 'political' grantees, whilst a seventh may have had a political motive for obtaining the land he bought. The case of Sir Arthur Darcy, who received the largest of these grants and probably got the most favourable terms has already been referred to. He was a man in a strategic political position in 1536, and this must surely have something to do with his success, even if the particular suggestion made earlier is rejected. He was also a man looking for advancement, for he was one of the younger sons who had to make their own way. He entered royal service about 1518, and in 1532 he was reminding Cromwell that for his fourteen years of faithful service he had had only small rewards (including, incidentally, a few grants of wardships).[1] When his moment came he was able to establish an estate of his own worth as much as that which his father shortly afterwards lost. The Earl of Cumberland and the Earl of Shrewsbury were also men of key importance in 1536; indeed, but for their loyalty the crisis would have been much greater and its outcome far less sure. Cumberland wanted the estates of Bolton Priory, which his ancestors had founded, and he was allowed to buy most of them. It was so much to the King's advantage that he should be strengthened in this way that he was even allowed £1,000 towards the purchase price, calculated as usual at twenty years' value. The situation is analogous to that in Devon where the King made an outright gift of an extensive estate to Lord Russell in order to buttress his position in the West Country.[2] By the time he died in 1542 the first Earl of Cumberland, having added the Percy fee as well as Bolton to his patrimony, was in control of over

---

[1] *L.P.* V, no. 1288. In 1524 he had received an annuity of £20 from Brierley (W.R.), during the minority of Lord Mounteagle's heir (IV, i, no. 1298); in 1531 he had the wardship of Walter Strickland with an annuity of £13. 6s. 8d. (V, no. 80(33)); and in 1535 he got the wardship of the heiress of Sir John Dunham with an annuity of £40 (VIII, no. 802 (4)).

[2] J. A. Youings, art. cit., p. 23.

a third of all the land in the wapentake of Staincliffe. Shrewsbury's acquisitions, in Yorkshire at least, were less spectacular: but the lordship of Rotherham was nonetheless a valuable addition to the Talbot domains in Hallamshire and Strafforth.

John, Lord Latimer's grant of Nun Monkton's estates in February 1538 (at the usual purchase price) is less easily explicable in these terms, for his loyalty in 1536 was marred by a lengthy hesitation. He was said to be out of favour in the middle of 1537, and was forced to surrender his London house to the King.[1] But by the time of the grant he seems to have satisfied Henry that he would be trustworthy for the future. The growing importance of York as a focus of Northern politics may well explain Latimer's desire for an estate near to the city. The same consideration seems to have been in the mind of Sir Thomas Tempest, sergeant at law and a member of all the Councils in the North from 1525. He was the third of four sons of the Tempest family which lived at Holmeside, County Durham, and in 1538 neither he nor his nephew Robert seemed to have any hope of ever succeeding to the family inheritance. He became an influential lawyer, and it was in this capacity that he served on the Council. In 1537 he complained in a letter to Cromwell that he found regular attendance at York expensive, and a month later he got the lease of Synningthwaite Priory, which was well situated for frequent visits to that city. The following year he converted his title into a freehold one by purchasing the same property in the name of his nephew.[2]

The sixth of the 'political' purchasers was Sir Marmaduke Constable the elder. Younger son of old Sir Marmaduke Constable of Flamborough (died 1518), he had by this time acquired Everingham and other manors by his marriage to the heiress of Sir John Sothill. Sothill's ancestors had been the founders of Drax Priory, and this was no doubt one reason why Constable wanted to buy the site and demesne of that house. But it was his political soundness, not his claim as heir to the 'founder', that got him the preferment: in this he contrasts sharply with his brother Sir Robert

---

[1] *L.P.*, XII (ii), no. 14.
[2] *L.P.*, XII (ii), no. 152. Sir Thomas died in 1546; P.R.O.: E 150/241/11.

Constable who supported Darcy in the affairs of 1536-7.[1]
Sir Robert's son, Sir Marmaduke Constable the younger,
might have made his own excursion into the monastic land
market, for he had obtained a lease of Nun Monkton and
its demesnes in September 1536; but any plans he may have
had to convert this into a freehold title were thwarted by his
father's attainder and execution. Another man who wanted
an estate in the Ainsty because of the political development
of York was Sir Thomas Wharton, also a member of the
Council in the North, whose main estates lay far afield.[2]
Wharton, created a baron in 1544, did not make his purchase
of Healaugh Priory direct from the Crown, and as we have
seen he may have had to pay more for it than the Augmentations price. He had already got the lease as early as July
1536, which may well have been a small bribe in view of the
political situation, and in view of his loyalty later in the year
it is a little surprising that he was not able to secure a grant of
the freehold of his estate directly from the Crown. Certainly
it was to the King's advantage to strengthen this man's hand
in Yorkshire, and that was the result of the purchase.
Wharton's interest in the Healaugh lands arose from the fact
that some years earlier, as a favourite of the sixth Earl of
Northumberland, he had received a gift of the Percy estates
in Healaugh and Catterton. He was therefore in a sense heir
to the founder of the nearby priory.

The next four names are those of what might be called
'administrative' grantees: men whose connections with the
movement against the monasteries before 1536, or with the
Court of Augmentations after that date, made them almost
inevitable purchasers of monastic property. Three of them
we have already met: Leonard Beckwith, William Blythman
and James Rokeby. The fourth, Sir Thomas Legh, is well
enough known for his part in the visitations of 1535 and for
his public career thereafter. Between them these eleven
'political' and 'administrative' men bought lands worth
£950 a year: a substantial proportion of the total amount of

[1] Sir Marmaduke Constable the elder actually sat on the commission to suppress
the lesser religious houses in Yorkshire in 1536, and remained loyal in the Pilgrimage
of Grace; *L.P.*, X (i), no. 721 (5); XI, nos. 581, 728, 1046.
[2] His career is recounted in the *Dictionary of National Biography*.

revenue which passed from the Church to private lay ownership during these years.

Another group of men who made some substantial
purchases were merchants and financiers, four of whom come
next in the table. A fifth man who might almost be counted
in this group was Henry Goodrick, a younger son from a
Lincolnshire house, whose career is meagrely documented
but whose marriage to the daughter of Christopher Rawson,
merchant of the Staple, probably means that it was city
money which enabled him to buy Ribston Preceptory.[1]
The largest purchase of all in the West Riding before 1546
was that of Fountains Abbey and much of its central estate
by Sir Richard Gresham. He was one of the richest men in
London in 1540, as well as one of the most influential in
matters of government finance, and his career need hardly
be recapitulated here. Coming as he did from Norfolk, he
had no known interest in Yorkshire lands before this time,
and one can only assume that he bought Fountains because
he believed it would prove a lucrative investment. All the
evidence suggests that it was.[2] Robert Fermour, a leather-
seller and warden of his company in 1540 and 1547, bought
property in various parts of England and his interest in the
West Riding was likewise that of an investor: he bought
the manor of Hambleton, valued at £25 in 1540 but at £43
by 1549.[3] At this point it is worth mentioning another
transaction involving city men which does not appear in the
table. In August 1540 the Crown made a series of grants of
monastic property as security for a loan: that is, a royal
mortgage. Two of the patents included West Riding property worth £96 a year.[4] It was stated in each grant that if
the money were repaid within a year it would be null and
void, but as no repayment seems to have taken place the
patents presumably took effect as straightforward grants,
leaving the merchants who had made the loan to divide the
lands amongst themselves. One of the West Riding manors

[1] Surtees Soc., xli, p. 40, and Harleian Soc., xvi, p. 144.
[2] Cf. supra, p. 240, where the increase in value of the estate is referred to.
Gresham's career is covered in detail by the *Dictionary of National Biography*.
[3] P.R.O.: Wards 9/135/f. 103; cf. W. H. Black: *History and Antiquities of the
Worshipful Company of Leathersellers*, p. 64.
[4] *L.P.*, XIX (ii), 166 (45–6).

mortgaged in this way was Bolton-upon-Dearne and in 1574 it was still in the possession of Francis Trappes, heir of the goldsmith Robert Trappes who had participated in the loan.[1]

The other two merchants in the table were Yorkshiremen who were in the process of establishing themselves as landlords: Richard Pymond and Hugh Wirrall. Pymond was a Wakefield merchant who sold a variety of commodities, including wool, cloth, woad, foodstuffs and wine; and if we can believe some of the accusations made against him in proceedings in Chancery he was not above sharp practice in order to advance his fortune. On two occasions he tried to coerce Wakefield dyers into buying woad from him rather than from other merchants, by taking what they regarded as unreasonable legal action against them in connection with their debts. The proceedings suggest a man of some power in Wakefield town affairs, but there are no town records of the period to tell us more about him. He made his first purchase of land in 1528, a tenement in Wakefield, and in 1537 he became farmer of Sandal Park, to which he subsequently added the farm of South Kirkby tithes. Then in 1543-4 he bought some monastic lands in Wakefield together with the rectories of Batley and South Kirkby. This interest in tithes is not surprising, for it was an easy way of obtaining grain supplies which as a merchant he could sell to his own profit. He might, in other circumstances, have founded a new gentry family in the vicinity of Wakefield, but he had no offspring and may not even have been married, so that when he died in 1546 his estate had to be divided amongst his three sisters.[2] Hugh Wirrall has appeared before in this chapter, and as the son of a merchant he was one generation further along the road towards gentility. He was richer than Pymond, having more lands but possibly less valuable goods at the subsidy of 1546.

The remaining thirteen people in the table were established landowners, but not men of great political weight. They ranged in wealth from mere yeomen to substantial gentry. Three were knights. Sir William Fairfax, who was

[1] P.R.O.: Wards 9/140/f. 445.
[2] Y.A.S.R.S., ii, p. 51; L.P., XII (ii), no. 1150 (27); P.R.O.: SC 6/Hen VIII/4579; C 142/74/70.

presumably the real purchaser of the property formally sold to his son Guy, was the son and grandson of judges, and his uncle was Sergeant Thomas Fairfax of Finningley. He was thus the first of his family to be a landed gentleman rather than a lawyer with an estate, and he had not lost the habit of adding to his estate whenever the opportunity arose. His wife was the heiress of John Thwaites of Denton, who left West Riding land worth £70 when he died in 1512, and Sir William bought for his sons not only the monastic site of Nun Appleton and its demesnes, but also the manor of Toulston which his neighbour Sir Oswald Wilstrop was compelled by financial difficulties to sell in 1541.[1] The contrast between Wilstrop and Fairfax in these years epitomizes the contrast between rising and declining families, which probably had more to do with personal wisdom at this period than with great social movements. Another of the three knights was Sir George Darcy, who as the eldest son of Lord Darcy one might expect to have been too well established to have much interest in buying lands. But he was cut off from his father's estates by the attainder of 1537, except for the parks of Rothwell and Roundhay held on perpetual lease. He had married an heiress, the daughter of Sir John Melton, but did not inherit the full Melton estate until 1546 when Sir John died. In the meantime he had purchased several estates: in addition to the religious property for which he is noticed in the table, he bought the manor of Swillington in 1543, and probably other land. By the time he was restored to the barony in 1548 he had an established position and was at least as wealthy as his father had been.[2] Thus as in the case of Fairfax, the Darcy purchases fit into the pattern of a rising family fortune. The third knight was not a West Riding resident but lived just across the Nottinghamshire border at Hodsoke: Sir Gervaise Clifton had, however, a growing interest in Yorkshire, having become Steward of the Crown's lordship of Cowick and Snaith in 1538. He got the lease of St. Mary's Abbey's

[1] P.R.O.: C 142/26/4; Y.A.S.R.S., ii, p. 93. Wilstrop's financial difficulties were alluded to earlier, *supra*, p. 219.

[2] Both Sir George and Lady Dorothy Darcy died in 1558, leaving between them lands in the West Riding valued at £196 a year, and also property in the East Riding. P.R.O.: C 142/116/14 and 57.

demesne at Airmyn in 1540, and the freehold two years later. Its value of £31 a year was not very great by comparison with the estate he had just inherited from his father, which the feodary had declared to be worth £268.[1] Another man who should be placed on much the same level as the knights was John Tempest, the second son of Sir Richard Tempest of Bolling; he was faced with some of the same problems as Sir George Darcy, even though his father was not actually attainted, as well as with the more common problems facing a younger son. He managed to get the farm of several mills in the lordships of Bradford and Slaidburn, where his father had been Steward, in 1539; and two years later he bought ex-monastic land in Wilsden and Cullingworth. A promising start for a younger son, but the sequel is different from many because in 1545 his elder brother Sir Thomas died and John was his heir. Significantly he immediately sold his recent purchases and was content with his family inheritance. About the same time he was knighted, and in due course he followed in his father's footsteps as steward of Wakefield.[2]

At the other end of the scale were the yeomen, like Thomas Stevenson of Whitgift, who bought land that had been in his own tenure there and who was taxed on lands worth £9 in 1546; or William Dyneley of Bramhope, who before he purchased a monastic estate there was assessed on goods worth £10 in 1545 and on lands of £5 in 1546; both bought their land through agents, not as direct recipients of letters patent.[3] The most remarkable case of a rising yeoman was that of Richard Paver. His origins are unknown, but in 1527 he became farmer of the manor of Pannal (a possession of St. Robert's Friary at Knaresborough), and about the same period he married one of the three heiresses of Elizabeth Brigham; she had died in 1519 leaving lands in Braham and Spofforth worth £14 a year or more, so that the marriage must have brought Paver a small estate immediately. By 1543 he was living at Braham and over the next four years he bought out the other shares in the Brigham property from the husbands of the other two

---

[1] *L.P.*, XII (i) no. 795 (13).
[2] Cf. *supra*, p. 158.
[3] *L.P.*, XXI (ii), nos. 200 (50) and 476 (107); P.R.O.: E 179/207/192, 200.

heiresses. In 1543 he bought religious land in the same vicinity, with the result that by 1547 he had an estate worth at least £50 a year. Yet in 1612 his descendant still failed to convince the King's herald of his claim to bear arms: rising into the gentry was after all not so easy as buying land.[1] Other men with £50 a year, like John Lambert of Calton and Arthur Kay of Woodsome, were already established as middling gentry—that is, as esquires. It is a pity that we do not know why they bought land when so many others like them did not do so. The reason must surely have been a combination of personal inclination and family finances. The most curious case is that of Brian Sandforth. Between 1539 and 1545, Brian (acting on the first occasion with his father Edmund) made three mortgage arrangements with William Hewett, a London cloth merchant, the mortgaged property being the manor of Harthill, some other lands there, and the manor of Thorpe Slaven. On its own this might well be interpreted as an indication of financial difficulty. But in 1545 Brian Sandforth bought Thorpe Rignall Grange, which he still held at his death in 1553 along with a reversionary interest in other lands, because his father was still alive. The arrangements of this family must have been very complicated indeed. A Chancery case belonging to a date sometime between 1538 and 1544 offers part of the explanation, for it arose out of a suit by Brian Sandforth against one A. Barley of Derbyshire to obtain moneys promised at the time of his marriage.[2] If he won, he would have money to buy land; but on the other hand he might well have needed to borrow in order to pay for the litigation. The case is a useful reminder that to classify families into 'rising' and 'declining' categories can be highly misleading.

To sum up, the transfer of monastic land to lay ownership did not take place according to any easily identifiable rules. The desire for land, the ability to pay for it, and access to favours, were all factors which might have bearing on particular cases. Sometimes land was purchased in order to

---

[1] P.R.O.: SC 6/Hen VIII/7304; E 150/221/4; Y.A.S.R.S., ii, pp. 116–7 and 128; P.R.O.: E 179/207/191.

[2] P.R.O.: C 1/1063/1–4; Y.A.S.R.S., ii, pp. 87, 117.

strengthen an established family, but the men who chose to do this were in a minority amongst their class. Very often purchases were made either to establish a family on the land for the first time, or to further such an establishment already in progress. Occasionally land was bought just as an invest-ment. However, to quote Tawney, 'the fruits of confiscation do not always rest where they first light'. Once bought, the former religious estates took their place in a land market that was becoming increasingly fluid in the 1530s and 1540s. The analysis which has just been attempted concerns only the period before Henry VIII's death, which was merely a prelude to the era over which there has been most contro-versy. Subsequent development was not necessarily along the same lines as those discussed here. What we have been deal-ing with are the first reactions to the Dissolution, and we must remember that an event with such devastating conse-quences as the suppression of all the English monasteries could take place once and only once.

CONCLUSION

No simple formula will enable us to sum up in a few crisp words the relationship between land and power in the reign of Henry VIII. By the mid-seventeenth century, when Harrington and Hobbes were elaborating their political theories, it was probably true that 'Riches joined with liberality is power, because it procureth friends and servants'.[1] And since property in land was at that time the greatest source of money income, the distribution of property was a major factor in the distribution of power. The relationship was clearly appreciated by Harrington, whose theory of the 'balance of property' was one worthy of the age of geometry in which he lived. But neither property nor money had always played this key role in political life. Historians have criticized frequently the calculations which Tawney made after reading *Oceana*, but all too often they have missed the most important point. Tawney's idea that the social framework of mid-Stuart politics was very different from that of the mid-Tudor period was sound; but statistics of land-ownership were not necessarily the most important feature of the contrast. A great deal of land did change hands in the century before 1640, and it has still to be disproved that at the end of that period the gentry, however defined, had a larger share of the nation's wealth than at the beginning.[2] Yet our analysis of the statistics of land-ownership in the West Riding around 1535 suggests that even before the Dissolution the gentry as a class probably owned as much as half the land of

---

[1] Thomas Hobbes: *Leviathan* (Everyman edition, 1914), p. 43; this is not of course the whole of Hobbes' definition of power, but it is one of the points he places first.

[2] There is one table in the 'gentry controversy', which has so far gone unchallenged, which shows conclusively that 688 manors in thirteen counties belonged in 1558 to families ennobled before 1602; by 1602 those families owned only 456 of these manors, and in 1640 only 329. The number of families involved declined from sixty-four in 1558 to sixty in 1602, and to fifty in 1640. Even so, one can show from these figures that the number of manors owned *per family* fell from 10·75 in 1558 to 7·9 in 1602, and to 6·6 in 1640. L. Stone: 'The Elizabethan Aristocracy —a Restatement', *Econ. Hist. Rev.*, 2nd ser., iv (1951–2), 321.

England, possibly more. It is unlikely that their share rose
to more than three quarters during the century that followed.
The question one must ask is: what power could they enjoy
as owners of 75 per cent of the land of England which they
could not have enjoyed with only 50 per cent, *if everything
else remained the same?* On its own it does not seem likely
that this change would explain very much. But of course
other things did not remain the same, and the changing
'balance of property' must be seen against the background of
other, perhaps more significant changes.

It was not merely the distribution of land which was
being transformed during 'Tawney's century', but the whole
relationship between society and the land. Tawney might
have done better had he explored not the *balance*, but the
very *idea* of property, which was far more clearly defined by
the middle of the seventeenth century than it had been a
century before; indeed one of the reasons for the development
of the concept was the 'rise of capitalism' which so much
interested that author. If one goes far enough back, one
eventually reaches a period when control over the land was
not measurable in money terms, and when the essential
factor in the relationship between land and power was not
property and money income but lordship, tenure and
obligation. It will be recalled that in Chapter II the pattern
of control over land in the West Riding was analysed in
two quite different ways, the first based on the principle of
territorial lordship, the second on the concept of property
and income. In the earlier part of the sixteenth century, both
patterns were found to have some relevance, for it was a
period when England was in the middle of a transition from
the 'medieval' to the 'modern' system of control over land.
The former was characterized by lordship and tenure, and
was a system held together by custom; the latter was a system
whose most important feature was ownership, and whose
economic relationships tended to be determined by specific
contracts. Lordship meant in effect control over people as
well as over land. But the ancient jurisdictions upon which
such control depended had been gradually eroded by the expansion of royal justice, and so lordship was gradually undermined. At the same time, custom began to be undermined

18

by the increasing use of money; and lords demanded money from their tenants more often than the performance of service. One may trace the origins of the trend back to at least the thirteenth century, perhaps the twelfth, but it took several centuries for it to completely transform man's relationship to land. Money tended at first to flow along lines determined by custom and by the framework of lordship, and feudalism was 'bastardized' before it finally declined.[1] It was not until the sixteenth century, when inflation compelled landlords to increase their money income by every means they could, that money began to dominate the system. The changing balance of property was not a fundamental cause of this change, but rather another reflection of it, for with the inflation of prices those who ran into financial difficulty had to sell their land to others who managed their affairs in a more business-like way. Nor was it the flow of property in the land market which most seriously damaged the position of the nobility (or aristocracy) in this transformation. In political terms their most serious loss is to be measured not in terms of a declining number of manors or in declining revenues, but in terms of their loss of authority over people whose ancestors had once been attached by tenure and obligation to great territorial lordships. The gentry, as a social class, originated as the mesne lords of manors whose ultimate lordship had belonged traditionally to the honours and baronies of great noble houses. What happened between the thirteenth and the seventeenth century was that they became emancipated from the 'medieval' system of lordship over land; within the 'modern' system, as property-owners, they became the equals of the nobility before the law, differentiated from them only by the fact that most noblemen had larger estates and more revenues than most gentry. (The nobility of course retained their special position in Parliament and in relation to criminal law.) In the time of Henry VIII the emancipation was not yet complete. One of the features of the 'medieval' system to survive longest was wardship, and if one seeks a terminal date for the transition from medieval to modern land

---

[1] The process was analysed, and the phrase invented, by K. G. McFarlane 'Bastard Feudalism', *Bull. of the Institute of Historical Research*, xx (1943–5).

systems, one will find it in the Parliamentary abolition of
military tenures and of wardship, in 1641. The present
study has sought to demonstrate that the patterns of both
economic and political life in the West Riding in the years
about 1540 are only fully intelligible if they are related to
the much earlier patterns from which they had evolved.
Even on the level of economic activity and the pattern of
production, not all the diversity within the Riding can be
explained in terms of the straightforward effects of physical
geography. The location of rural industries, for example,
seems to have been partly the product of differences in
ancient custom between certain upland areas and the remainder of the Riding, as well as of more specifically
economic factors in the environment. As for the pattern of
politics and control over lordships, the framework had
originally been shaped by the arrangements made in the
aftermath of the Norman Conquest: some features can be
explained only by going back beyond Domesday Book.
That ancient framework was in decline, but its traces are
still to be found in the records of the reign of Henry VIII;
and the very form of the records themselves often reminds
us that they were originally devised by administrators of
the thirteenth and fourteenth centuries. Much that historians have regarded as 'medieval' was still very much alive in
the period with which we have been dealing. Thus Honours
like Pontefract and Knaresborough, although absorbed into
the domains of the Crown, were not yet dead institutions.
They still had castles, supposed to be maintained in some
degree of military preparedness, and as steward of Pontefract a man like Darcy still had the duty of overseeing some
of the military arrangements of the Honour. At Skipton,
again, there was a castle with defences still capable of with-
standing a local siege and with a lord, the Earl of Cumberland, whose 'power and worship' was seldom challenged in
the surrounding Honour. Even where the local castle was in
decay, as at Spofforth, the ancient connection between the
barony and its member-manors was continually being
recorded in such documents as inquisitions *post mortem*, and
some of the holders of those manors were still employed as
officials of the barony by the sixth Earl of Northumberland.

Another feature of territorial lordship to survive into the sixteenth century was the memory that the lord of the castle or barony was often heir to the foundership of the local monastery, and several West Riding men recalled the fact in letters to Cromwell when it looked as though the monasteries might be dissolved.

In the longer term the effect of the development of a monetary economy and of the 'capitalist spirit' would be to make economic interest a conscious motive in politics: Tawney's central purpose indeed was to explain how that came about. But one must be careful how one applies this generalization to landownership. Economic interest tended to break into politics through the activity of organized groups of men with common interests to protect; but it was in the fields of trade and industry that this happened, not in the field of land and agriculture. Already by the reign of Henry VIII, Miss Miller has shown how London merchants and financiers operated a lobby in the House of Commons, which although not very successful in attaining its ends, foreshadowed the growth of more effective business pressure-groups in later reigns.[1] But landowners never had that kind of role in politics: the power which their land gave them, whether by virtue of lordship or of property, was never the power of a pressure group. Their power was (or seemed to be) a part of the natural order of the world. What was changing in the sixteenth century was the way in which they exercised that power, which was indeed conditioned by the economic framework of society.

As far as the power of land was concerned, the most important change was the transformation of territorial lordship, whose decline we have observed, into a more fluid system of patronage depending on access to royal favours and control over appointments to offices: the patronage which was the 'cement of politics' in England from the mid-sixteenth to the later eighteenth centuries. In that system, men's choice of patron depended only to a very limited extent on the tenure of manors from a great

[1] Helen Miller: 'London and Parliament in the Reign of Henry VIII', *Bull. Inst. Hist. Research*, xxxv (1962), 128–49.

territorial magnate, and far more on the power at court or in
the county of a given individual. It was a system which was
often bound up with monetary corruption, and we can
already see the beginnings of it in the activities of men like
Sir Leonard Beckwith after the Dissolution of the monasteries. In the disposal of monastic property we see land not
as a sacred trust but as the object of multifarious transactions
whose ultimate object was to gain more wealth. The King
himself set the trend in motion, for it was in order to
increase his wealth that he dissolved the monasteries in the
first place. The whole sequence of events which followed
the suppressions must be seen as a factor of the greatest
importance in the transformation of men's attitude to land
and wealth. It is a case in which political motive underlay
both economic and political change.

The transitional nature of early sixteenth-century society
is also apparent when we look at the character of opposition
to the Crown. One of Tawney's motives in studying the
balance of property was to discover how and why the Great
Rebellion against Charles I differed in its social dimensions
from the dynastic conflicts of the fifteenth century. A
similar theme occurs in his *Agrarian Problem in the Sixteenth
Century*, where he contrasted two major rebellions of the
sixteenth century: the Pilgrimage of Grace and the rebellion
in Norfolk of 1549. In the latter he found an example of
conflict between the commons and the nobility and gentry
and he related it to the general thesis of his study: that
the inflation of the sixteenth century forced landlords to
respond by raising entry fines, enclosing common lands, and
generally challenging ancient custom, so that traditional
bonds of lordship and natural obedience were strained and
finally broken. In other words, he was trying to see in the
rebellion of 1549 an early example of class conflict. By
contrast the Pilgrimage of Grace, and also the Rising of the
North in 1569, appeared to Tawney as the last examples in
English history of revolt dominated by feudal ties of lordship, in which the commons followed the overmighty
subjects who were their 'feudal' masters. In the Pilgrimage
the commons of central and eastern Yorkshire certainly
ended by accepting the leadership of noblemen, even if they

did not begin by following the secret instructions of Lord
Darcy and the Percy clients. At the same time the evidence
from the North-West supports the idea that even in 1536
there was an element of conflict between lords and commons
over such issues as enclosure and gressums. But this contrast
between the events of 1536 and those of 1549 should not be
emphasized to the exclusion of an attempt to trace back
the 'class-conflict' type of rebellion beyond the sixteenth
century. The first important revolt of that kind was surely
the Peasants' Revolt of 1381, which sprang from an earlier
situation of economic conflict, in which the issues were
villeinage and freedom of labour. It is necessary to push back
the origins of modernity beyond the sixteenth century, as
well as to recognize the survival of medieval features of
lordship well into that century.

There is, however, another sense in which the Pilgrimage
of Grace reflected the transitional nature of society, one which
Tawney did not remark upon. The 'feudal' rebellions of the
fifteenth century were essentially dynastic in motive: that
is to say, their leaders simply wanted to seize the throne,
and no major constitutional issues were involved. But in
1536 there were very important issues of principle at stake,
and one might even say that had events developed in a
different way the Pilgrimage might have been the prelude to
England's first 'war of religion'. It was of course no more
purely religious in character than the wars of sixteenth-
century Germany and France, but without resentment
against Henry VIII's religious policies it would not have
taken the form it did, and might even not have happened at
all. The issues were not yet so clear-cut as they became later
in the century, and it was still possible for a conservative like
Darcy to attract the support of a reformer like Sir Francis
Bigod; but both men acted much more out of idealism than
out of a desire to change the dynasty. Moreover, the religious
element was an additional bond between lords and commons
in the revolt: some rebels may have acted only out of a
desire (or necessity) to follow their natural leaders, but
others were infected by a religious enthusiasm of their own.
Possibly the most significant feature of the rebellion was
that the traditional framework was not strong enough to

contain it: even if Lord Darcy began by using the commons, he thereby encouraged a trend which carried with it a very untraditional view of politics and society. Ideology is a much abused word, and purists will doubtless object that its use should be restricted to writings about the age which produced it, our own. But it was in the issues of principle in political conflicts of earlier centuries that ideology was born.

In a traditional society political choices are for the most part determined by formal relationships, sanctioned by the tradition and its religious beliefs, the most important such relationship in medieval England being that between lord and vassal or tenant. By the time of the Pilgrimage of Grace the traditional framework was already breaking down, and such things as personal conscience and economic interest were beginning to influence political decisions: in that revolt, some men acted according to traditional loyalties, but others took sides according to religious belief or an idealistic view of law; and indeed Lord Darcy himself was strongly influenced by such things. Once again, it will be remarked that there were earlier instances of revolts that involved issues of principle: those of the thirteenth century, in which groups of barons sought to force royal acknowledgement of law; and that of 1381 in which John Ball and Wat Tyler put forward demands for a whole new conception of the social order. By the reign of Charles I, the traditional framework had broken down almost completely, and the modernity of the civil wars in his reign consists very largely in the fact that they were fought by men opposed to one another on grounds of interest or principle rather than of allegience. The Pilgrimage of Grace, far from being the last purely feudal revolt in England, represents an important step in the transition from tradition towards modernity in political life. To say that by 1536 ideology had begun to count as a factor in politics is to draw attention to a neglected but very important aspect of the decline of feudal lordship.

That decline was initially counterbalanced by an increase in the power of the monarchy. Henry VIII countered the rebel oath of the Pilgrims with an oath of supremacy which most of his subjects had already taken towards himself, and which the majority were unwilling to break. The importance

of the oath in sixteenth-century England is a subject which
demands further study; it was probably bound up with the
tendency of the Tudor monarchy to rely on the concept of
divine right, where previous dynasties had been more content to regard ecclesiastical sanctions as their effective
religious base. The first two Tudor sovereigns did much to
encourage the notion of the 'divinity that hedgeth kings'.
By insisting on the swearing of allegiance by all his subjects,
Henry VIII probably broke once and for all the bonds of
private lordship which had threatened royal power for
centuries past. Yet in the long run it would not be the
monarchy that would gain most from the change. The
Pilgrimage of Grace failed because the 'feudal' power of
overmighty subjects was no longer an adequate basis for
successful rebellion; and because devotion to a principle
was not in itself sufficient basis for a movement powerful
enough to defeat the Crown. But in time the gentry and the
Commons would together find in Parliament a focus for
opposition to the monarchy on grounds of principle. That
was the true significance of the 'rise of the gentry' in the
sixteenth and seventeenth centuries.

APPENDIX I

SOME PROBLEMS CONCERNING SOURCE MATERIALS

I

THE present chapter will probably be found tedious by the reader who is interested only in results and not in the methods by which they were obtained. But it will be judged essential by those who wish to criticize the statistical content of Chapters II, III and VI, either in general or in detail. A certain part of the source material used in this study may be described as conventional, in the sense that it consists of letters, narrative reports, court proceedings and so on, of the kind familiar to all workers in the early Tudor period. No special commentary on such sources seems called for here, though the problems in handling records of litigation should not be under-estimated. But the sources which have been used to measure such quantities as income from land, the value of estates, or the assessment of taxable wealth, are in many cases very technical, in the sense that they can only be used and compared if they are seen in the context of the administrative machinery which produced them. I propose to deal with four categories of such material, and then to discuss more generally the question of the valuation of land in the sixteenth century.

I. *Exchequer Records*

Early Tudor financial arrangements have been studied in some detail by Professor Richardson and by Dr. Elton, and the particular aspect of subsidy assessment and collection by Dr. Schofield.[1] I cannot do more than stand on their shoulders and peer cautiously into the small corners of the Tudor financial courts which were dealing with the West Riding. All the records concerned are in the Public Record Office, and the reference numbers given are to the class lists of that repository.[2]

[1] G. R. Elton: *The Tudor Revolution in Government* (Cambridge, 1953); W. C. Richardson: *Tudor Chamber Administration 1485–1547* (Baton Rouge, 1952), and *History of the Court of Augmentations 1536–1554* (1961). R. S. Schofield: 'Parliamentary Land Taxation, 1485–1547 (Unpub. Thesis, Ph.D. Cambridge 1963).

[2] A general summary of the classes of public records used will be found in M. S. Giuseppi: *Guide to the Contents of the Public Record Office*, volume i (revised edition, London, 1963); more detailed lists are published in the series *Lists and Indexes*, or are available in typescript at the Record Office itself.

(i) Lay Subsidy Records:

The most important class of records used in the present study are the
Subsidy Rolls (E 179). Nine subsidy acts were passed by Parliament
during Henry VIII's reign; four in the period 1512–15, one in
1523, one in 1534 and the last three between 1540 and 1545.
Although some assessment rolls for the West Riding have survived
from the earliest period, and also some for the years 1540–1, the most
important bodies of material of this kind were compiled under the
statutes of 1523, 1543 and 1545. In each of these three statutes,
provision was made for more than one collection; and there was to be
a separate assessment for each collection. In principle the most
interesting records are those for the collections which affected most
people. For example, the third and fourth collections under the 1523
statute were limited to people with lands or goods worth over £50;
whereas the first assessments under that act, made in early autumn 1523
and 1524, covered everyone with lands worth £1 a year, or goods
worth £2, or wages worth £1 a year. It is these latter assessments
which have been most frequently used by writers on the society of
this period.[1] It is noticeable that the assessment was to be made in
Autumn, before Martinmas, and the collection had to be completed by
the following February: in other words, the assessment was to take
place just after the harvest when everyone was in possession of most
goods, and collection was to be made in winter, before most of the
fields were sown. The dates of the surviving rolls suggest that the
statute was not always exactly adhered to; they also suggest a need to
examine each roll individually before deciding whether it represents
the actual assessment-roll or the roll copied from the assessment-roll
and used at the time of collection. To the principle of using assessments which covered the most people must be added the practical
consideration of how many rolls survive. There is at least one roll
for each of the administrative divisions of the West Riding for one
or other of the years 1523–4: to use the assessment of those years
for an analysis therefore would be quite feasible.

But it is not the only possibility. Under the statute of 1543,
assessments were to be made in the autumn of 1543, 1544 and
1545, with collections in February 1544, 1545 and 1546. The West
Riding rolls which survive under this statute were mostly made in
1545, but they did not all belong to the last assessment and collection.
The following sequence of events, indicated by the collector's rolls
from Agbrigg and Morley Wapentakes, shows that what actually

[1] See the works by W. G. Hoskins and J. C. K. Cornwall cited in footnote 1,
page 96.

APPENDIX I 265

happened was yet one degree more complicated.[1] On 20 June 1545, an indenture was signed between four of the subsidy commissioners assigned to Morley wapentake (led by Sir Henry Savile) and Robert Furness of Mirfield, collector for Morley wapentake. It stated that the persons named in the annexed schedule had lands worth £5 or more, or goods worth at least £10, and that they were to pay the subsidy before the following 15 July (i.e. 1545). This must have been a delayed collection, theoretically due to be made the previous February. A similar indenture was made between the commissioners assigned to Agbrigg and the collector for that wapentake. What is more noticeable than the delay, however, is the fact that the minimum values of land and goods stated in this indenture are not those contained in the statute; they are higher, which suggests that the commissioners themselves divided their work into two parts, collecting the tax of those more richly assessed separately from that of poorer folk. This is confirmed by the fact that on 26 October 1545, the commissioners made a further indenture with the same collector, for both wapentakes, and to this is attached a schedule giving the names of men assessed on lands between £1 and £5, and on goods between £1 and £10. This may well have been the assessment roll for the collection due the following year. Be that as it may, the point to which I would draw attention is simply that in order to get a full picture of the assessment of 1545, whether late or not, it is necessary to have both rolls for each wapentake. It so happens that for all the divisions of the Riding at least two rolls survive for 1545, and in some cases three. This means that coverage is probably complete for that year: but on closer examination it turns out that some townships are missing from some rolls, whilst others are partly illegible.

The last collection of taxes due under the 1543 statute was still unfinished when the first assessments under the statute of 1545 were due to be made. The most complete set of rolls for the West Riding was made under this statute, in February 1546. In this case the delay was only slight. Unfortunately however the lists for this assessment were less lengthy than those of June and October 1545 combined, because the minimum qualification for contribution was higher under the statute of 1545 than under the previous one. As was noticed in Chapter III, only 4,631 inhabitants of the Riding were assessed in February 1546, compared with thrice that number the previous year.[2]

Since hardly anything is known about methods of assessment, the

[1] *Statutes of the Realm*, iii, pp. 938–51 and 1019–32, for the subsidy acts of 1543 and 1545; the rolls for Agbrigg and Morley for 1545 and 1546 are printed in *Thoresby Miscellanea*, vol. iii, (Thoresby Society publications, vol. ix, 1899), pp. 311–16, and *ibid*, vol. iv (Thoresby Soc., vol. xi, 1904), pp. 101–29 and 333–68.
[2] See Table VIII, and the accompanying observations on page 97.

question of reliability cannot be answered with any confidence. How-ever, a comparison between the rolls of 1524 and those of 1545–6 can be made, and it is quite clear that in the latter year far more people found themselves entered on the subsidy rolls than twenty years before. Thus in thirty townships of the Ainsty, 346 names appear on the roll of 1524, compared with 541 names in 1545–6.[1] The difference is found throughout the Riding. It could be due simply to the fact that the 1523 statute, although including men with wages worth £1 a year, laid down a minimum qualification of £2 for assessment on goods; whereas in 1545 (that is, in the statute of 1543) the minimum value of goods liable to assessment was only £1. Or the increase could be due to population growth, to inflation, and to increased adminis-trative efficiency. Whilst not wishing to rule out any of the other factors, that of greater efficiency seems to me a very likely reason for the increase in numbers; at all events, the rolls of 1545–6 seem a more promising source than those of 1524, at least as far as Yorkshire is concerned. That is why they have been used in Chapter III.

In addition to the subsidy assessment (or collectors') rolls, the Exchequer records also include subsidy accounts. They are to be found in the enrolled accounts of the Lord Treasurer's Remembrancer (E 359). They cannot be used for the analysis of social structure, but as a general measure of wealth they have been used for a regional analysis in Table III (page 29). They are compared there with the yields normally expected from the fifteenth of moveable wealth granted to Edward III in 1334. These did not vary in principle, and were still being granted by statute in the early sixteenth century, although there were occasions when remission was made of all or part of the tax due from a particular village—often because of plague or some other disaster. A convenient list of total theoretical yields survives from the year 1415.[2]

(ii) Clerical Subsidies and the *Valor Ecclesiasticus*

The clergy were taxed separately from the laity, and their subsidies were granted by the Convocations, not by Parliament. Fewer assess-ment rolls have survived, but there is one for part of Yorkshire (the Archdeaconry of Richmond) made in 1523.[3] Apart from that record, the only thorough survey we have of clerical wealth for taxation purposes in this period is that made in 1535 for the tenth granted the previous year. In its fullest version, this is known as the *Valor Eccle-siasticus,* whose twenty-two volumes and three portfolios include a

---

[1] P.R.O.: E 179/217/92; 109–110.
[2] P.R.O.: E 164/7.
[3] P.R.O.: E 36/149.

very large part of the country. For the rest we must fall back on a summary version of the survey which gives only the net value of each religious house or benefice, the *Liber Valorum*. Both records have been printed, to give a full survey of the country, and they have been analysed in great detail by Savine.[1] Little need be said about them here, beyond the observation that it is possible to check a great many of the *Valor* figures by comparisons with the Augmentations estate records to be discussed below. In the present study information about land revenues has been taken from the latter source as far as possible, and the *Valor* has for the most part been used only for its information about the secular clergy, especially parochial incumbents and chantry priests.

(iii) Other Records

The Exchequer records include a number of series of accounts of medieval origin, whose style changed little over the centuries. The accounts of the sheriffs were entered on the great roll of the pipe each year, and the Remembrancers kept their memoranda rolls in meticulous detail. These records do contain some information about individual counties, and the pipe rolls have been mentioned briefly in Chapter IV. But the amount of information is not great, by comparison with other series available; and in view of the pitfalls involved for anyone who has not mastered all the details of the Exchequer system, it was decided not to try to use them for this study.

In addition, the Exchequer records include a great deal of miscellaneous material, some of it connected with the estate administration to be mentioned below. Amongst the other records to be found there are muster rolls (not a separate series, but there are West Riding rolls in E 36/43 and E 101/58); papers relating to the suppression of monasteries, the sale of lands, and so on. Such material has been used where relevant references have come to light, but it is impossible to be sure that every possible record relevant to an individual county has been found.

II. *Estate Records*

The accounts, surveys, rentals, court rolls, made in the administration of estates in the first half of the sixteenth century still in many cases followed a form or style which had been developed in the thirteenth or fourteenth century. The class of records known as

---

[1] *Valor Ecclesiasticus*, ed. J. Caley, published by the Record Commission, (London, 1810–34): vol. v covers the Diocese of York; A. Savine: *The English Monasteries on the Eve of the Dissolution* (Oxford Studies in Social and Legal History, no. i, 1909).

'ministers' accounts', for example, was compiled according to rules of accounting appropriate to the reign of Edward I, and those rules must be understood before the records can be made to yield any information about the actual yearly revenues from a particular estate or manor. It is also essential to understand the accounting structure of the whole estate, from the receivers and receiver-general down to the bailiffs of individual manors. On the one hand, there is a danger of over-estimating income if one fails to appreciate that an item of revenue could appear on the 'revenue' part of the account long after it had been reduced in value or ceased to bring in revenue at all. On the other hand, the total revenue from an estate is liable to appear too low, if only the receiver-general's account is used at a period when it was customary for lesser receivers to make important payments of expenditure before the revenues reached the owner of the estate or his receiver-general. For these reasons it was deemed necessary, in using this material for the calculations made in Chapter II, to take each manor or township separately and to make a careful investigation of the annual income from each part of a small estate. As was mentioned in that chapter, the method is not perfect since it does not enable one to deduct the expenses of estate administration; in any case, the dividing line between estate expenses and the patronage of the large landowner is not an easy one to draw.[1]

The practice of surveying estates, in the sense of making an extent to discover their annual value, also goes back to the thirteenth century, as does the making of custumals to record the obligations of the peasantry which at that period were more complicated than simple money payments. The changing meaning of the word 'survey' when applied to records of this kind is not without significance: whereas a thirteenth-century survey or extent would merely list holdings (often in bovates) and the obligations due from the holders, we should expect a seventeenth-century survey to give a more detailed description of the land and its value. The development of surveying as a professional art during the sixteenth century has been described in an article of Professor E. G. R. Taylor.[2] By the end of the century the standard of accuracy was quite high, and surveys were often accompanied by carefully drawn maps. But the parallel evolution of the custumal was its development into a rental, and very often rentals of the later

[1] See above, pp. 66–7. The complexities of estate administration have been explored in relation to a number of particular estates which included West Riding lands, e.g. Sir Robert Somerville: *The Duchy of Lancaster*, i, 1265–1603 (London, 1953); and J. M. W. Bean, *Estates of the Percy Family 1416–1537* (Oxford, 1958). See also C. D. Ross and R. B. Pugh: 'Materials for the Study of Baronial Incomes in Fifteenth Century England', *Econ. Hist. Rev.* 2nd ser. vi (1954).
[2] E. G. R. Taylor: 'The Surveyor', *Econ. Hist. Rev.*, xvii (1947).

sixteenth century give no more than a list of names and the rents due from them. Both changes had begun by the period with which we are dealing here, although the most striking technical advances came only in the second half of the century.

Court rolls of manors have not been used to any great extent in this study. By the sixteenth century they dealt mainly with manorial customs concerning responsibility for fencing open fields, or the commoning of beasts on manorial pastures; or else with transfers of holdings. Neither subject can be taken very much further than it was taken by Tupling in his study of Rossendale, in neighbouring Lancashire, though of course there were differences of detail between the various physical regions.[1] But the main reason for not trying to use these records is that they do not survive in sufficiently large quantities for statistical use to be possible. There was, however, another kind of court record, in which the disputes are often of more intrinsic interest: namely records of the courts of the large estates, to which tenants could appeal when the manorial court either had inadequate jurisdiction or when its judgement was contested. Such was the Court of Duchy Chamber in the Duchy of Lancaster, which we have seen at work in cases of enclosure disputes in the West Riding. But the strength of the Duchy Court is not unrelated to its position as virtually a royal court. By the sixteenth century the powers of private estate courts of that kind were probably in decline, though they have left few records. The position of baronial and honorial courts was different: these were courts to which mesne lords owed suit, and their decline was an aspect of the general decline of territorial lordship over free tenants. Free tenants had ready access to the King's courts.

(i) Crown Estate Records:

A large proportion of the estate records used in Chapter II are in the Public Record Office: they cover not only the Crown estates of 1535 but also monastic estates confiscated after 1536, together with such estates as that of Lord Darcy which came to the Crown as a result of attainder. The table overleaf summarises the main classes of records used under this head.

(ii) Private Estate Records:

The survival of estate records other than those made by the royal officials and carefully preserved in government offices is rather a matter of chance, and not surprisingly there is much less material in private collections for earlier periods than for the seventeenth century

[1] G. H. Tupling: *Economic History of Rossendale*, Chetham Society, n.s. vol. 86 (Manchester, 1927). That work showed that there was a very active traffic in copyhold land throughout the sixteenth century.

Responsible authority	Ministers' and receivers' accounts	Surveys and rentals
Duchy of Lancaster	DL 29: Ministers' and Receivers' Accounts of Honours of Tickhill, Pontefract, and Knaresborough	DL 43: Rentals and Surveys of individual manors and lordships DL 44: Special Commissions, including some surveys, e.g. of castles in the Duchy
General Surveyors of Crown lands	SC 6/Henry VIII: Ministers' accounts of: (a) Duchy of York Lordships: Conisbrough, Hatfield, Wakefield (b) Attainted lands, including estates of Darcy, Hammerton, etc. (c) Percy estates, inherited in 1537	SC 11 and 12: Rentals and and surveys of particular manors, etc.; occasionally such records are found in Exchequer Misc. Books (E 36)
Court of Augmentations	SC 6/Henry VIII: Ministers' Accounts of all monastic property confiscated, except where it was granted out immediately	SC 11 and 12: Rentals and surveys of monastic property E 315: Miscellaneous Books of the Court, including some rentals, surveys, accounts, etc.

and later. One reason is that by and large it was only during the course of the sixteenth century—and more especially after 1550—that gentry landlords took to making careful records of estate administration (as opposed to deeds and other records of title).

The monasteries were amongst the earliest keepers of records on their estates, and some of the most famous thirteenth- and fourteenth-century surveys and accounts were made by the estate officials of religious landowners. But the archives of monasteries were frequently dispersed after the Dissolution. The Augmentations officials made their own survey of the confiscated property, and were not much interested in older records once the operation was completed. With occasional exceptions, the only monastic records to be taken to the Exchequer as a matter of course were leases and records of title. Therefore it is to private collections that one must look for surviving monastic estate accounts and surveys. Very few have come to light in the West Riding, but one example which should be mentioned is the series of Selby Abbey accounts in the Londesborough Collection at Beverley (East Riding Record Office). They show, what no Augmentations account shows, how the monastic administration worked; but for the purpose of a township-by-township survey of the

Abbey's possessions they are less useful than the records made after the Dissolution.

A number of local collections contain family estate archives of this period. The most notable is the Skipton Castle MSS, now preserved by the Yorkshire Archaeological Society at Leeds. The same repository has a number of other collections which contain West Riding rentals, surveys and accounts, and there is also some useful material in the Gascoigne Collection and in the Vyner MSS at Leeds City Library. At Sheffield, there is a little material in the Wentworth Woodhouse muniments, and in the local Sheffield collection; but the Arundel Castle MSS which include some Talbot estate papers are not very helpful for the period at present being studied. Wherever rentals and surveys could be found for gentry estates, they were used; but the greater part of the information about gentry income from West Riding land had to be drawn from wardship records.

III. *Wardship Records*

(i) Inquisitions *Post Mortem:*

The inquisition *post mortem*, another type of record whose origins go back to the thirteenth century, was compiled by the escheator of the county (or occasionally by a special commission) in response to a writ of *diem clausit extremum* issuing from Chancery. Such a writ would be issued whenever a man died who may possibly have held land by military tenure from the Crown (either in chief or from a royal barony or honour), in order to discover what lands he held, from whom he held them, their value, and the age of his heir or heiress. In theory an inquisition was held in every county where the deceased man held land, so that the Yorkshire escheator's inquisitions do not include lands lying outside his county, nor are they limited to men who resided in Yorkshire. (There was only one escheator for all three Ridings.) When the record had been made it was sent back to Westminster to be filed in Chancery, and it is in the archives of that court that the principal series of inquisitions survives (C 142). A copy was normally made for the Exchequer (E 150); and where a wardship was revealed, a third copy was sent to the department responsible for wards, after 1540 the Court of Wards. Between them the three series have preserved a large number of the inquisitions made: about 350 were used in compiling the tables of income distribution in Chapter II.

The inquisitions *post mortem* have been held in contempt by biographers of later medieval and sixteenth-century landlords.[1] There

---

[1] e.g. C. D. Ross and T. B. Pugh in the article cited in footnote 1, page 268; the opinion is frequently expressed by those concerned with writing biographies for the sixteenth century volumes of the *History of Parliament*, not yet published.

can be no doubt that, like all records which give annual values of land, by the later sixteenth century the inquisitions did not pretend to give realistic values. Everyone knew that land was worth much more than the sums collected in annual rents, the difference being made up by fines paid on entry into new tenancies; but no attempt seems to have been made to bring the records of land values made by royal officials into line with the new state of affairs. This objection naturally applies far less strongly to the first half of the sixteenth century than to the second. Doubts about the reliability of fifteenth-century inquisitions on the other hand, could well be applicable to those of Henry VIII's reign. Nevertheless, it should not be imagined that escheators of the latter period merely repeated the values given in fifteenth-century inquisitions. There is clear evidence in some cases that the attempt of the early Tudor monarchs to increase the efficiency of the government machine at least led their officials to do their own valuation work and not rely on out-of-date precedent. For example, Carleton-by-Snaith was valued at £28. 12s. in 1485, but at £82. 19s. 4d. in 1550; and Beamsley and Gargrave were put at £50 in 1541 compared with only £23. 6s. 8d. in 1517.[1]

The procedures which the early Tudor escheator followed in order to arrive at his estimate of the value of this or that manor or parcel of land cannot be reconstructed in detail. In theory his inquisition merely reproduced the sworn evidence of the jury which was summoned in accordance with the writ *diem clausit extremum*. The document begins with a statement that the inquisition was held at a certain time and place, lists the names of the jurors present, and then proceeds, with the phrase '*qui dicunt super sacrum quod . . .*', to enumerate the details demanded by the writ. The original inquisitions which survive in Chancery, however, frequently contain internal evidence that the jurors were not the escheator's primary source of information. In many of them there is a difference of ink, even sometimes of hand-writing, between the text of the main body of the document (including the details of land, tenure and valuation) and the jurors' names. The latter, together with the date of the hearing, bear every sign of having been written in at a later stage than the compilation of the substance of the record. This suggests that the function of the jury was merely confirmatory, except perhaps in cases where some dispute had to be settled. In the majority of cases, especially where no wardship was involved, it seems highly likely that the substance of the inquisition was worked out by the escheator in direct negotiation with the family of the deceased. If this was the case, then it might be of some significance

---

[1] *Calendar of Inquisitions Post Mortem: Henry VII*, i, no. 97; P.R.O.: E 150/245/12; E 150/220/7; and E 150/239/8.

that the escheator was usually a youngish man of a lesser gentry family, often a man who later went on to become a lawyer.[1] He would not be in a very good position to gainsay a more influential knight. On the other hand, as we shall see later in the chapter, he had some idea of how much land was worth and could not easily be deceived by figures that were utterly unreasonable.

Since comparison with other records is not usually possible there is no direct evidence whether the figures for land values contained in the Yorkshire inquisitions of this period were reliable or not. It is very likely that they were reasonable but not perfect; the imperfection does not seem to have been extreme. It is as well to bear in mind that its consequences for the tables in Chapter II do not seriously affect the arguments put forward there. Of the four categories of landlord only the fourth is affected by the imperfection of the wardship records. The point of Table V (page 73) was to show that the fourth category, the gentry, already had a higher proportion of landed income before the confiscation and sale of church lands than is often supposed. The initial calculation presented in that table showed that the gentry had at least 49 per cent of temporal land income in 1535; any imperfection of the valuations given in wardship records merely means that that percentage should be increased.

One other point about the values in inquisitions must be taken into consideration when they are being used in conjunction with figures drawn from estate records. It was noticed that in using the latter for township-by-township surveys of land-ownership, it is impossible on large estates to take account of all estate expenses: the figures used therefore must be regarded as 'gross' rather than 'net'. The escheator, however, was instructed to report the value of lands' *ultra reprisis*': that is after the deduction of all charges on the revenues. Usually such charges represent no more than normal estate expenses; but sometimes they also include annuities payable to other members of the deceased man's family, and this might reduce the figure for annual value considerably. Thus in May 1554 an inquisition *post mortem* on the lands of Christopher Mallory valued his manor of Studley Magna at £40 a year; two years later, a further inquisition on his lands reduced this figure to a mere £6. 13s. 4d. By a lucky accident a paper concerning the Mallory estates in 1547 has survived in the records of the Exchequer, which records the annuities due out of Studley and other manors at the time when Christopher entered his inheritance: they

---

[1] There is a typescript list of sixteenth-century escheators in the Public Record Office. Amongst the young lawyers who held the position were Leonard Beckwith (in 1521), Thomas Gargrave (1519), Thomas Grene (1526, 1532 and 1536). One escheator, Anthony Hammond, held this post in 1534 then became feodary of the West Riding in the following year.

amounted to the whole of Studley's annual value of £40. Perhaps one of the recipients died during the next few years, which explains why Studley was not said to be worth nothing at all in 1556.[1] Unfortunately it is seldom possible to correct this kind of imperfection in the escheator's figures; but again it works in the direction of minimising the share of gentry income in the overall calculation.

(ii) Feodaries' Surveys

The feodary made a survey of an estate only when a wardship was actually declared and the question of its disposal had to be decided. There was a separate feodary for the West Riding, and presumably he was instructed by the Master (and later the Court) of Wards to make a survey of the ward's lands within the Riding. But not only do we have no information about how he went about his work: not even the original surveys sent in by him have survived. Without exception the feodaries' surveys used in the present study (and those for all other counties at this period, it would seem) are the copies entered into registers by the Court of Wards (Wards 9).[2] They cover whole estates, not just returns from individual counties. In the absence of precedent books, and of any local papers giving clues about his work, the feodary's methods must remain obscure. Bell, in his study of the Court of Wards, suggested that the valuations of land given in feodaries' surveys were likely to be more accurate than those of the escheators' inquisitions. But he was writing chiefly of the early seventeenth century and all the examples he cites belong to the period after Sir Robert Cecil became Master of the Wards in 1599.[3] There is other evidence which points in the opposite direction, suggesting that the feodary was less efficient than the escheator. An enquiry into the whole problem of financial administration in 1553 produced an observation that it was unwise to leave the full survey of wards' lands to the feodaries on the grounds that he might later be responsible for accounting for the revenues of those lands, if they were not sold, and that he would consequently be tempted to undervalue them in his return. What is more, the commissioners in the enquiry suggested a more

[1] P.R.O.: C 142/102/59 and 105/47; Wards 9/137/f. 139; and E 314/132/f. 57.

[2] Wards 9 in the P.R.O. covers the whole series of Miscellaneous Books of the Court of Wards: feodaries' surveys for the period 1513–79 are bound. For later dates the surveys are not bound. The series of feodaries' accounts (Wards 8) begins in 1540; it is valuable for understanding the administrative work of the feodary, but does not add much information about the lands for which he was accounting.

[3] H. E. Bell: *Introduction to the Court of Wards and Liveries* (London, 1953), p. 56; cf. also J. Hurstfield: *The Queen's Wards* (London, 1958), p. 233.

rigorous use of escheators' inquisitions to counterbalance this danger.[1]

The best way to settle the question whether the feodary was more reliable as a valuer than the escheator, in the period with which we are dealing, is to make comparisons between their respective records in the West Riding in this period. A sample of forty-three items which appeared in both an inquisition *post mortem* and a feodary's survey between 1520 and 1550, in connection with the same wardship, showed that in nineteen cases the valuations in the two records were identical; in eight cases there may have been minor adjustments, or the entries do not allow direct comparison; and in sixteen cases there was a completely independent valuation by the feodary. (In Chapter II, where a revised valuation is found in the feodary's survey, it has of course been used in preference to the escheator's figure.) A similar series of comparisons in the period 1550–60 showed fourteen cases of identical valuation out of twenty-six. But in the period after 1560 the practice of independent valuation by feodaries seems to have died out altogether. Out of twenty cases where inquisitions and surveys can be compared in the West Riding between 1561 and 1579, not a single one shows any evidence of revision by the feodary. It would be inadvisable to attempt a generalization for the whole of England on the basis of Yorkshire evidence alone, but it will not escape the reader's notice that 1560 was the year in which Sir William Cecil (Lord Burghley) became Master of the Wards; nor that it was immediately after he was succeeded by his son Sir Robert that Bell began to find evidence of revision of escheators' values by feodaries. This could, possibly, be yet another example of the way in which the inflation tended to assist administrative corruption, for Lord Burghley is known to have made sizable profits from his tenure of the mastership.[2]

IV. *Patents, Deeds, etc.*

The records which were regarded as most precious in the sixteenth century (indeed perhaps in any age) were records of title. They are of little help in compiling statistics about the value of land, but essential for the study of the land market. They are highly technical documents, and a full understanding of their meaning depends on a full knowledge of the land law, which by the sixteenth century was extremely

[1] 'Remembrances and notes made by commissioners . . . upon examination of the King's courts of revenue', British Museum, Harl. MS. 7383. I owe this reference to Dr. Schofield.
[2] J. Hurstfield: op. cit., pp. 266–8.

complex.[1] But without them it is impossible to trace the descent of any parcel of land, or to measure the flow of property from one kind of owner to another. There exists no systematic study of manorial descents in the West Riding, and it was beyond the scope of the present study to trace the history of individual ownership of all the land. For this reason no attempt was made in Chapter II to distinguish between different sorts of gentry. There is of course a large body of material which falls into the category of 'deeds' in the various collections of family archives in the West Riding, and in due course it will no doubt be possible to trace the descent of most manors and lordships. In the present study, however, only two sets of records of title have been used: the patent rolls and the feet of fines. The former enable us to trace changes in ownership of ex-religious property after 1536; the latter were used for a very rough measurement of the volume of the land market in Chapter VI. The patent roll was of course the highest form of enrolment of title in the realm.[2]

II

The rule which has been applied throughout the statistical sections of this study is that land cannot be measured in any terms other than financial. Insofar as control over land is a measurable quantity at all, it must be measured as income. The source materials just summarized may for this purpose be said to fall into two types: those which make statements about the actual passage of revenue from tenant to land-lord, and those which indicate the annual value of given quantities of land in a rather more abstract way. The former kind of record is the earlier in origin, its most reliable form being the annual estate account. But already by the latter part of the thirteenth century administrators were beginning to think in terms of land having a theoretical annual value. A document preserved in the 'Annals of Burton' appears to be a set of instructions directed to an escheator in 1259. It tells him to discover how much arable meadow and pasture was contained in the demesne of a manor, and how much an acre of each was worth; which must surely mean that the writer envisaged an abstract value that

[1] R. B. Pugh (ed.): *A Calendar of Antrobus Deeds before 1625* (Wilts. Arch. Soc., Record Branch, iii, 1947) gives some indication of the complexity of the subject. It is unfortunate that the West Riding volumes of the *Victoria History of the Counties of England* have not yet appeared, or even been begun: that series is the only work which sets out to supply a systematic survey of manorial descents for every township in the county concerned.

[2] The *Calendar of Patent Rolls* published by the Public Record Office covers the reigns of Henry VII and Edward VI, but not that of Henry VIII: the patent rolls for the intervening reign appear, year by year, in the *Letters and Papers of the Reign of Henry VIII*, edited by J. S. Brewer, J. Gairdner and R. H. Brodie (1862–1932).

could belong to any acre of a given type and quality of land. The fact
that demesne is specifically referred to seems to suggest that the
method had been devised to deal with the problem of recording an
annual figure for land kept 'in hand' by its owner, which did not yield
income in the form of rent. However the inquisitions of the period
show that sometimes the idea was extended to the lands of tenants; it
is stated that there are so many bovates in a given manor, worth say
3s. a bovate.[1]

For the administrative official, of the sixteenth century as of the thirteenth, there were two possible methods of obtaining information about
the value of land. The older of them was the enquiry upon oath, whose
great prototype is seen in the Domesday Book, but which was still used
by Tudor officials in such cases as the holding of an escheator's inquisition. In itself this method could never yield more information than the
owner himself had about his land, and in general it seems to have been
directed towards obtaining evidence about rents and obligations
rather than about theoretical annual values. Its natural extension was
the inspection of estate records by the official making the enquiry, and
indeed an Elizabethan precedent book concerning the escheator's work
says that he had the right to demand production of rentals when
making an inquisition.[2] The second method was that of actually
visiting the lands in question and making a survey of them. Professor
Taylor's study of the progress of this method from the thirteenth to
the seventeenth centuries has already been mentioned. It became
increasingly important as the great inflation developed, for by the reign
of Elizabeth even the landlord himself had to make an external enquiry
in order to arrive at an estimate of the difference between his tenants'
income from their holdings and the rents they were paying. In the
period before 1550 this was less necessary. But the appreciation that
such a survey was possible, and that the theoretical value of land might
be calculated, may well have made it possible for escheators, subsidy
commissioners and others to make a rough decision about whether
the information laid before them was reasonable or not.

Already by this period, books were being published about the art of
surveying. But they do not offer great assistance to the modern
reader, either in his enquiries about what land was actually held to be
worth by the acre or in the matter of how sixteenth-century surveyors
arrived at their estimates of land values. Richard Benese in 1537

[1] The instructions of 1259 are printed in Hubert Hall: *Formula Book of Legal Records* (London, 1909), p. 70; there is a good example of bovates valued at 4d. per acre, with 9 acres in each bovate, in the inquisition on the lands of Edmund de Lacy who died in 1258, printed in *Lancashire Inquests*, Lancashire and Cheshire Record Society, xlviii (1903), p. 213.
[2] P.R.O.: Index 17396, f. 63.

published a table giving values per acre for land, but on closer examination it turns out to concern only acreages of woodland. Nearly a century later, we find Aaron Rathborne advising his readers to inform themselves of the general value of different sorts of land, but he adds the tantalizing remark, 'by the best means you can, which I hold not fitting here to relate'.[1] His method, alas, must remain a professional secret. All we have are the results of the administrators' and the surveyors' efforts: the records themselves. These can be made to yield a little information, and it was a comparative examination of inquisitions *post mortem*, feodaries' surveys, and a selection of estate accounts and surveys, which led me to the conclusion that wardship records are not so utterly unreasonable as sources for land values as some writers have assumed.

The estate records which can be used to discover how much land was worth by the acre are surveys of demesnes made from time to time, notably on the occasion of the suppression of the monasteries, and accounts (or sometimes leases) which give details of the acreage of large farms as well as of the rents paid for them. The question of undervaluation of monastic demesnes at the Dissolution was raised briefly in the last chapter. Here, Table A gives the results of a sample analysis

TABLE A

Average Values of Different Types of Land on Twelve Monastic Demesnes, 1536-9

	Average value per acre	Range of values per acre
Arable	8*d*.	5*d*.–18*d*.
Pasture	11*d*.	3¾*d*.–16*d*.
Meadow	24*d*.	17*d*.–34*d*.

of information concerning twelve monastic demesnes valued by the Augmentations officials at that time. The range is quite striking, and as we saw before, the lower values per acre probably represent serious if not deliberate underestimations; the average figures given therefore must also be lower than they would have been had all the demesnes been 'valewed to the uttermost,' as Pontefract was. Table B seems to confirm the impression that the monastic demesne valuations were faulty. It analyses a sample of twenty large farms which in 1535 (or at some date close to that) were leased to tenants so that the estate accounts or surveys record an actual money income from them. The

[1] Richard Benese: *The Maner of Measurynge of all Maner of Lande* (supposedly of 1537: copy in British Museum); and Aaron Rathborne: *The Surveyor* (London, 1616), p. 216.

TABLE B

Variation in Value Per Acre of Arable/Pasture Amongst Twenty Farms Let at Rent, c. 1535

Rent per acre	Number of farms in each range	Acreage involved
8d.–11½d.	5	491
12d.–13d.	4	1,493
14d.–18d.	6	2,018
18d.–23d.	2	289
24d. and over	3	225

information about them is less detailed, in that whilst acreages are given for arable, pasture and meadow separately, only one figure is given for the rent paid. It will be evident from Table A that arable was usually worth slightly less than pasture, and that meadow was worth double the latter or more. The figures in Table B are for the mean value per acre of arable and pasture, calculated on the assumption that meadow was worth twice as much per acre. They are therefore only approximate. The average rent for the twenty farms was probably about 15d. per acre. A comparable figure for the monastic demesnes would be 10d. per acre of arable/pasture. These figures are fairly comparable, moreover, to the extent that they all relate to land which was at one time or another kept as demesne by substantial owners: it was not likely to be land of poor quality, but would rather be the best land on the manor or estate.

The evidence from inquisitions *post mortem* is contained in Table C.

TABLE C

Variations in Valuation Per Acre of Arable/Pasture, in Inquisitions Post Mortem, 1509–47

Range of values per acre	Number of items in each range
under 2d.	4
2d.–3½d.	12
4d.–5½d.	20
6d.–7½d.	25
8d.–9½d.	23
10d.–11½d.	17
12d.	16
12½d.–15d.	11
15½d.–18d.	6
over 18d.	4

Eighty West Riding inquisitions were examined, belonging to various
dates in the reign of Henry VIII, and from them 138 individual
items (often whole manors) were extracted, in each case there being
both acreage and value recorded in the inquisition. Again it was
necessary to seek a figure for arable and pasture together, and to assume
that meadow land had double value. There was an additional factor
making for distortion in many cases: the description of a whole manor
would give not only acreages but also messuages or tenements, and it
was not possible to allow for these. The average figures analysed in
Table C therefore are slightly higher than they should be, but the
error is probably not great. The results show that the median value
for arable and pasture, according to these records, was between 6*d.*
and 8*d.* per acre. A little lower than the monastic figure, and considerably lower than the average for the twenty farms. But then we are
dealing here not with demesnes, where the quality of land was surely
very high, but with whole manors. The range of quality would be
greater, and one would expect the average therefore to be lower. It
would be natural for the lowest rents to be paid for land on the margin
of cultivation. It may not be out of place therefore to observe that in
the lordship of Wakefield new takings were let at a normal rent of 4*d.*
per acre, though there was also an entry-fine of 20*s.* per acre to be paid
since the tenure was subsequently secure and fines probably fixed.[1]
4*d.* an acre is even lower than the average figure emerging from the
inquisitions analysis, and if that is taken as a lower limit, then an
average of 8*d.* per acre for an estate including more poor quality land
than good does not seem unreasonable. On the other hand in the
sixteen cases where the average value indicated by the escheator's
record was lower than 4*d.* it seems almost certain that there was undervaluation. Perhaps we have here a rough yardstick by which to decide
whether any particular inquisition is to be taken as giving a reasonable
valuation. But no attempt has been made in this study to revise the
valuations of West Riding inquisitions. Since they have been used only
en masse, to estimate the extent of the possessions of a whole class of
landlords, we need do no more than register the conclusion that
whilst in some cases the values cannot be accepted, in many the
values given in wardship records are not at all unreasonable.

The whole concept of the value of land, like the concept of a rental
is a reflection of the growing importance of money as the measure of a
man's wealth and position. Indeed it was one of the first consequences
of the 'rise of a money economy', and its beginnings can be seen in the
thirteenth-century rule about distraint of knighthood, which insisted
that a man should become a knight if he had lands worth £40 a year.

[1] Survey of c. 1545, P.R.O.: SC 11/991.

By the sixteenth century it had become perfectly usual to think in such terms. Yet at the same time, if it is necessary to sum up the character of the source materials available for the study of land and social structure in Henry VIII's England, the most important point that must be made is that a great many of the records are still 'medieval' in form—and also in handwriting—a significant reminder that the 'modernity' of the post-Reformation or post-Renaissance period was not achieved at one bound.

APPENDIX II

Principal Lordships of the West Riding before 1535

Centre	Type of lordship	Chief lord in 1535	Vills in hand	Mesne vills	Other features, notes
I. *Wapentake of Strafforth and Tickhill*					
Tickhill	Honour and Liberty	Duchy of Lancaster	2	26	Castles at Tickhill and at Laughton-en-le-Morthen. (Additional dependencies in Notts.)
Conisbrough	Lordship	Crown (Duchy of York)	3	2	Castle and Park at Conisbrough
Doncaster	Borough	Crown	3	?	Charters of incorporation, 1194 and 1467
Hatfield	Lordship	Crown (Duchy of York)	5	—	Included Hatfield Chase
Bawtry	Lordship	Clifford, E. of Cumberland (Clarence inheritance)	2	—	
Maltby	Lordship	As last	2	4	Included Kimberworth and its dependencies
Roche	Monastic estate	Roche Abbey	6	—	Initially granted out of Maltby Lordship?
Sheffield	Lordship	Talbot, Earl of Shrewsbury	7	6	Also known as Hallamshire Castle at Sheffield; Forest or chase at Bradley
Hooton Pagnell	Lordship	Fitzwilliam, Earl of Southampton	1?	?	
II. *The Central Wapentakes*					
Snaith	Lordship	Duchy of Lancaster	2	7	Park at Phippin
Airmyn	Liberty	St. Mary's Abbey, York	5	?	Also known as Marshland

Pontefract	Honour	Duchy of Lancaster	13	26	Castle at Pontefract, with Park. The 39 vills counted here are the part of the Honour that was in Osgoldcross, Barkston and the east of Agbrigg Wapentakes; the Honour also had dependencies in Staincross Wapentake; and in Agbrigg Morley and Skyrack the lordships of Kippax, Barwick, Leeds, Rothwell and Almondbury were attached to it.
Kippax; Barwick	Lordship	Duchy of Lancaster	7	18?	Small castles at Kippax and Barwick. Probably originally one or more lordships, absorbed by the Honour of Pontefract during the middle ages. Leeds was also in some way associated with Barwick, and is counted as one vill 'in hand'
Rothwell	Lordship	Duchy of Lancaster	2	5?	Part of the Honour of Pontefract by the sixteenth century. Large Park at Rothwell Hay.
Almondbury	Lordship	Duchy of Lancaster	2	6	Small castle at Almondbury, with small park. Attached to the Honour of Pontefract by the sixteenth century
Monkhill and Ledsham	Monastic estate	Pontefract Priory	3	—	Granted out of Honour of Pontefract. The Priory also had an important estate at Barnsley, in Staincross Wapentake.

APPENDIX II

APPENDIX II—*continued*

Centre	Type of lordship	Chief lord in 1535	Vills in hand	Mesne vills	Other features, notes
Monk Bretton	Monastic estate	Monk Bretton Priory	4	—	Probably also granted out of the Honour of Pontefract, but in Staincross Wapentake
Brierley	Lordship	Stanley, Lord Mounteagle	4	9	The whole lordship was held of the Honour of Pontefract; it lay entirely in Staincross Wapentake
Wakefield	Lordship	Crown (Duchy of York)	10	6?	Castle at Sandal; 'old' and 'new' parks at Wakefield. Holmefirth is included as a member, though an outlier away to the West
Sowerby	Lordship	Crown (Duchy of York)	3	3?	Forest in Sowerby, with park at Erringden. Closely associated with Wakefield from early times. Sometimes known as Sowerby-shire
Elland	Lordship	Savile of Thornhill	1	6?	A group of townships within Wakefield and Sowerby lordships over which Sir Henry Savile claimed the right to hold his own courts, a claim disputed by the Crown. Savile also held Thorn-hill, but from the Honour of Pontefract
Nostell	Monastic estate	St. Oswald's Priory	9	—	Probably granted out of the original lordship of Wakefield
Sherburn-in-Elmet	Barony	Archbishop of York	4	11	Castle at Cawood; park and lodge at Rest
Selby	Monastic estate	Selby Abbey	6	—	Granted out of Sherburn Barony

	Lordship / Monastic estate	Holder			Notes
Ouey			1	6	Attached to Barony of Sherburn
Headingley	Lordship Monastic estate	Archbishop of York Kirkstall Abbey	9	—	Possibly granted out of the part of the Honour of Pontefract which lay in Skyrack Wapentake and which included Kippax, Barwick and Leeds
Bardsey	Lordship	Divided into six parts between the Crown and noble families	6	2?	The vills 'in hand' were held in farm by Kirkstall Abbey, which paid rent to the six lords. Bardsey had a small castle
Harewood	Lordship	Divided between Redmayne and Ryther families	1	4	Possibly once associated in some way with Pontefract, but no trace of this was apparent in the sixteenth century
Bradford	Lordship	Duchy of Lancaster	3?	11?	Attached to the Honour of Tickhill in the sixteenth century; but the mesne lords in some cases owed suit to the court of the Honour of Pontefract
Bingley	Lordship	Astley family	?		The Astley family had its main estates in the Midlands, and nothing is known of its position in the West Riding; several small manors in the vicinity of Bingley are noted in inquisitions *post mortem* as held of that family

III. *Claro Wapentake and the Ainsty*

	Honour, or Liberty (or Soke and Forest)	Holder			Notes
Knaresborough	Honour, or Liberty (or Soke and Forest)	Duchy of Lancaster	5 (+17)	13	Castle at Knaresborough, with extensive Forest and parks. The Honour included the Lordship of Aldborough, and one of its dependencies was the Lordship of Scotton and Brearton; both included in the numbers of vills given here

APPENDIX II—*continued*

Centre	Type of lordship	Chief lord in 1535	Vills in hand	Mesne vills	Other features, notes
Spofforth	Barony	Percy, Earl of Northumberland	3	9	Included Ilkley and other outlying dependencies to the west. Castle at Spofforth, with park
Tadcaster	Lordship	Percy, Earl of Northumberland	1	7	Small Castle at Tadcaster. Healaugh Priory lay within the lordship but did not have an important compact estate around it
Thorp Arch	Lordship	Gascoigne of Gawthorpe	1	6	The remnant of a disintegrated lordship created by a post-Conquest grant to Osbern de Arches. Thorp Arch was held of the Earl of Derby's Lordship of Thirsk (N.R.), as were three other vills in the Ainsty
Great Ribston	Hospitallers' estate	Preceptory of St. John, Ribston	6	—	Originally belonging to the Knights Templar
Ripon	Liberty	Archbishop of York	7	10	The area in the immediate vicinity of the collegiate church of Ripon was a liberty in the fullest sense; the remainder was merely a lordship
Fountains	Monastic estate	Fountains Abbey	12	—	Granted out of the Lordships of Ripon and Kirkby Malzeard
Kirkby Malzeard	Lordship	Stanley, Earl of Derby	1	4?	Like Thorp Arch, this may have been at one time associated in some way with Thirsk (N.R.). Sometimes known as Kirkbyshire

20 IV. *Craven and Ewcross*

Skipton	Honour	Clifford, Earl of Cumberland	6	8?	Castle at Skipton; forest, and lodge, at Barden
Carleton	Lordship	Clifford, Earl of Cumberland	4	5?	Associated with Honour of Skipton by 1540, probably much earlier
Bolton in Craven	Monastic estate	Bolton Priory	7	—	Granted out of the Honour of Skipton, with the Lordship of Appletreewick as an outlying part
Settle; Gisburn	Lordship	Percy, Earl of Northumberland	4	10	Included the outlying Langstrothdale chase
Salley	Monastic estate	Salley Abbey	7	—	Granted out of the Percy Fee
Malham	Monastic estate	Fountains Abbey	8	—	
Barnoldswick	Lordship	Duchy of Lancaster	1?	?	Associated with Tickhill in the sixteenth century, and perhaps more anciently with Bradford
Bolland	Lordship or Forest	Duchy of Lancaster	2?	3	Entirely a forest area; attached from very early times to the Honour of Clitheroe in Lancashire
Burton-in-Lonsdale	Lordship	Stanley, Earl of Derby	1	?	Small castle at Burton; forest of Ingleborough. Formerly associated with lordships in Lancashire, and only added to Yorkshire in time of Henry I
Horton-in-Ribblesdale	Monastic estate	Furness Abbey	3	—	Possibly a grant from the Derby Fee in Ewcross
Dent	Lordship	Parr of Kendal	1?	2?	

APPENDIX III

Religious Houses of the West Riding

The principal sources used for the compilation of this list were: D. Knowles and R. N. Hadcock, *Medieval Religious Houses, England and Wales*, (London, 1953), *passim*; Suppression papers in the State Papers: P.R.O.: SP 5/2, 4; and records of surrenders summarized in *L.P.*, XII–XIV; also Augmentations Accounts of dissolved houses: P.R.O.: SC 6/Hen VIII/4452, 4460, 4471, 4476, 4482, 4522–3, 4534, 4539, 4542, 4579, 4584, 4590, 4595, 4606, 7304, 7454.

House and type	Founded	Size	Taxable income 1535	Gross income in West Riding at Dissolution		
				Temp.	Spirit.	Total
ARTHINGTON Cluniac Nunnery	c. 1154	11 nuns (1539)	£11	£18		£28
BOLTON Augustinian Pr.	1120 (at Embsay) (1154 at Bolton)	15 canons (1538)	£212	£232	£155	£387
DRAX Augustinian Pr.	c. 1130	10 canons (1536)	£92	£47	£43	£90
ESHOLT Cistercian Nun.	12th C.	11 nuns (1539)	£13	£34	—	£34
FOUNTAINS Cistercian Abbey	1132	32 monks (1539)	£1,004	£760	—	£760
HAMPOLE Cistercian Nun.	c. 1170	19 nuns (1539)	£63	£59	£35	£94
HEALAUGH Augustinian Pr.	c. 1180	6 canons (1536)	£72	£67	£28	£95
KIRKLEES Cistercian Nun.	12th C.	8 nuns (1539)	£19	£24	£6	£30
KIRKSTALL Cistercian Abbey	1147 (at Barnoldswick); (1152 at Kirkstall)	31 monks (1539)	£329?	£425	£17	£442

	Foundation	Community				
KNARESBOROUGH Trinitarian Friary	c. 1252	10 friars	£35	£45	£89	£134
MONK BRETTON Benedictine (orig. Cluniac) Priory	post-1153	14 monks (1538)	£239	£243	£84	£327
NEWLAND Preceptory of Order of St. John	post-1200	?	£129	£48	£67	£115
NOSTELL: ST. OSWALD Augustinian Pr. (with cells at Woodkirk and Skewkirk)	c. 1114	29 canons (1539)	£493	£402	£278	£680
NUN APPLETON Cistercian Nun.	c. 1150	19 nuns (1539)	£73	£46	£6	£52
NUN MONKTON Benedictine Nun.	c. 1147–53	12 nuns? (1536)	£75	£88	£16	£104
PONTEFRACT: ST. JOHN Cluniac Priory	c. 1090	13 monks (1539)	£340	£281	£153	£434
RIBSTON Preceptory of St. John (once of Templars)	c. 1217 (as Templar Prec.; refounded in 1312)	?	£207	£245	£16	£261
ROCHE Cistercian Abbey	1147	19 monks (1538)	£224	£163	£41	£204
SALLEY Cistercian Abbey	1148	21 monks (1536)	£147	c. £250	c. £50	c. £300
SELBY Benedictine Abbey (with cell at Snaith)	c. 1070	23 monks at Selby, 5 inmates at Snaith (1539)	£740	£292	£184	£476
SYNNINGTHWAITE Cistercian Nunnery	c. 1160	11 nuns (1536)	£61	£60	£5	£65
YORK: HOLY TRINITY Benedictine Priory	1089	11 monks (1538)	£169	£70	£88	£158
YORK: ST. MARY'S Benedictine Abbey	1089	51 monks (1539)	£1,650	£315	£47	£362

APPENDIX IV

Some West Riding Gentry and their Incomes

	Died	West Riding	Valuation of lands		Subsidy assessment (lands)
			Total	Source	
		£	£		£
Richard Aldburgh of Aldborough	1536	21	50	W9/129/267	24 (1524)
John Anne of Frickley	1544	45	—	E150/241/10	—
William Banester	1540	18	31	W9/130/231	—
Richard Beaumont of Whitley Beaumont	1541	59	—	E150/239/11	27 (1524)
Thomas Boswell of Ardsley	1541	86	86	W9/131/66	—
Richard Burdett	1547	30	—	E150/243/21	—
John Burton of Ingerthorpe	1530	22	—	C/142/51/37	10 (1524)
Sir Walter Calverley of Calverley	1537	50	—	E150/236/20	40 (1524)
Walter Calverley of Eccleshill	1539	15	15	W9/130/205	—
Christopher Clapham of Beamsley	1541	73	—	E150/239/8	24 (1524)
Sir William Compton of Compton Wynyates, Warwickshire	1528	90	1,650	W9/129/241 (1537)	—
John Copley	1543	78	—	C142/68/16 and E150/243/11	—
Sir John Dunham (left female heirs)	1534	45	211	W9/129/192	—
Anthony Eltofts of Bingley	1537	46	—	E150/236/8	10 (1524)
Sir Henry Everingham of Birkin	1547	122	137	W9/133/159	40 (1546)
Sir Thomas Fairfax of Walton	1521	87	—	E150/272/1	—
Alvered Fleming of Sharlston	1537	14	14	E150/236a/8	—
John Fleming of Crofton	1538	25	25	W9/129/281	—
William Franke of Alwoodley	1529	30	—	E150/231/11	20 (1524)
Sir William Gascoigne of Gawthorpe	1552	494	547	SC12/17/15	533 (1546)
John Gascoigne of Lazencroft	1558	62	—	C142/111/30	40 (1545)
William Gascoigne of Thorpe on the Hill	1539	26	—	C142/61/31	24 (1545)

| | Died | West Riding | Valuation of lands | | Subsidy assessment (lands) |
			Total	Source	
		£	£		£
Henry Gascoigne of Micklefield	1528	16	—	C142/48/135	—
John Greenfield of Barnbow	1541	14	—	E150/239/9	20 (1524)
Sir Stephen Hamerton of Wigglesworth	1537	125	—	E150/237/35	—
Sir Hugh Hastings of Norton	1541	129	289	W9/131/102	—
Sir Brian Hastings (?of Hatfield)	1537	17	?	W9/129/284	—
Walter Hawksworth of Hawksworth	1553	60	60	W9/135/273	40 (1545)
Ralph Hopton of Wortley	1533	41	—	C142/55/37	20 (1524)
William Ingleby of Ripley	1528	73	—	E150/230/11 and C142/48/160	160 (1524)
Sir Thomas Johnson	1544	96	143	W9/133/87	—
John Lacy of Cromwellbottom	1531	70	—	E150/232/4	27 (1524)
William Legh of Middleton by Rothwell	1541	62	—	C142/71/73	27 (1524)
Sir Richard Malleverer of Allerton Mauleverer	1521	over 76	—	E150/223/4	—
Sir William Malleverer of Worthersome	1551	84	over 154	C142/93/43	230 (1546)
Sir William Mallory of Gt. Studley	1547	97	—	E150/243/17	180 (1546)
Sir Nynyan Markenfield of Markenfield	1528	74	over 210	E150/230/7	67 (1524)
Sir Thomas Metham	1539	100	310	W9/130/224	—
Sir William Middleton of Middleton and Stockeld	1555	47	—	C142/105/62	267 (1546)
John Mountney of Cowley (near Sheffield)	1537	43	—	E150/236a/6	—
Sir Robert Nevill of Liversedge	1543	44	—	C142/68/41	50 (1524)
Lady Elizabeth, widow of Sir John Nevill of Chevet	1548	30	—	E150/244/27	60 (1546)
Sir John Norton	1520	over 32	—	E150/222/5	—
John Norton, son of last-mentioned, of Clother-holme near Ripon	—	—	—	—	67 (1524)
Arthur Pilkington of Bradley (near Huddersfield)	1539	45	—	E150/238/17	40 (1524)

	Died	West Riding	Total	Source	Subsidy assessment (lands)
		£	£		£
William Plumpton of Plumpton	1547	74	74	W9/135/6	53 (1546)
Henry Pudsey of Barforth (N.R.)	1544	82	156	W9/133/64	—
Ralph Pulleyn of Scotton	1539	38	—	E150/238/28	20 (1524)
Richard Redmayne of Harewood and Westmorland	1544	62	137	W9/133/101	—
Thomas Reresby of Thrybergh	1543	89	—	C142/69/124	—
Roger Rockley of Rockley	1534	9()	90	W9/129/199	—
Sir John Roecliffe of Cowthorpe	1533	86	—	E150/233a/4	100 (1524)
Robert Roos of Ingmanthorpe	1530	28	37	W9/129/75	30 (1524)
John Ryther (?of Ryther)	1528	148	187	W9/129/75	—
Sir Henry Savile of Thornhill and Soothill	1558	363	424		400 (1545)
Thomas Savile of Copley	1535	53	—	C142/82/43	20 (1524)
James Stansfield of Stansfield	1539	24	—	E150/238/5	13 (1524)
Sir Brian Stapleton of Carleton by Snaith	1550	113	—	E150/245/21	—
Sir Robert Stapleton of Wighill	1557	100	231	W9/137/209	160 (1546)
Sir Richard Tempest of Bolling	1537	117	—	E150/236/18	100 (1524)
Stephen Tempest of Broughton	1550	49	—	E150/245/12	72 (1546)
William Thwaites of Long Marston	1555	25	—	C142/105/54	48 (1546)
John Vavasour of Hazelwood	1524	130	—	E150/226/8	—
John Vavasour of Weston	1550	38	—	E150/245/14	20 (1546)
Thomas Vavasour of Denaby	1531	13	—	C142/52/38	—
Sir Robert Waterton of Walton (near Wakefield)	1541	53	—	E150/239/17	—
Thomas Wentworth of Wentworth Woodhouse	1549	59	—	C142/88/44	80 (1546)
Sir Thomas Wentworth of West Bretton	1543	40?	—	C142/68/17 and 111/65	—
Sir John Wentworth of North Elmsall	1544	141	—	E150/241/3	—
Guy Wilstrop	1521	86	—	E150/223/14 and 272/2	—

	Died	West Riding	Valuation of lands		Subsidy assessment (lands)
			Total	Source	
		£	£		£
Roger Wombwell of Wombwell (retired to a monastery)	(1531)	48	—	E150/223/15	—
Sir Richard Woodrove of Woolley	1522	56	—	E150/224/4	—
Thomas Wortley of Wortley	1544	68	68	W9/133/90	—

Sources: With one exception (Sir William Gascoigne of Gawthorpe), the figures for land-values are drawn from wardship records in the Public Record Office. References with the class numbers E150 or C142 are to inquisitions *post mortem*; those with the number W9 (in full, Wards 9) are to feodaries' surveys.

Figures for subsidy assessments are taken mainly from the records referred to at the foot of Table VIII (page) 97.

APPENDIX V

Chronological Summary of Events Mentioned in the Text, 1513–46

1513: Spring or Summer: Resistance to taxation in Craven and Ewcross, which continued through 1514.
September: Battle of Flodden: West Riding men took part, and eight of them were knighted.

1514: Thomas Wolsey became Archbishop of York.

1516: Fifth Earl of Northumberland examined in Star Chamber, on the subject of retainers.

1517: 8 June: Thomas Lord Darcy wrote to Wolsey that all was quiet in Yorkshire and the King's laws well observed.
October: Commissioners sat at York to investigate enclosures contrary to the statute of 1515.

1519–20: Bad harvests.

1523: Scottish campaign: West Riding men again participated, some of them under command of Lord Darcy.
August: Earl of Surrey reported that at York he found a feud between Henry Savile and Sir Richard Tempest.

1524: July: Lord Darcy again reported to Wolsey that the West Riding was in a good state of order.

1525: April: First reference to movement of tenants of Rothwell against Lord Darcy, owner of the Park there. (There is nothing to connect this unrest with the opposition to Wolsey's 'amicable grant' in Lincolnshire, East Anglia and Kent, in April and May of this year.)
July: Council of Duke of Richmond established, which was to sit part of the time at Sheriff Hutton and part at Pontefract.

1527: May: Death of Fifth Earl of Northumberland.

1527–8: Bad harvests and dearth.

1528: February: Proceedings against makers of sub-standard cloth in Yorkshire.
Conflict between John Norton and the Earl of Cumberland concerning commoning rights on Speldersden Moor and other matters.

1529: July: Lord Darcy drew up his list of grievances against Wolsey, who fell from power in October.
November: Reformation Parliament met: Yorkshire was represented by Sir John Nevill of Snape (later Baron

Latimer) and Sir Marmaduke Constable of Everingham. During this year, three local conflicts are referred to:

(i) The conflict between Lord Darcy and the tenants of Rothwell, who took the case to the Duchy of Lancaster court.

(ii) A conflict between John Frobisher and the tenants of Altofts, also in Duchy court.

(iii) An affray at Harewood between a chantry-priest and the servants of Sir William Gascoigne of Gawthorpe.

1530: April–May: Conflict between Sir William Gascoigne and John Saintpole, involving affrays at Carcroft.

June: Reorganization of the Council in the North, with Bishop Tunstall of Durham as its President. The personnel of the West Riding commission of the peace was also radically changed this year, following Wolsey's fall. November: Wolsey arrested at Cawood, where he had arrived the previous month. He died at Leicester, on the way South. His successor as Archbishop was Edward Lee.

1531: April: Affray at Kirkby Malzeard, arising from the conflict between John Norton and the Earl of Cumberland.

1532: Further references to conflict between Lord Darcy and the Rothwell tenants; and reference to conflict over enclosures on Winn Moor and at Kiddal.

Lord Darcy spoke out against the project for a royal divorce sanctioned by royal supremacy in spiritual affairs.

1533: January: Sixth Earl of Northumberland became the King's Lieutenant in the North, and president of the Council in the North; Thomas Lord Darcy and Sir Robert Constable apparently joined the Council at this time.

April: Commission to Sir William Gascoigne and others to examine William Legh and the tenants of Rothwell after their threat to pull down Darcy's enclosures.

September?: Commissioners sat at Leeds to enquire into the 'flocking' of cloth.

During the year, Sir John Nevill of Chevet became knight of the shire for Yorkshire, in place of his namesake of Snape, who became Baron Latimer.

1534: The conflict between Sir Richard Tempest and Sir Henry Savile was in full swing during this and the following year, with charges and counter-charges on various matters.

It was probably in this year that Cromwell received a
letter complaining of the deplorable state of law in Yorkshire, accusing Sir William Gascoigne, Sir Richard
Tempest and Sir Henry Savile of perverting the course
of justice.

July: Trial of Lord Dacre for treason, on the accusation
of the Earl of Cumberland.

September: Chapuys reported to Charles V that several
peers were disaffected, including Lord Darcy who had
plans for a revolt in the autumn. Darcy was prevented
from leaving for the North.

November: Oath of Supremacy administered.

December: Affray at Harewood, leading to Sir William
Gascoigne's imprisoning the constable at Gawthorpe.

During the year there were agrarian conflicts at Bishop-
laithes, near York, where a mob pulled down the enclosures of the Archbishop's farmers; and between the
tenants of Copgrove and those of Roecliffe, north of
Knaresborough.

1535: January: Commissioners sent out to compile the *Valor
Ecclesiasticus*, which was completed by early 1536.

Early in the year, Chapuys's letters indicate that there
was still disaffection against the King; but the Emperor
decided against taking any action.

February: The Earl of Northumberland agreed to disin-
herit his brother and make the King his heir.

June: Riots in Craven, especially at Giggleswick, where
enclosures of the Earl of Cumberland and of John
Lambert were pulled down.

August: Trial at York of George Lazenby, a Jervaulx
monk who had spoken in favour of the Pope; he was later
executed.

Summer?: Lord Darcy was permitted to return home; he
was certainly there by November.

September: Inhabitants of Halifax petitioned Cromwell
against their vicar, Robert Haldsworth, a protégé of
Sir Henry Savile, for trying to conceal his wealth from
the King's commissioners.

1536: January–February: Visitation of the Northern monasteries by Dr. Layton and Dr. Legh, to prepare their
compendium comperta for the Diocese of York, etc.

January: Litigation in progress between Sir Henry Savile
and Sir Richard Tempest, concerning the latter's stewardship of Wakefield and other matters.

1536:   March: Statutes for the Dissolution of monasteries worth less than £200 a year, and to establish the Court of Augmentations.

The Statute of Uses was also passed in this year.

March: Indenture granting Salley Abbey to Sir Arthur Darcy.

April: Subsidy commissioners reported trouble in making assessments in the North Riding, but there is no evidence of trouble in the West Riding at this point.

May: Knavesmire enclosure riot at York: directed against enclosures erected by the Mayor and Council of the City.

22 July: Death of the Duke of Richmond, which raised the question of gressums in Richmondshire.

August: Suppression of priories of Synningthwaite (3rd), Healaugh (9th), and Drax (24th).

September: Suppression of Nun Monkton Priory. In June Sir William Gascoigne sought 'preferment' to it.

28 September: Suppression commissioners met resistance at Hexham Priory.

Late September: Beginnings of revolt of commons in Dent and Sedburgh.

1–4 October: Beginnings of rebellion in Lincolnshire, initially at Louth and Horncastle. The Lincolnshire revolt began to wane about the 12 October.

5 or 6 October: Archbishop Lee heard that the Earl of Shrewsbury had set out against Lincolnshire, and wrote to York, Beverley and Ripon to stay the commons there.

8 October: Rising at Beverley; report at Lincoln that the Halifax area had risen.

10–13 October: Rising of Howdenshire, Marshland and Snaith led by Robert Aske. Archbishop Lee fled to Pontefract, where Darcy was in command of the castle.

11–12 October: Rising of Mashamshire, Coverdale, Middleham, Nidderdale, Kirkbyshire, and probably Ripon.

12 October: Salley Abbey reoccupied by rebels.

13 October: Risings in Richmondshire, and round Malton.

16 October: Robert Aske entered York, which went over to the rebellion; he devised the Pilgrims' oath. The same day the Earl of Cumberland was forced to retreat to his castle, after setting out for Hexham; the rebellion in Craven appears to have begun at this time.

1536:   17 October: Rising round Bishop Auckland: Bishop
Tunstall fled to Northam. Rising also occurred in
Westmorland about this date.

19 October: The Earl of Derby decided to obey the
King.

20 October: Rebels from north entered York; Hull fell to
the rebels.

21 October: Lord Darcy surrendered Pontefract Castle
to Aske and Sir Thomas Percy.

22–3 October: Some of the rebels advanced to Went-
bridge and Hampole, in the direction of Doncaster.
Meanwhile Sir Stephen Hamerton and Nicholas Tempest
went into Blackburnshire, to forestall the advance thither
of the Earl of Derby.

24 October: Muster of Pilgrims, estimated at 30,000 near
Doncaster. The Earl of Shrewsbury meanwhile was at
Rossington, just south of Doncaster, and others of his
force at Tickhill.

27 October: Parley at Doncaster Bridge between the
Pilgrims' leaders and the Duke of Norfolk: truce agreed
upon, whilst two rebel leaders went to London to see the
King

28 October: Lancaster taken by rebels from Westmorland and Dentdale; but Carlisle still held out against those
of Cumberland.

1 November: Sir Henry Savile, who had fled South, was
back at Dewsbury threatening to take action against those
who had supported the rebellion.

Early November: Sir Brian Hastings reported disturbances in Marshland and plundering of the King's game
in Hatfield.

18 November: Darcy and Aske, at Temple Hirst,
received an invitation from the King to send 300 men to
meet Norfolk again at Doncaster.

19 November: Sir Henry Savile sent word to followers
at Wakefield to join him (at Rotherham), but they were
prevented by Thomas Grice.

21 November: Council of Pilgrims met at York, to
choose representatives to meet Norfolk at Doncaster.

27 November: Sir George Darcy was succeeded as
Sheriff of Yorkshire by Sir Brian Hastings.

2–4 December: Council of Pilgrims at Pontefract, to
draw up the articles to be presented to Norfolk. A
'convocation' of northern clergy also met at Pontefract.

6 December: Second meeting between Pilgrim leaders and Norfolk at Doncaster. He accepted the articles and promised they would be submitted to a Parliament. The rebels agreed to disperse.

13–16 December: The King's pardon was read by Clarencieux King of Arms at Halifax, Bradford, Leeds and Skipton.

Late December: A number of West Riding gentlemen went up to London, notably Sir Oswald Wilstrop, Sir George Darcy, Sir Nicholas Fairfax, and Robert Aske. The latter was received by the King on 12 December. About this time Sir Richard Tempest was ordered to hand over Sandal Castle to Sir Henry Savile.

1537: 10 January: Lord Darcy and Sir Robert Constable received a royal summons to London, but excused themselves.

12–13 January: Bills appeared on church doors round Leeds, Harewood, etc.; and further restlessness in Kirkbyshire.

16–20 January: Abortive East Riding revolt led by John Hallom and Sir Francis Bigod.

18–20 January: Further unrest in Richmondshire.

4–6 February: Further unrest round Jervaulx, led by Ninian Staveley.

5 February: Duke of Norfolk arrived at York, to carry out his functions as Lieutenant of the North, and to pacify the country. New members were appointed to the Council in the North, including the Earl of Cumberland, and Bishop Holgate of Llandaff.

14–15 February: Norfolk proceeded from York to Fountains Abbey and Ripon, thence to Richmond, on his way to Carlisle. He sent Sir Arthur Darcy to recover control at Salley Abbey.

17 February: Battle of Carlisle, where Lord Clifford defended the town successfully against the rebels. Norfolk arrived there on the 19th.

10 March: Abbot of Whalley executed at Lancaster.

24 March: Robert Aske rode up to London, where he was arrested on the 7 April. Darcy set out for London at the end of March, and was also arrested; the same thing happened to Sir Richard and Nicholas Tempest, and Sir Stephen Hammerton.

Early May: Grand juries sat in Yorkshire to indict the rebels.

15–16 May: Lord Darcy and other rebels tried at Westminster.

26 May: Robert Haldsworth reported the recent execution of Sir Stephen Hamerton, Nicholas Tempest and others.

2 June: William Thirsk, *quondam* Abbot of Fountains executed, along with Abbot of Jervaulx, the Prior of Bridlington, and Sir Thomas Percy.

29 June: Death of the Sixth Earl of Northumberland, leaving his lands to the King under an agreement completed on the 3 June.

30 June: Execution of Lord Darcy.

12 July: Robert Aske executed at York.

July: Hearings and correspondence concerning the money of Robert Haldsworth, vicar of Halifax, which his enemies alleged to be treasure trove.

25 August: Sir Richard Tempest died in the Fleet prison.

1538: January–May: Sir Henry Savile, having succeeded to Lord Darcy's position as steward of Pontefract, surveyed the castles there and at Sandal.

June: Robert Holgate, Bishop of Llandaff, became president of the Council in the North, an office he held until 1550.

June: Sir John Nevill reported the willingness of the Prior of Monk Bretton to surrender his house, and sought preferment to the demesnes.

In the same month, Roche Abbey was surrendered to William Blytheman and other commissioners.

November–December: Monk Bretton Priory, and the friaries of Knaresborough, Pontefract and Doncaster surrendered to Sir George Lawson, William Blytheman and others.

1539: January: Bolton Priory surrendered.

May: Statute vesting all monastic property in the Crown.

August: Surrender of Esholt Priory.

29 November: Surrender of St. Mary's Abbey, York, which became the seat of the Council in the North.

November–December: Surrender to Drs. Layton and Legh of the monasteries and nunneries of Nostell, Kirkstall, Hampole, Pontefract, Kirklees, Fountains, Arthington, Nun Appleton and Selby.

December: First commission appointed for regular sales of monastic property.

1540:   November: Preceptory of the Order of St. John at Ribston surrendered to the Crown; the preceptory of Newland also surrendered at some time during the year.

1541·   March–April: Discovery of Wakefield plot, for a rising at Pontefract Fair at Easter; the leaders were arrested.

17 May: William Legh of Middleton and several others were arrested for their part in this plot.

15 June: Sir John Nevill of Chevet executed for failing to act on his first intimation of the conspiracy.

August to October: the King visited Yorkshire; he was at Pontefract from the 23 August to the 3 September, and at York from the 16 to the 27 September. Rumours that he might meet James V of Scotland were not fulfilled. He received the humble submission of the Yorkshire gentry. The harvest appears to have been poor in Yorkshire this year, and plague was reported at Foulby and Wragby, near Wakefield, and deaths were high in Morley Wapentake.

1542:   January: Parliament met; the Yorkshire knights were Sir Ralph Ellerker and Sir Robert Bowes; Ellerker was later replaced by Thomas Waterton, esquire.

October–November: Norfolk led a campaign in Scotland, culminating in the Battle of Solway Moss.

1543:   Dispute between Sir John Wentworth and the tenants of Morley and Gildersome, after he had ploughed up part of their commons.

A statute was passed prohibiting the manufacture of coverlets outside York.

1544:   Spring: Further campaign in Scotland: at least seven West Riding gentlemen, and 700 soldiers, took part.

Death of Archbishop Edward Lee; he was succeeded by Robert Holgate.

1545:   January: Instructions to the Council in the North to take action against enclosures of commons and extreme increases in fines and rents.

February–March: The King and the Archbishop of York made an exchange of lands, in which the latter lost many of his West Riding temporalities, in return for various spiritual possessions.

Statute for the suppression of the chantries. There is evidence of private disendowments in the West Riding in the 1540s.

1546:   February: Commissions appointed to survey the chantries. Subsidy assessments made in the West Riding: those used in Chapter III.

INDEX

Wapentake boundaries
Other boundaries
▲CLARO Meeting-places of Wapentakes
Honour of PONTEFRACT
■ Centres of principal Lordships
● Other Lordships
TICKHILL Honours of the Duchy of LANCASTER
O Townships pertaining to Otley
S Townships pertaining to Spofforth

0   10   Miles   20   30
0   10   20   30   40   50
          Kilometres